Dedication

This book is for you, dear colorist.

May your time spent coloring these pages
bring you joy, plus lots of fun
mixed in with plenty of relaxation..

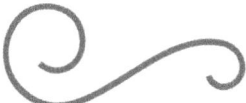

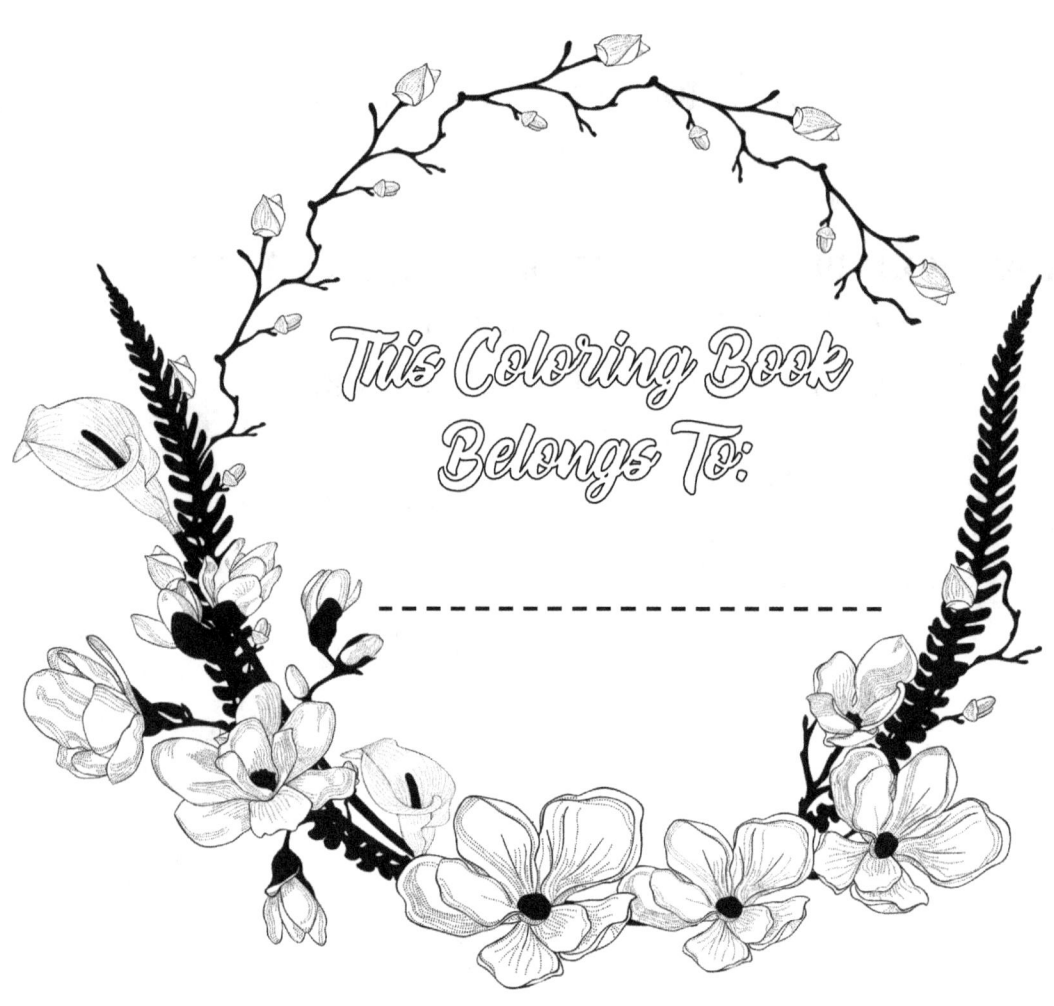

This Coloring Book
Belongs To:

_____

Sample Colors

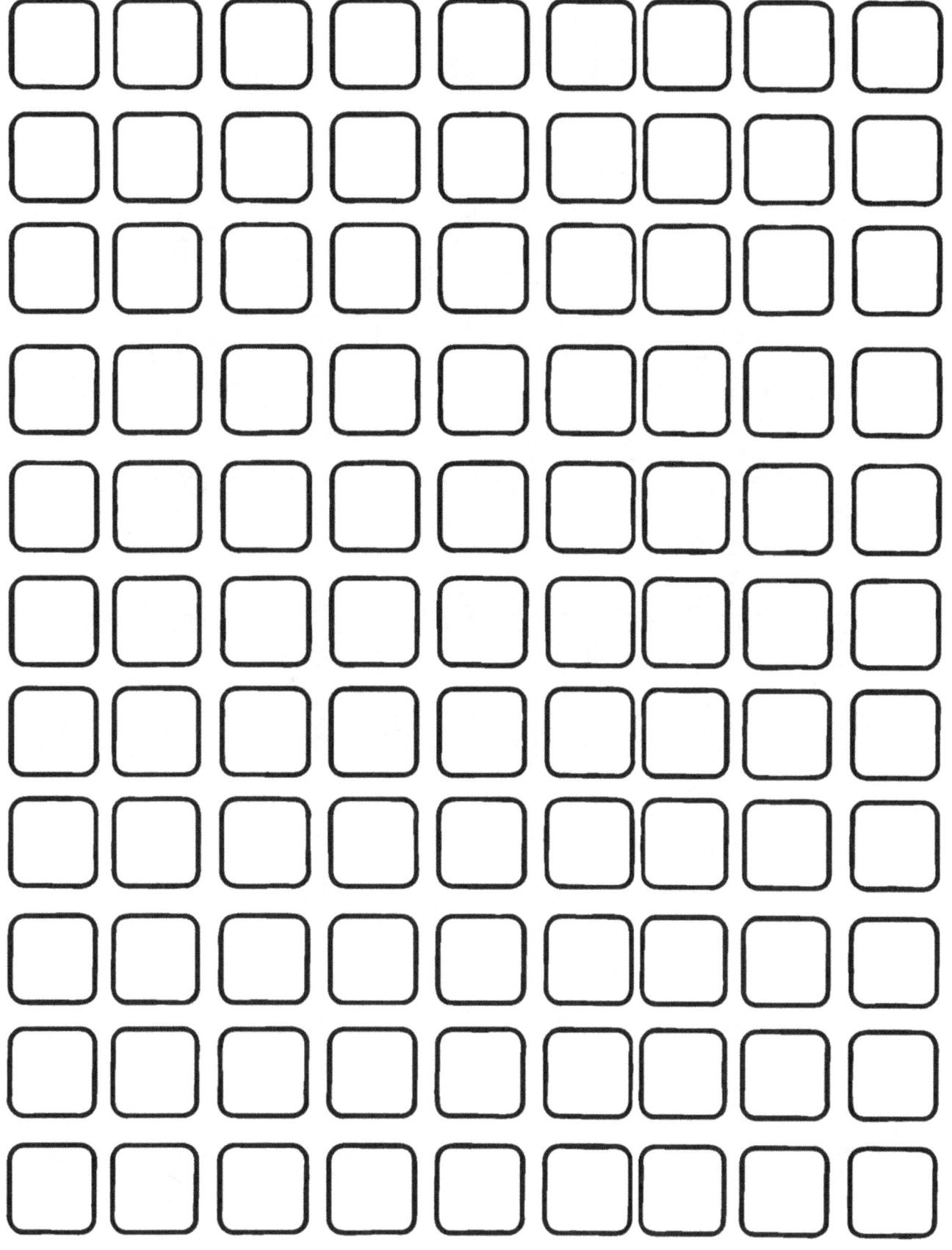

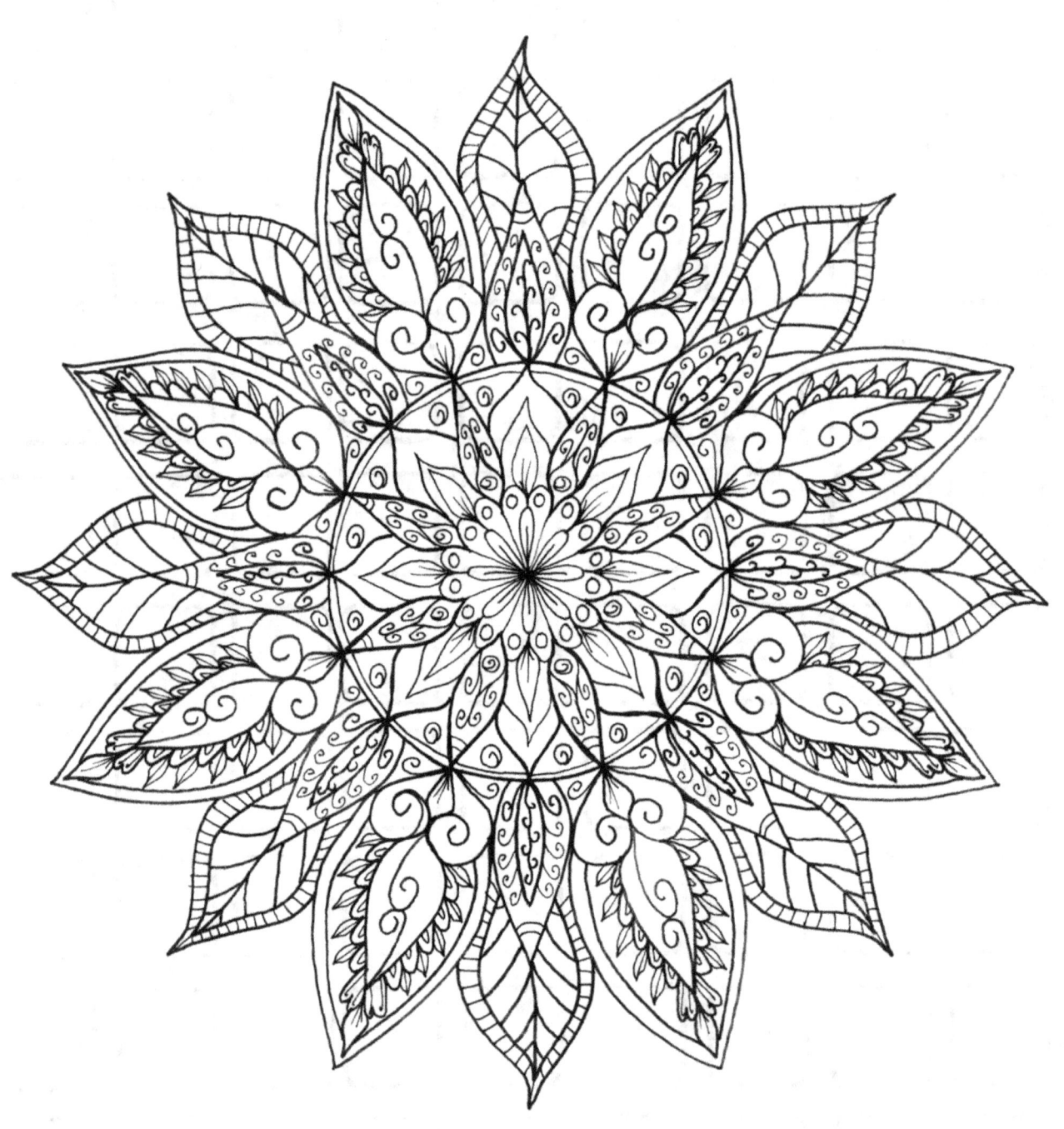

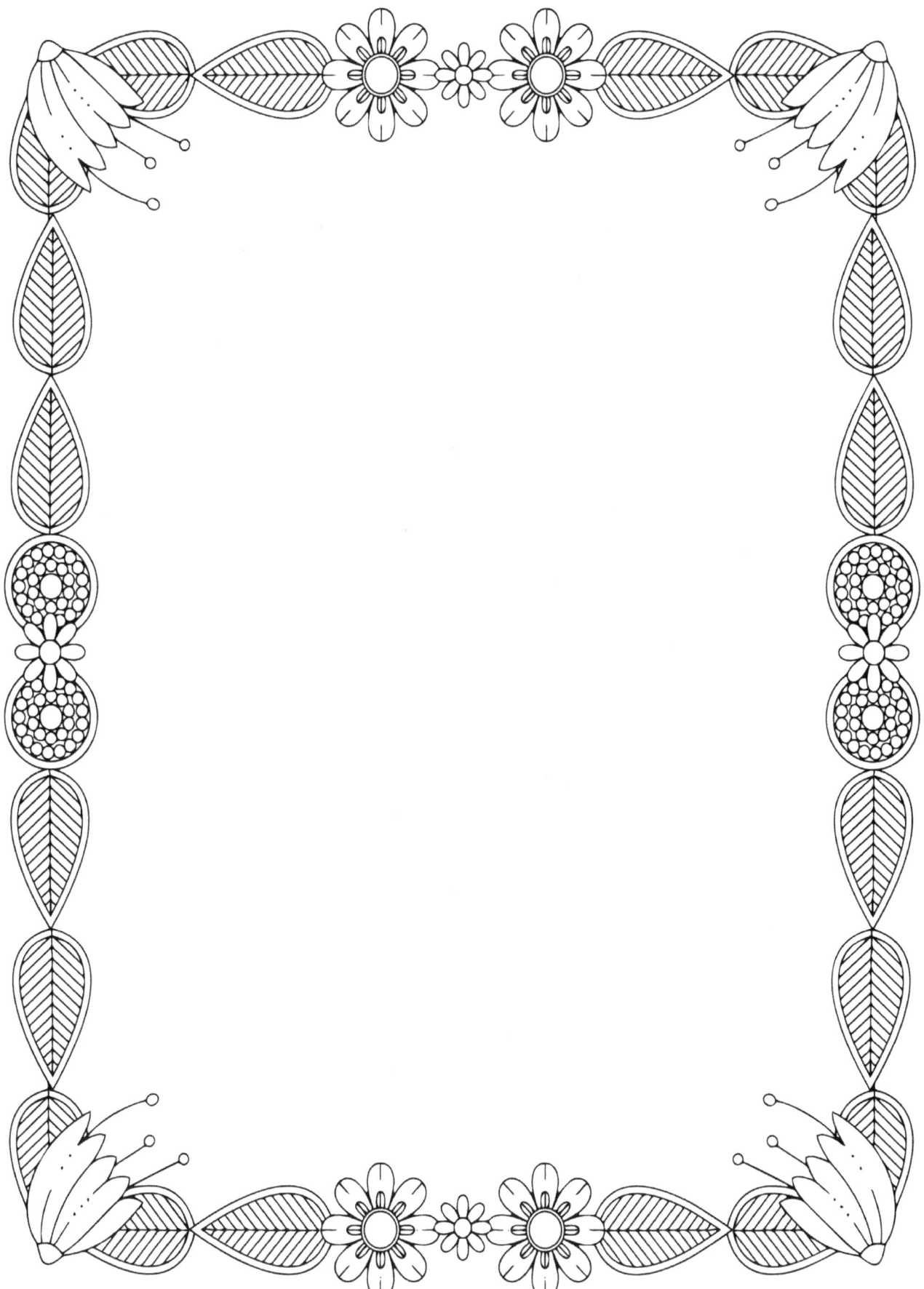

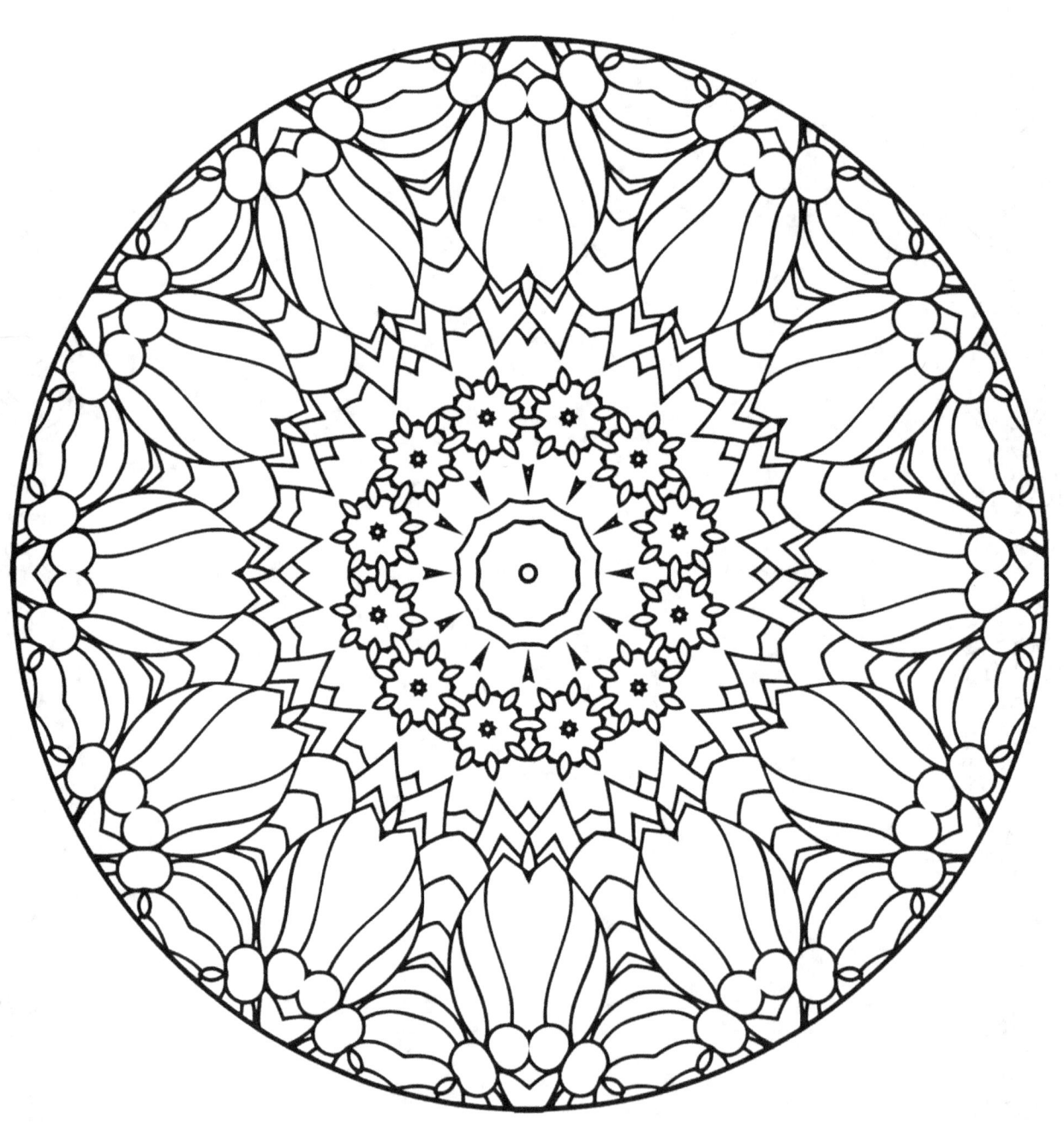

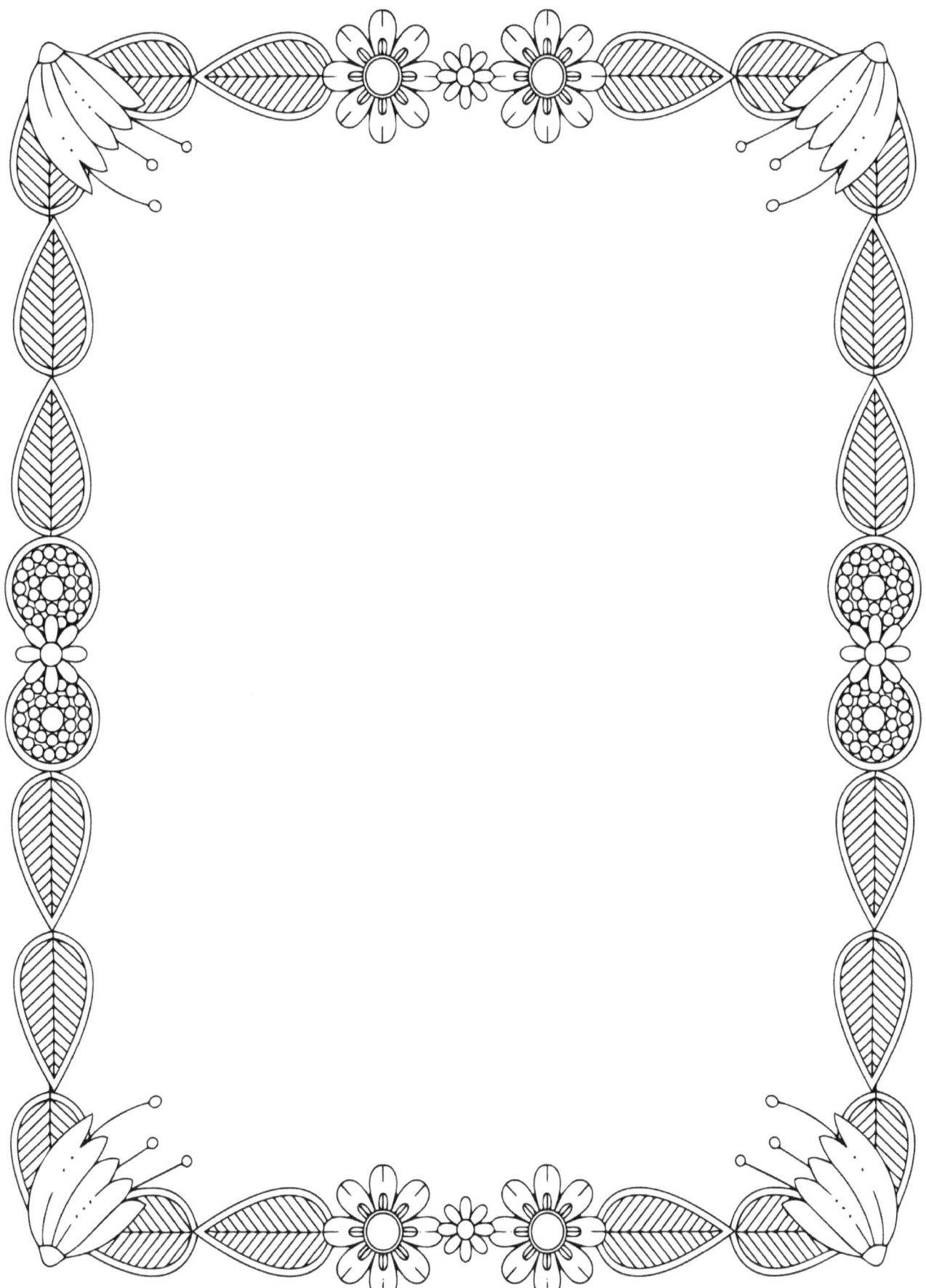

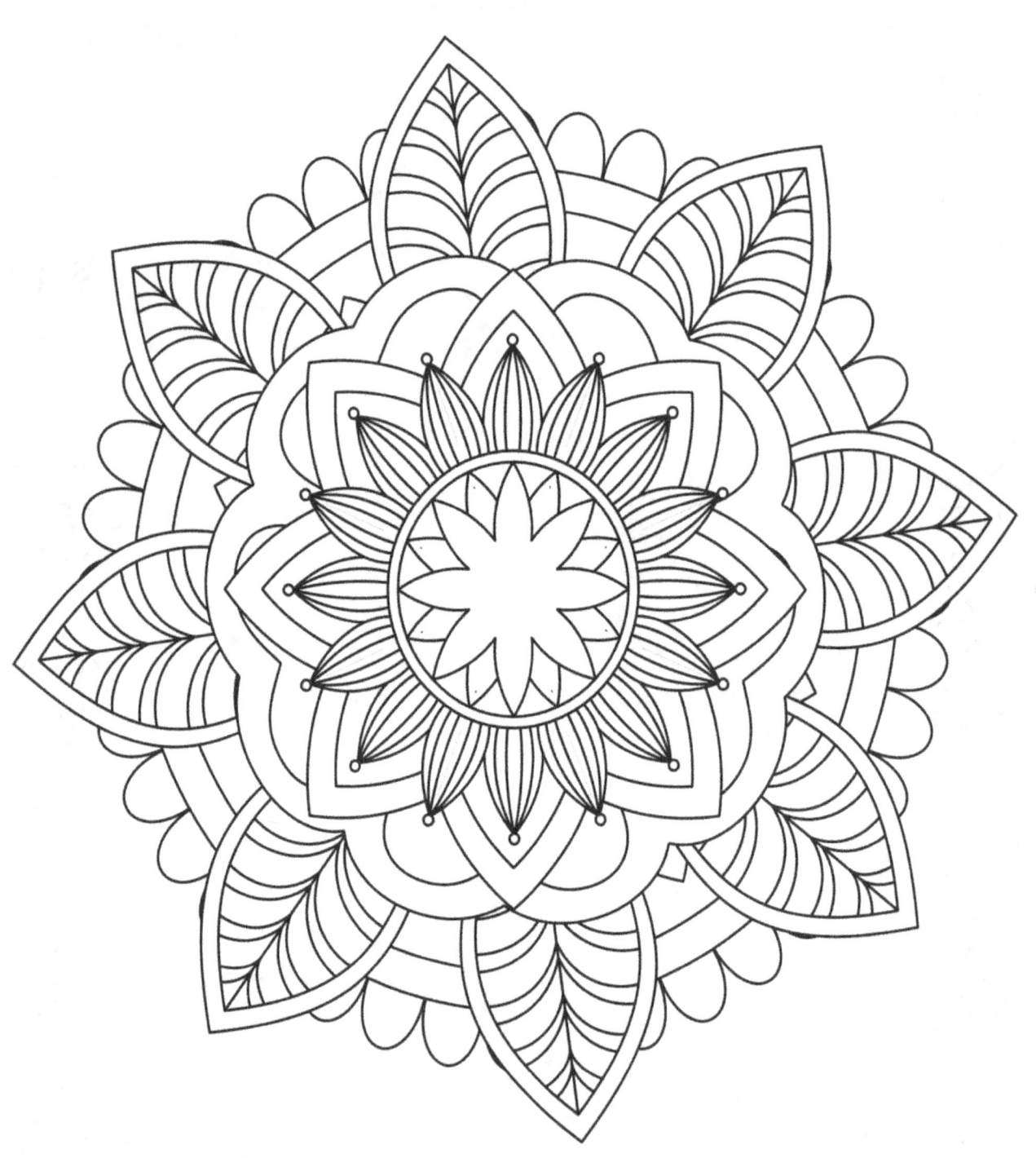

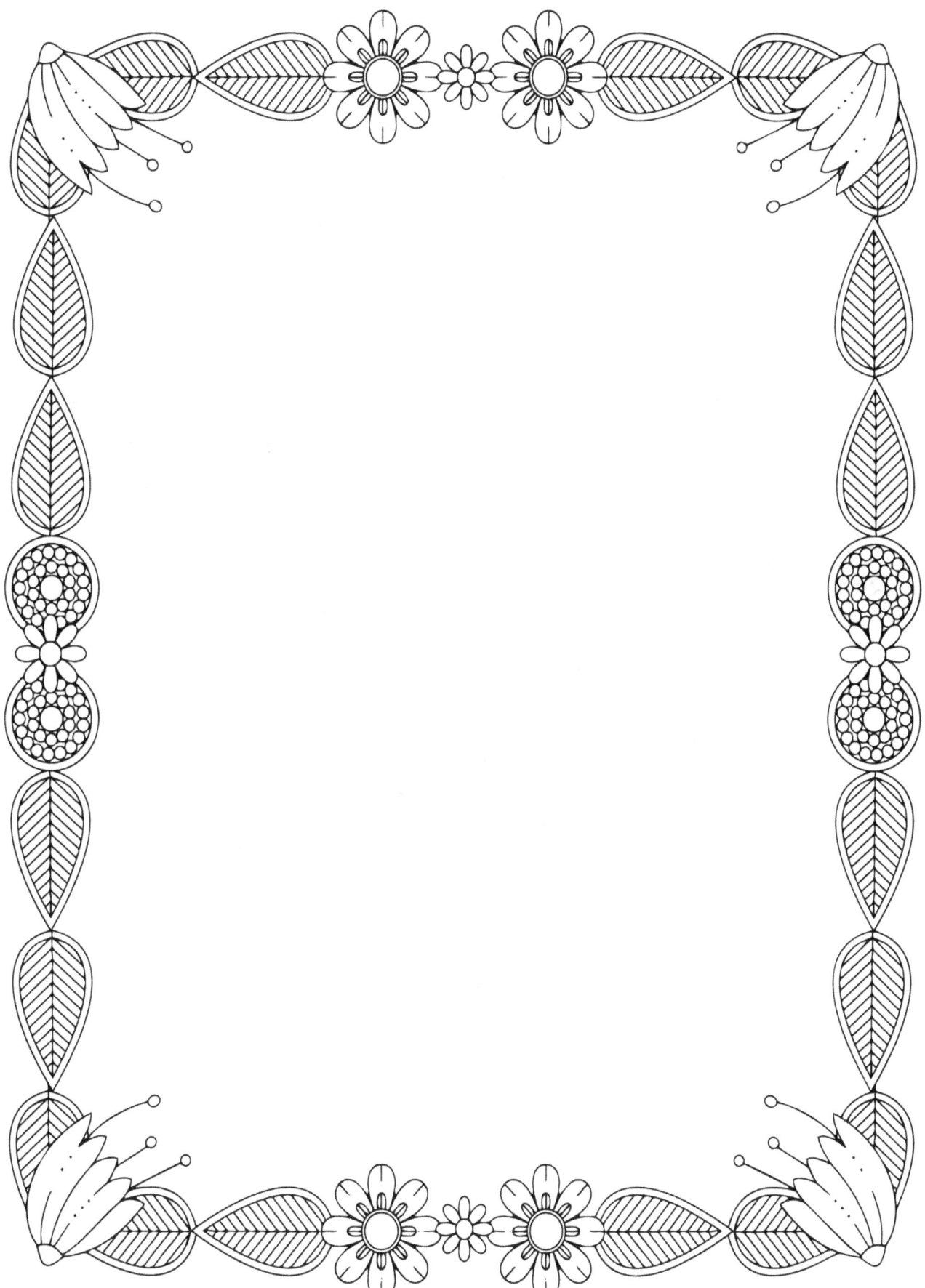

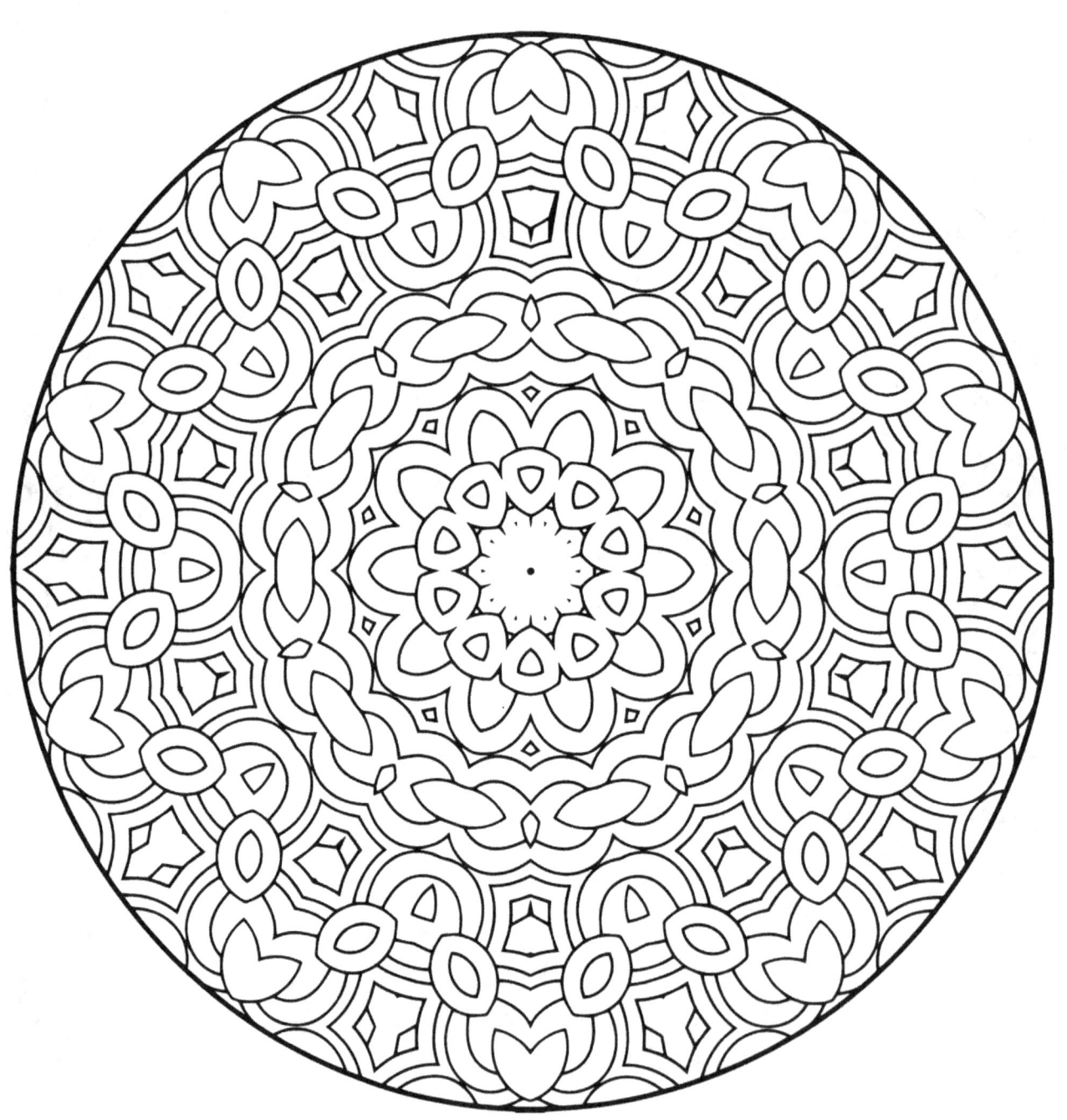

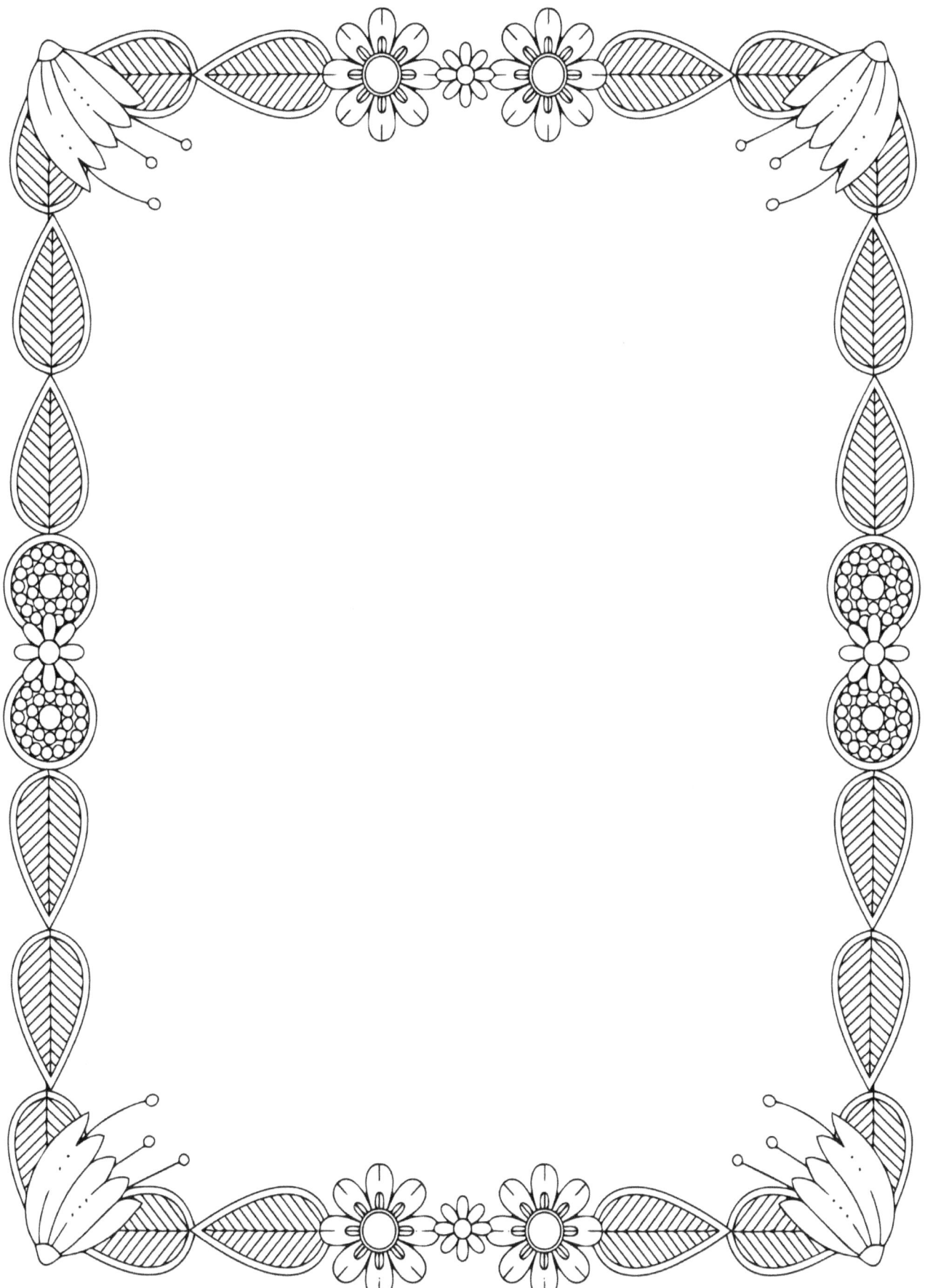

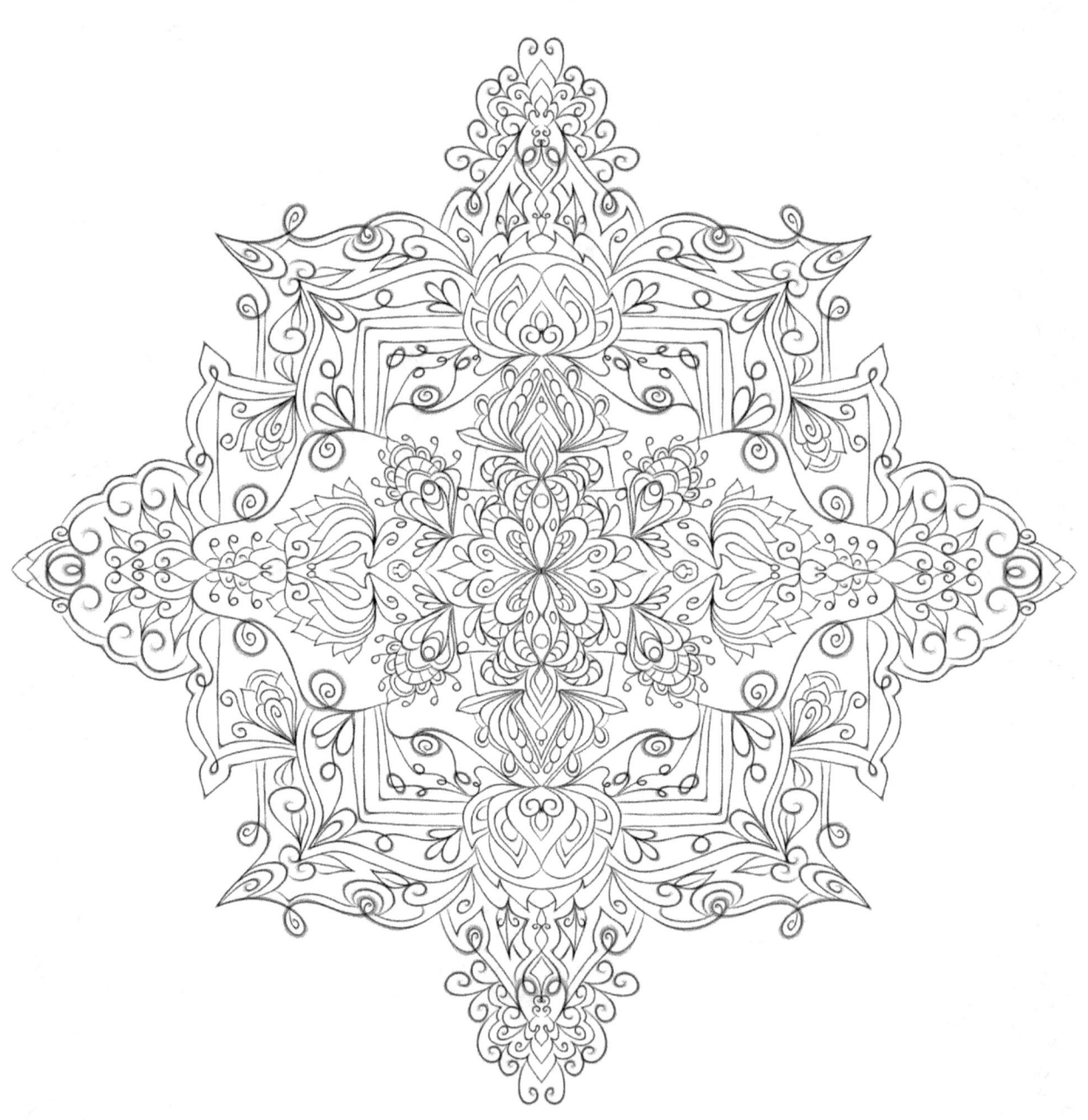

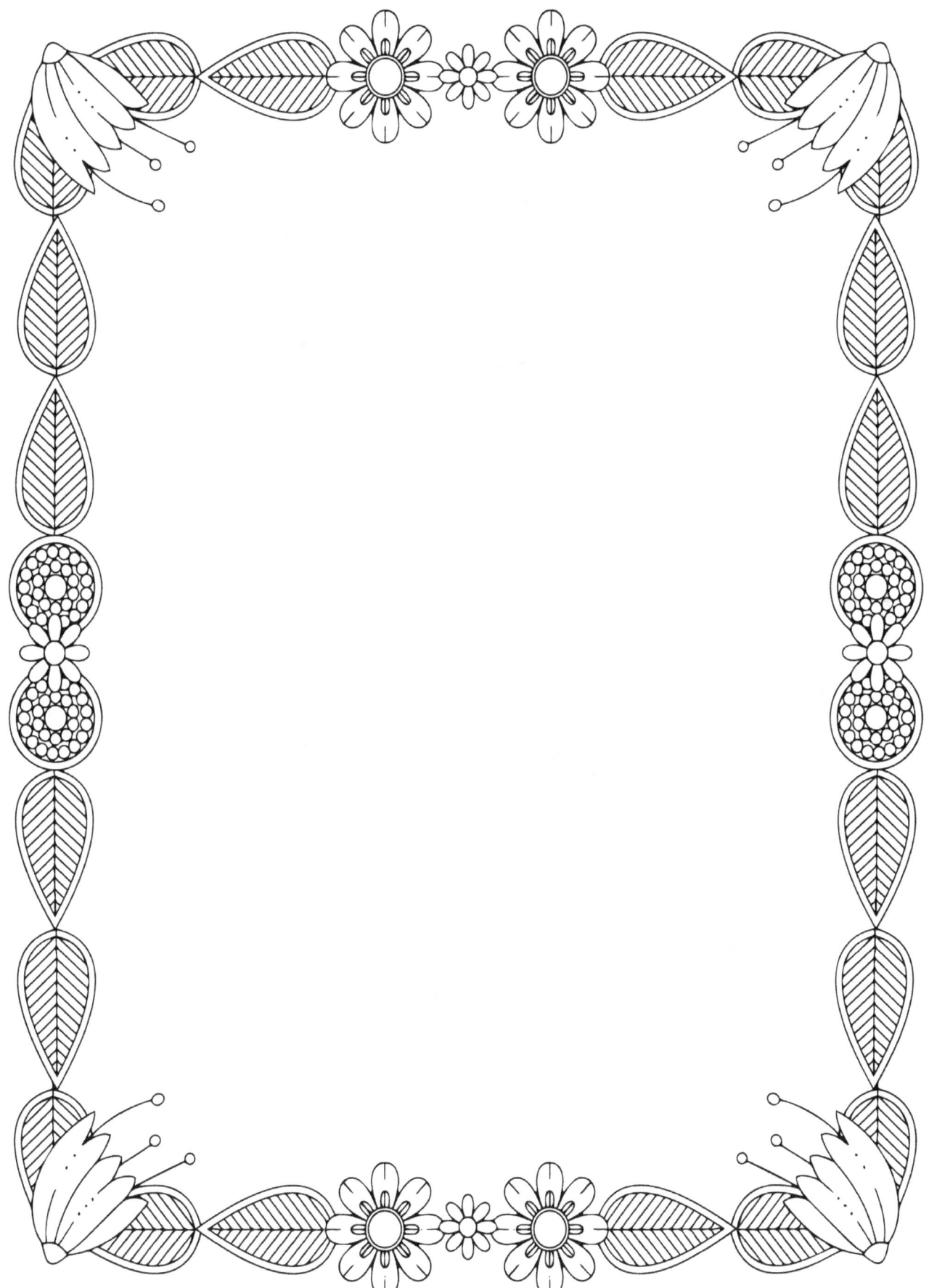

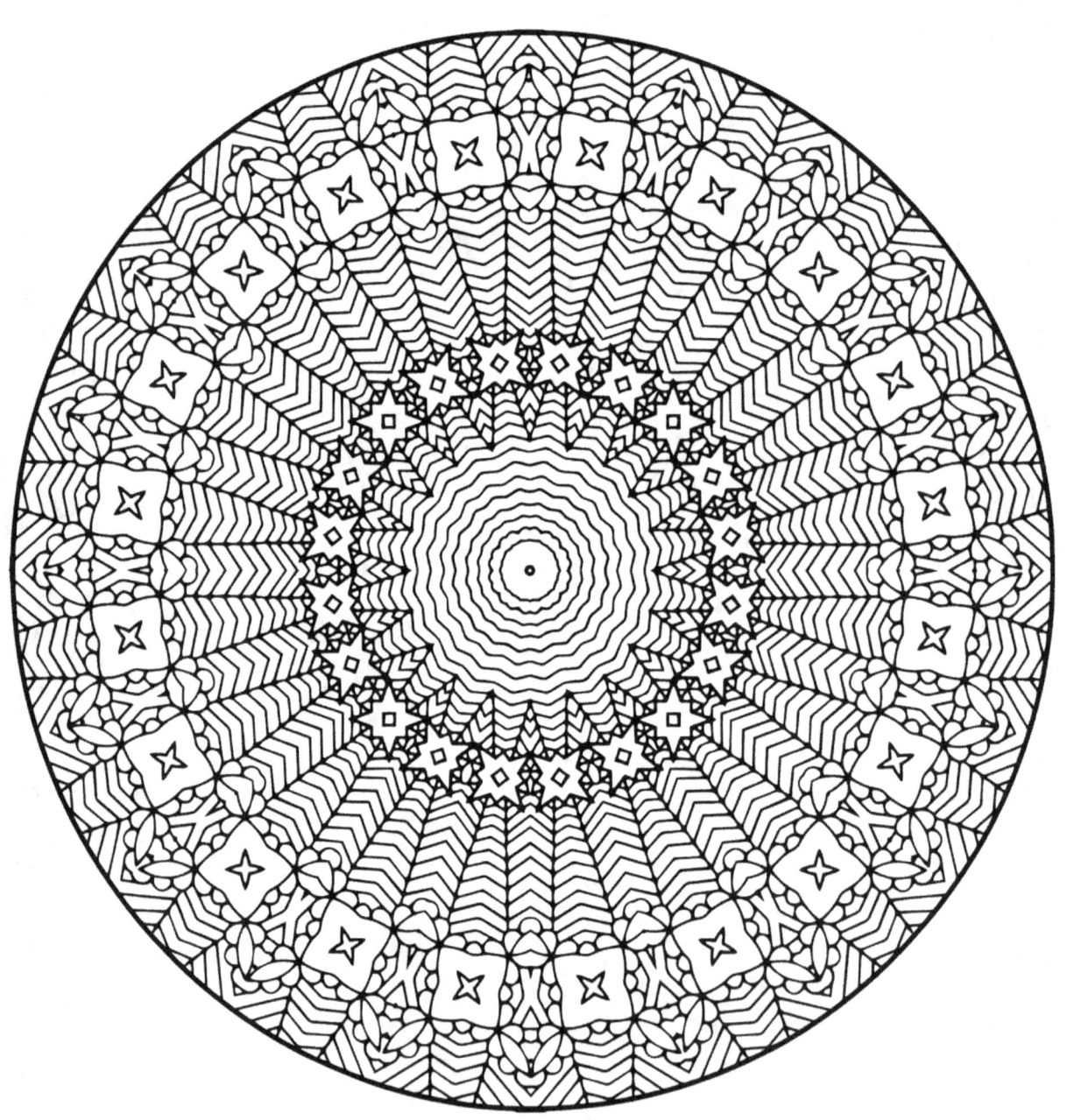

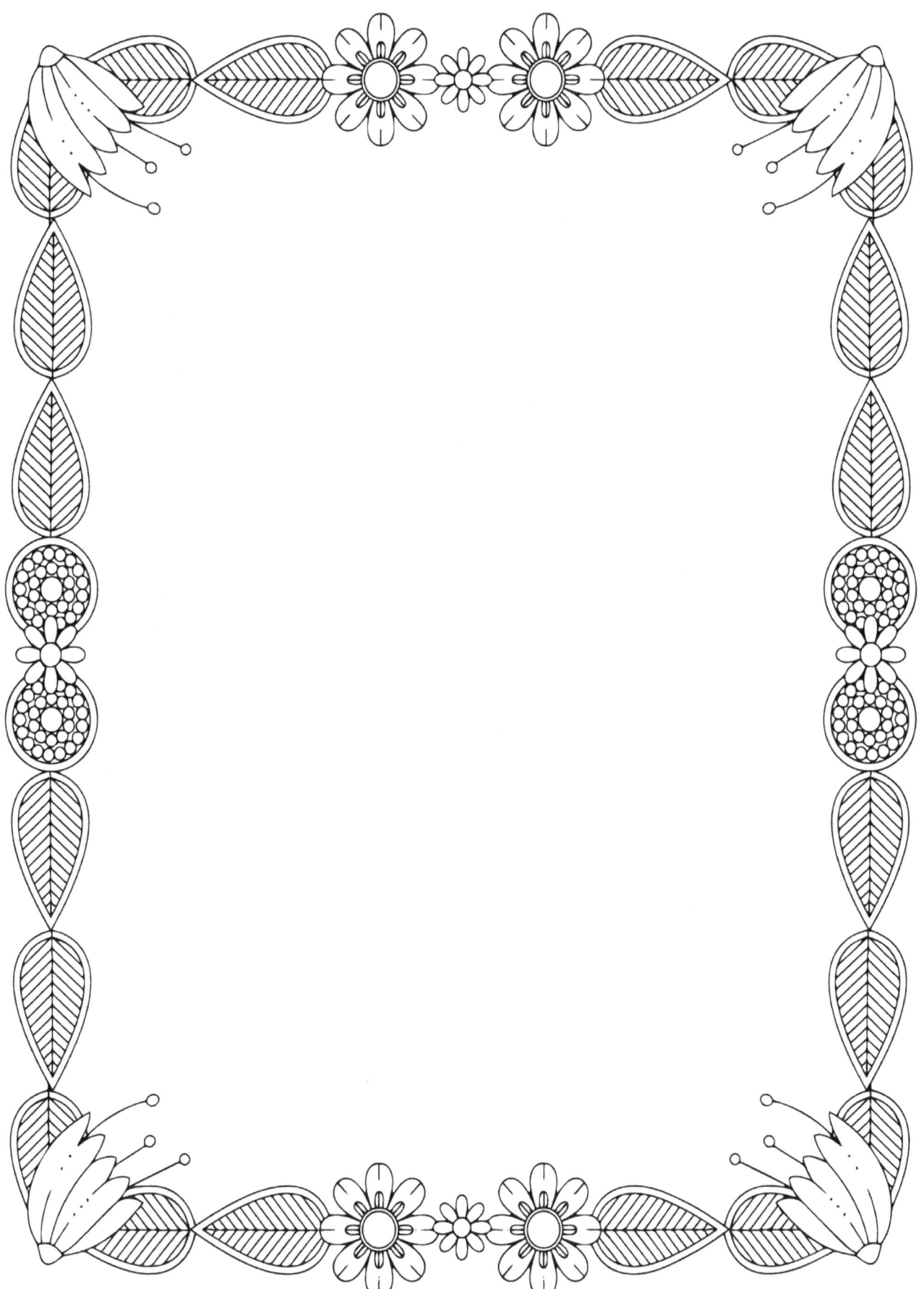

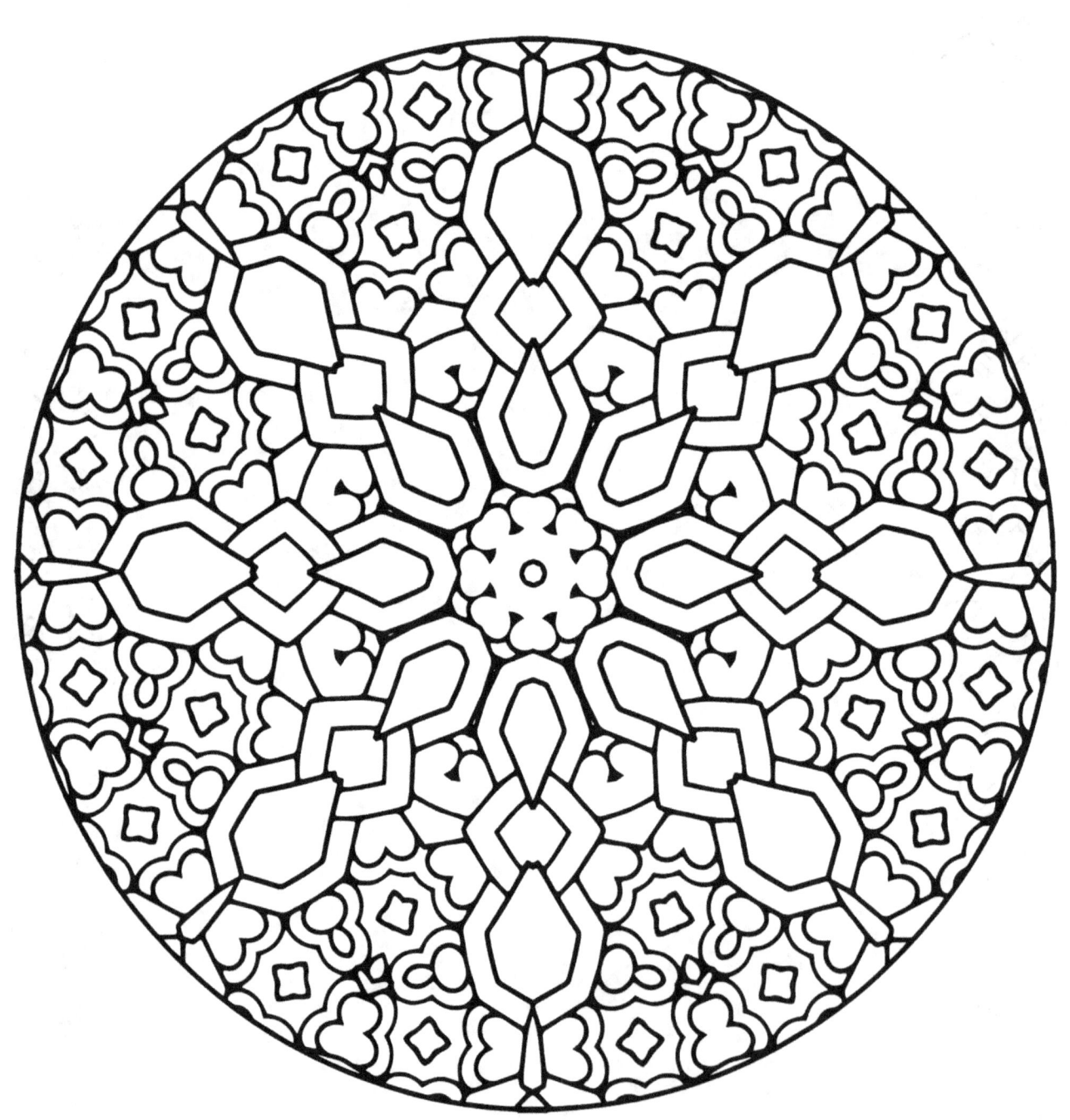

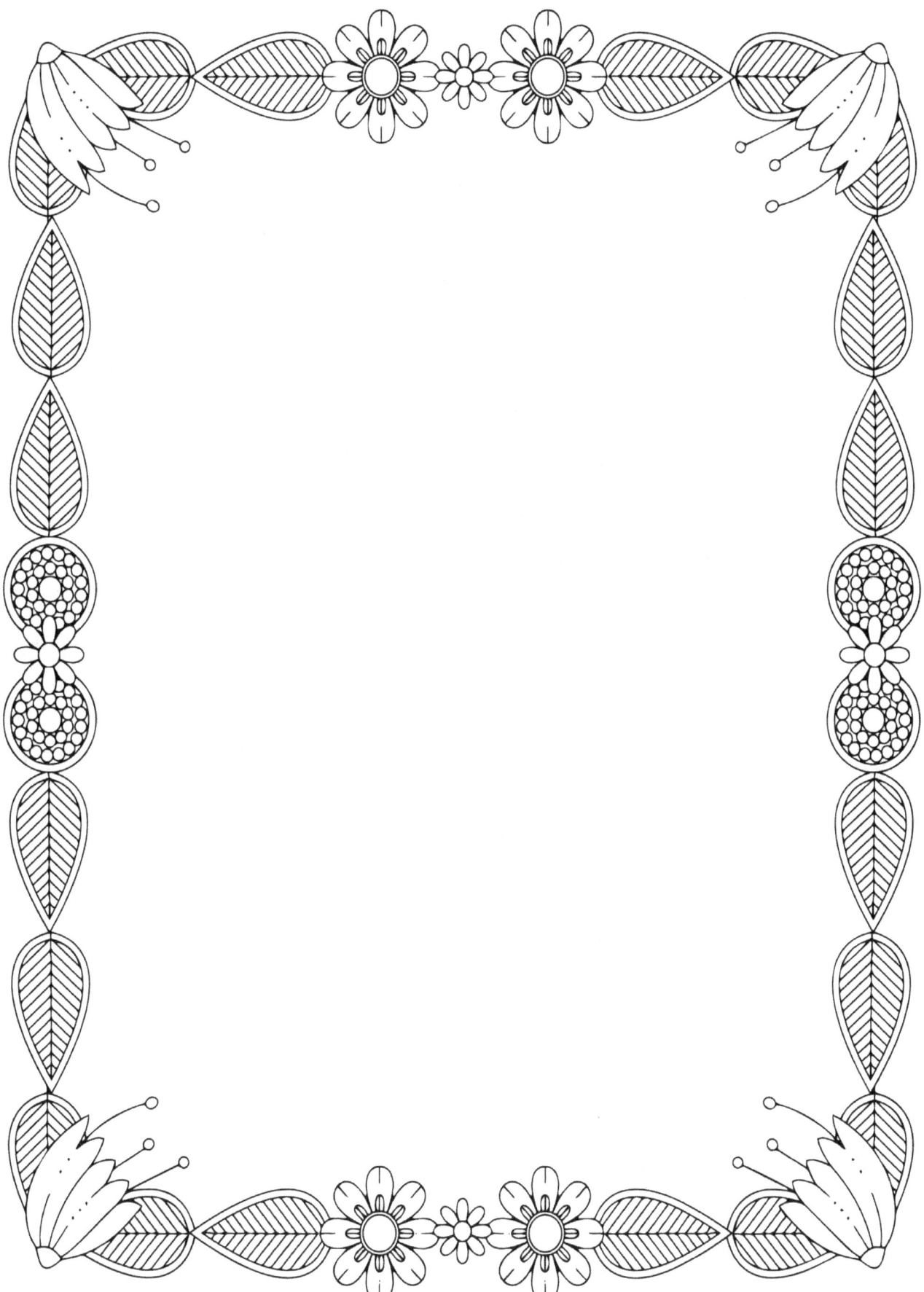

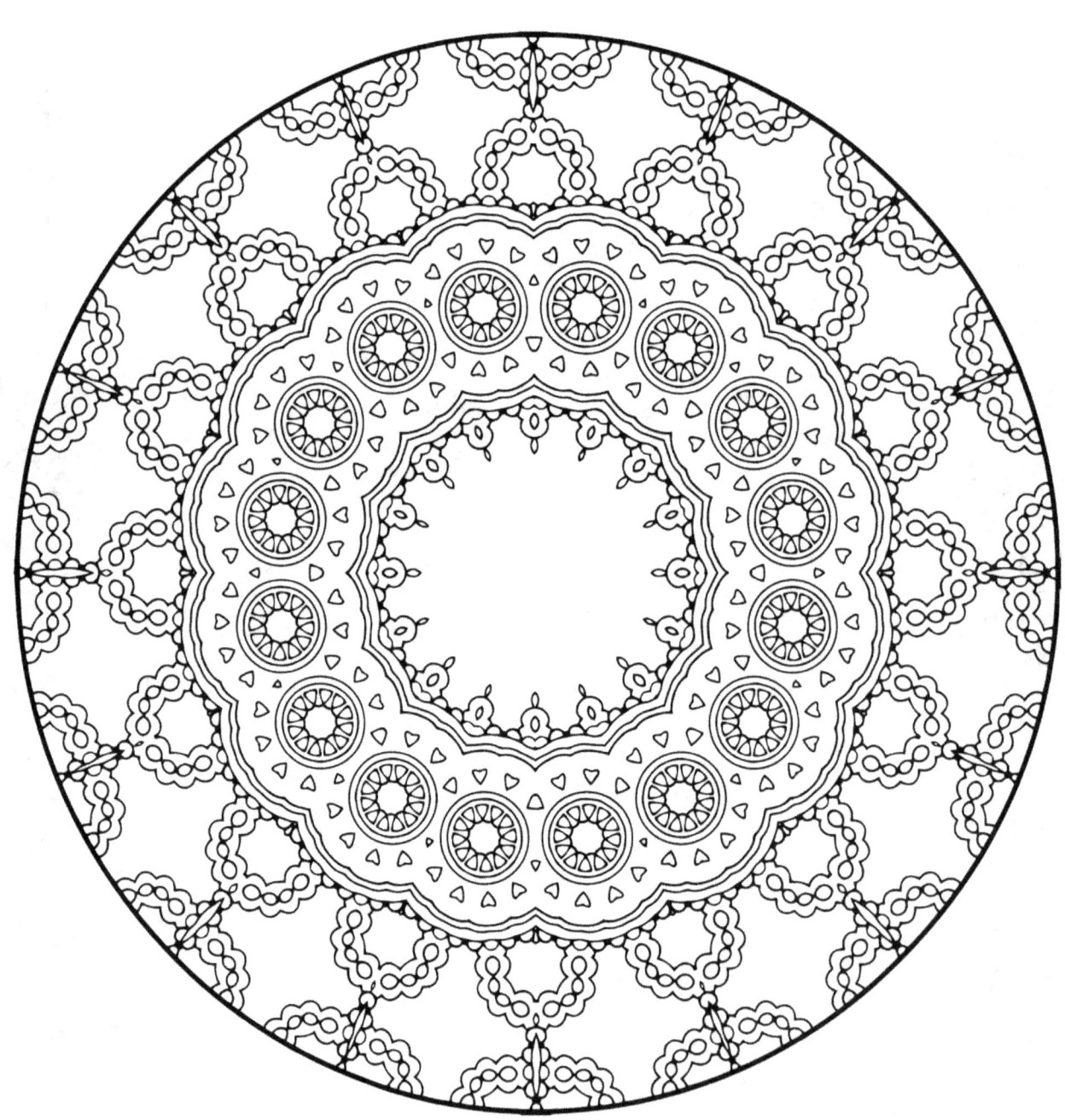

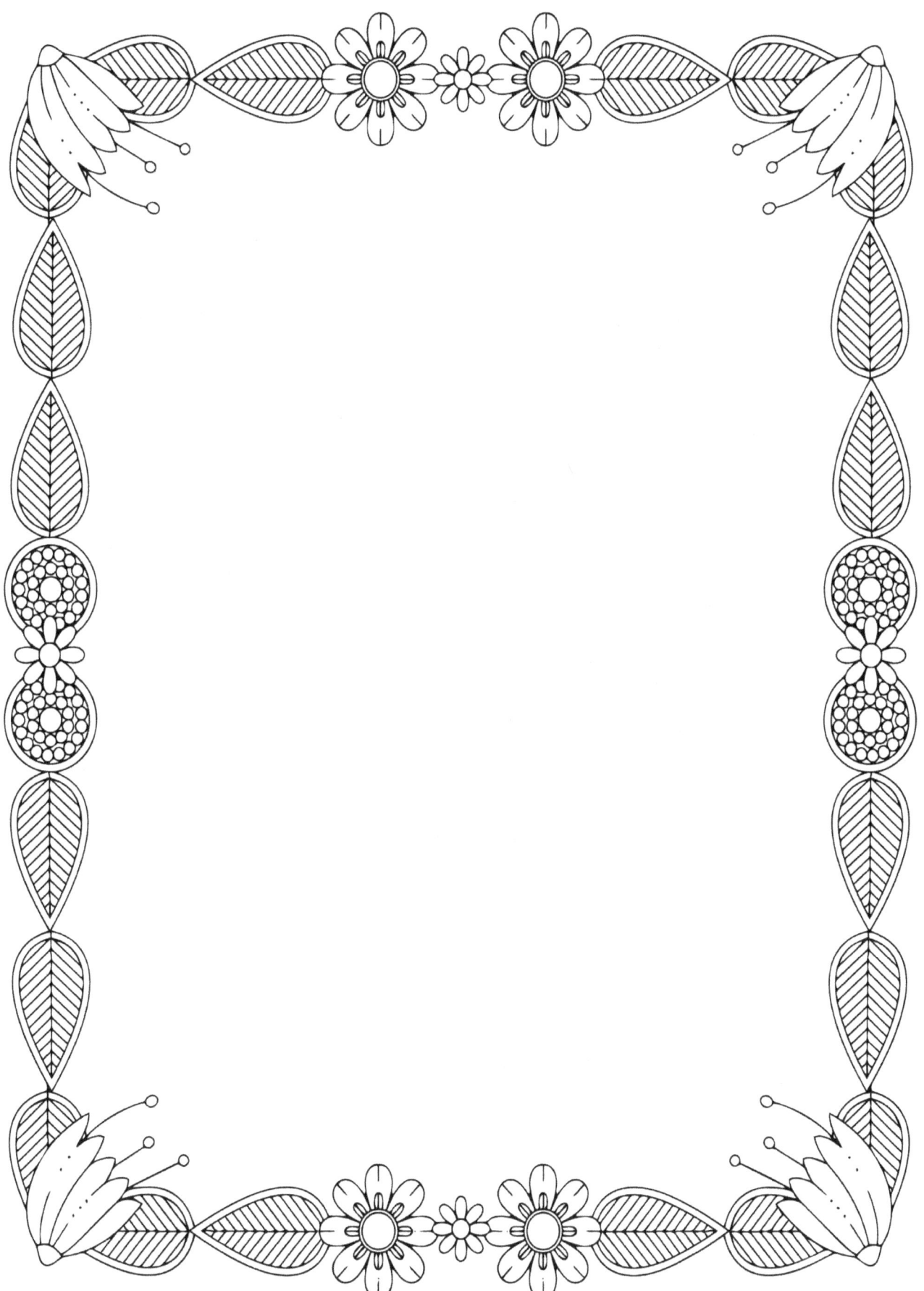

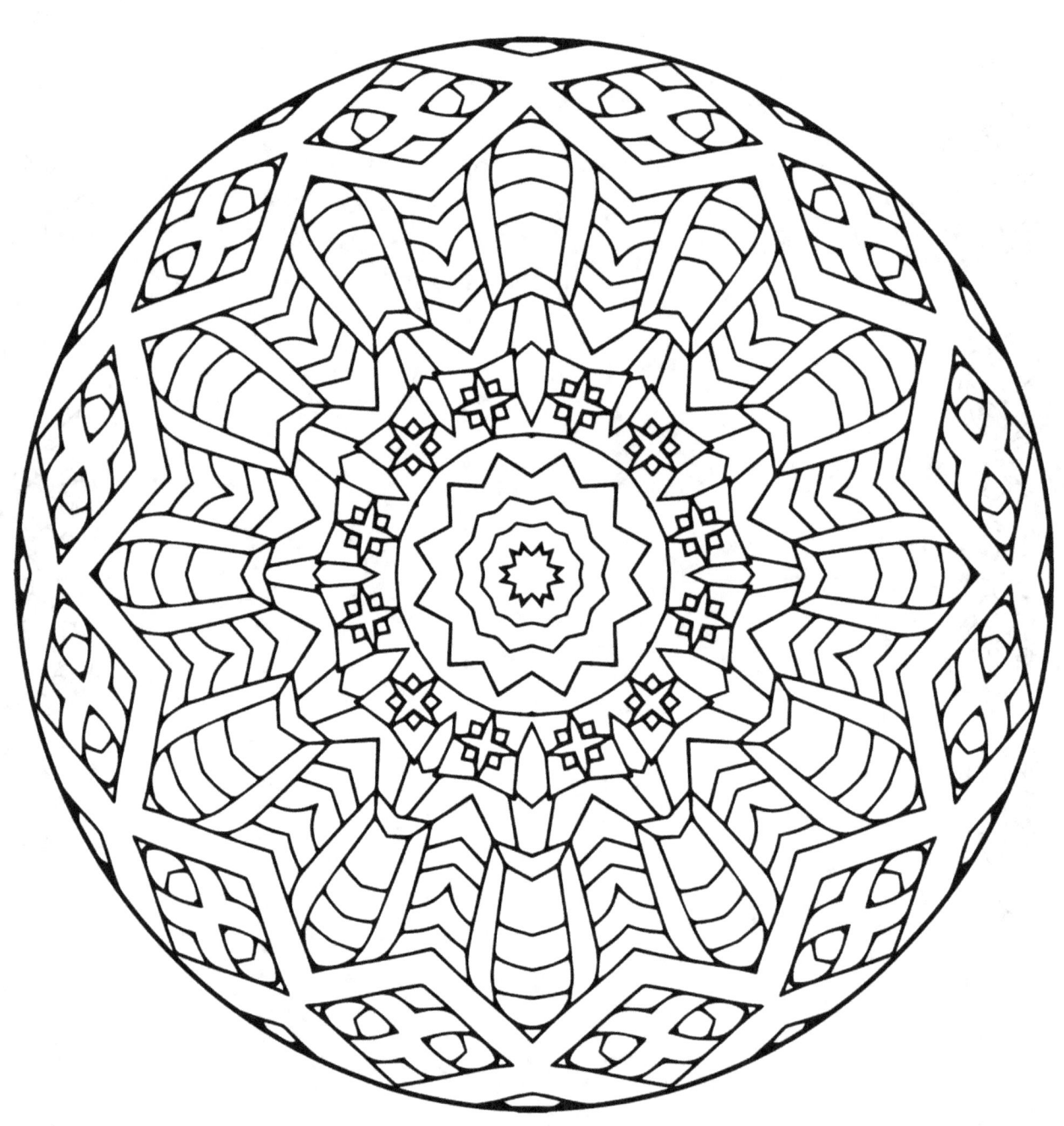

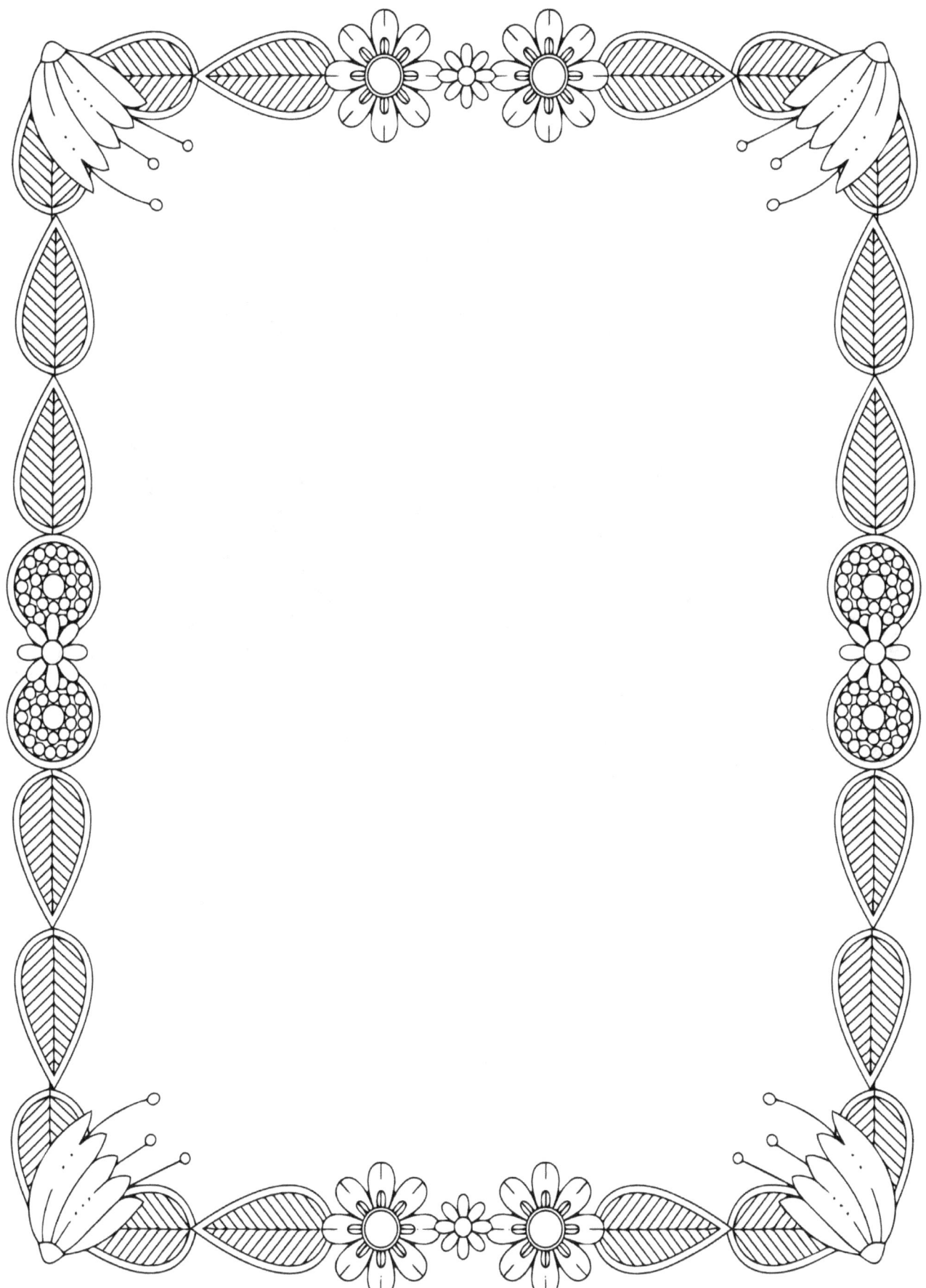

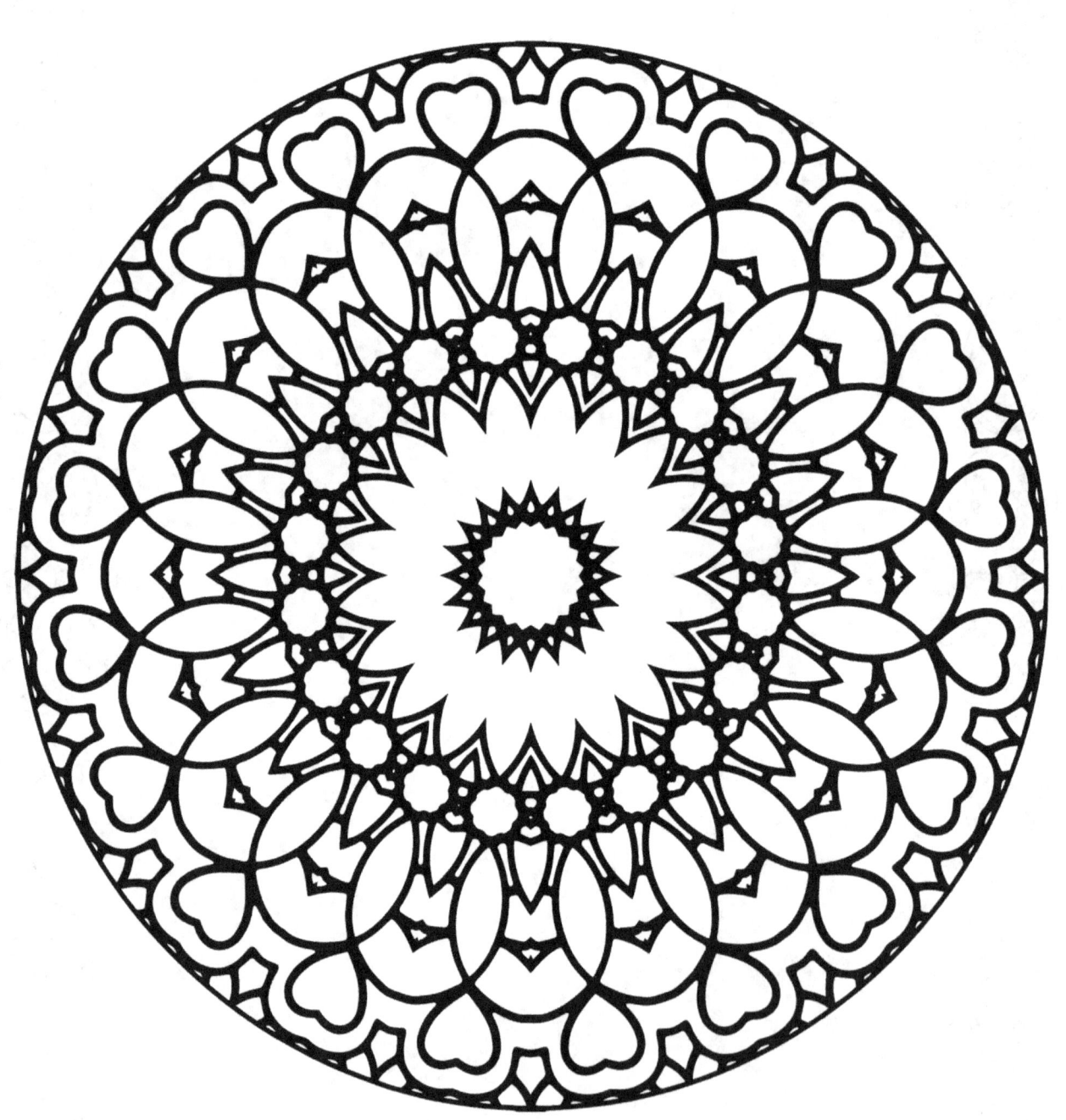

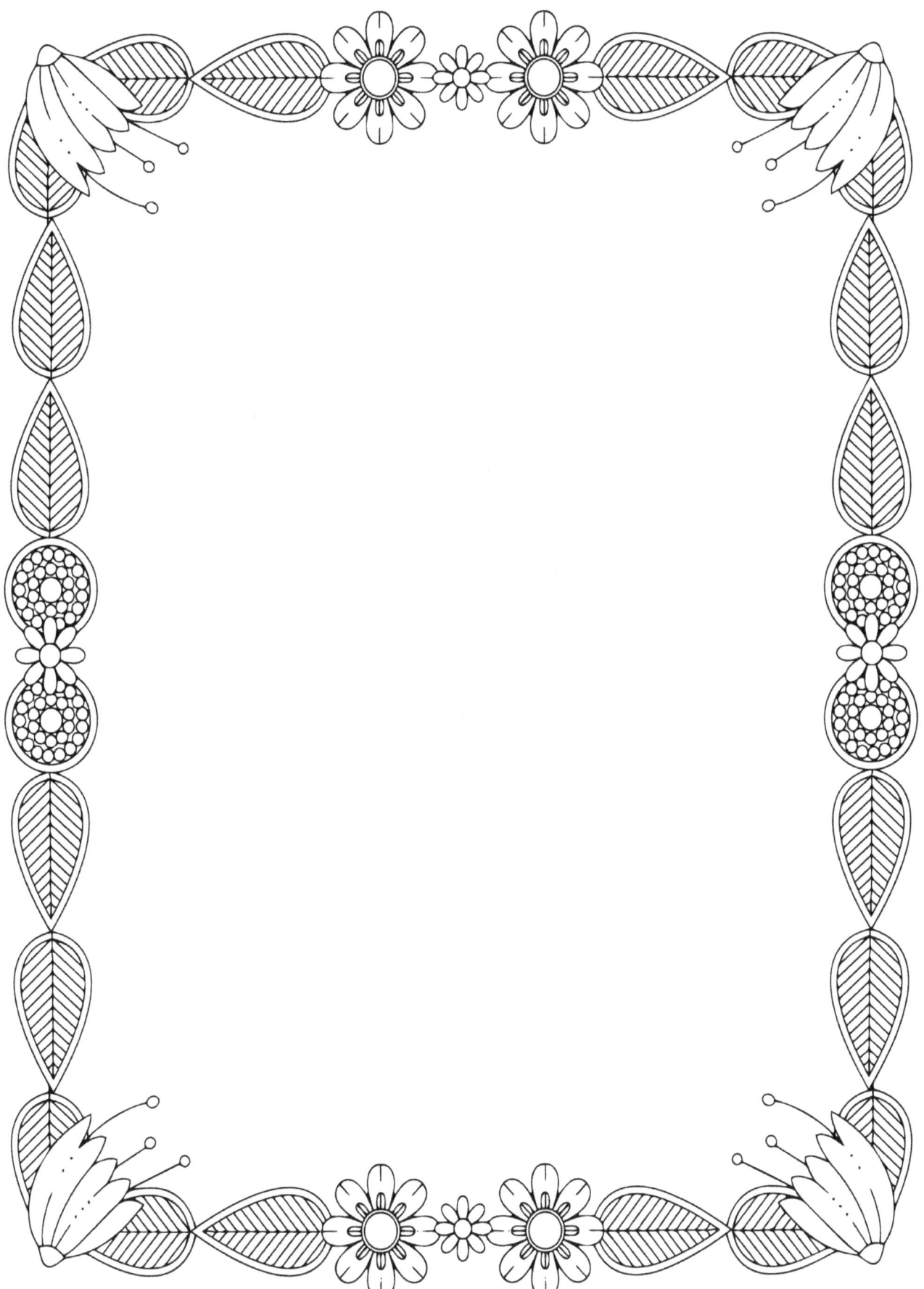

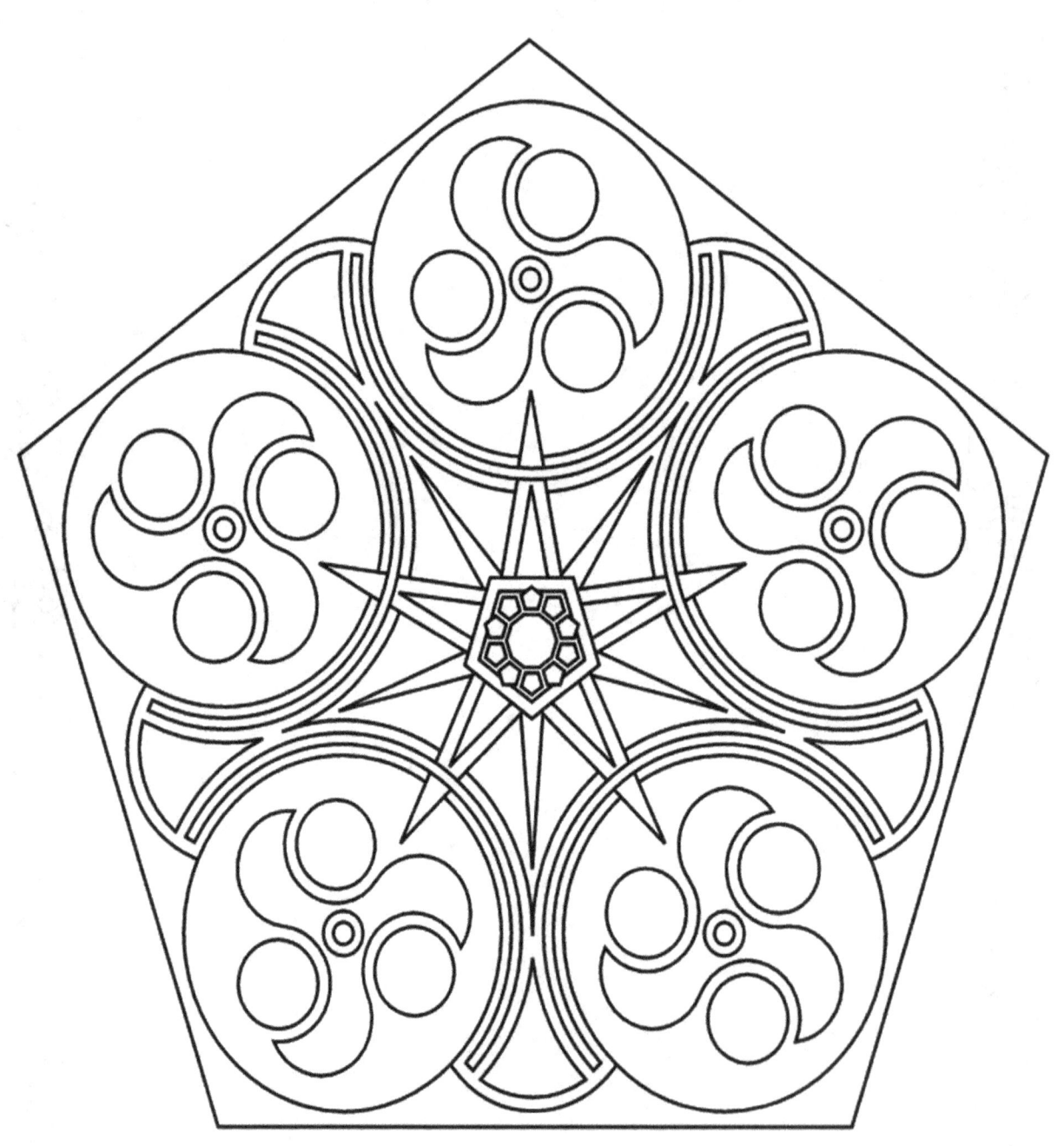

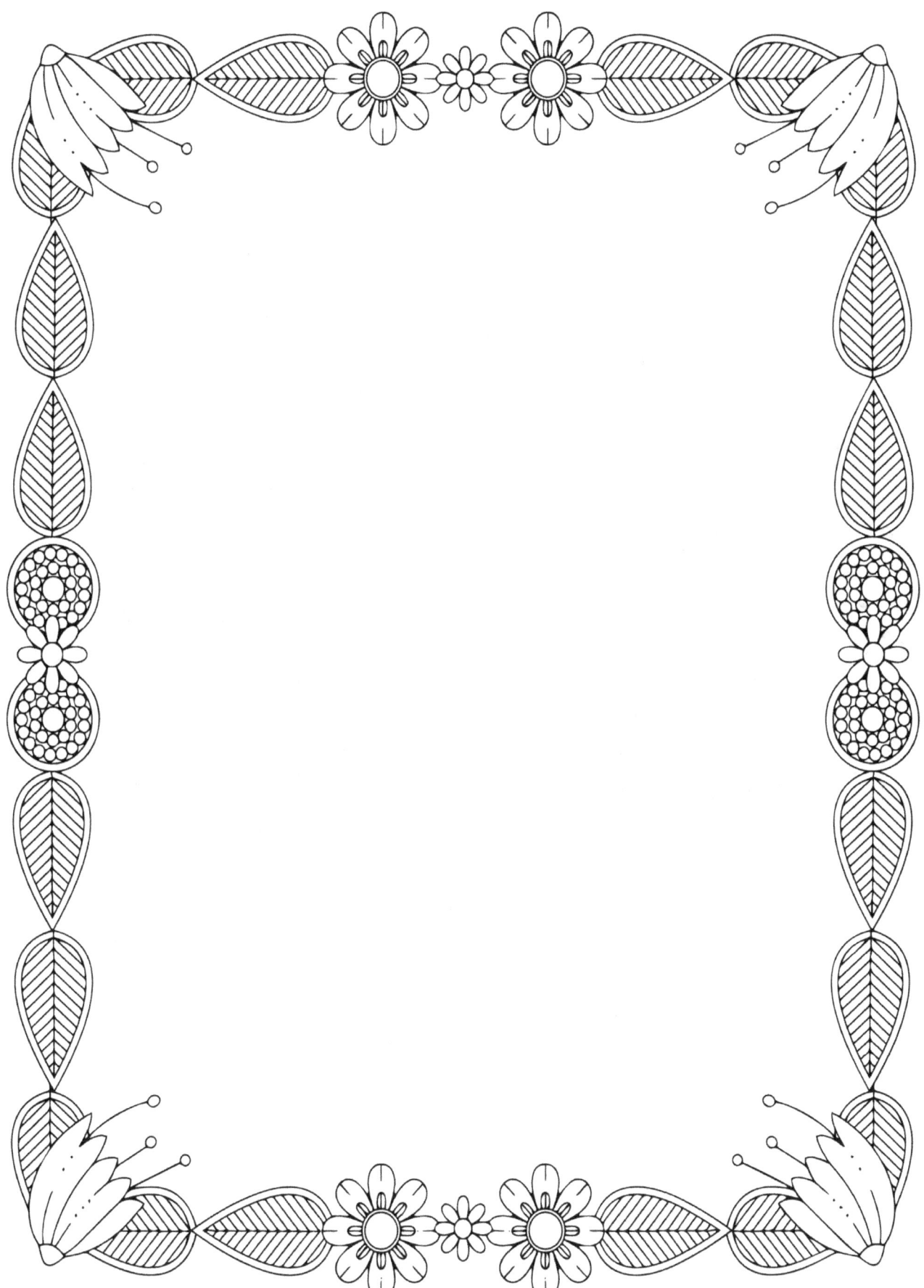

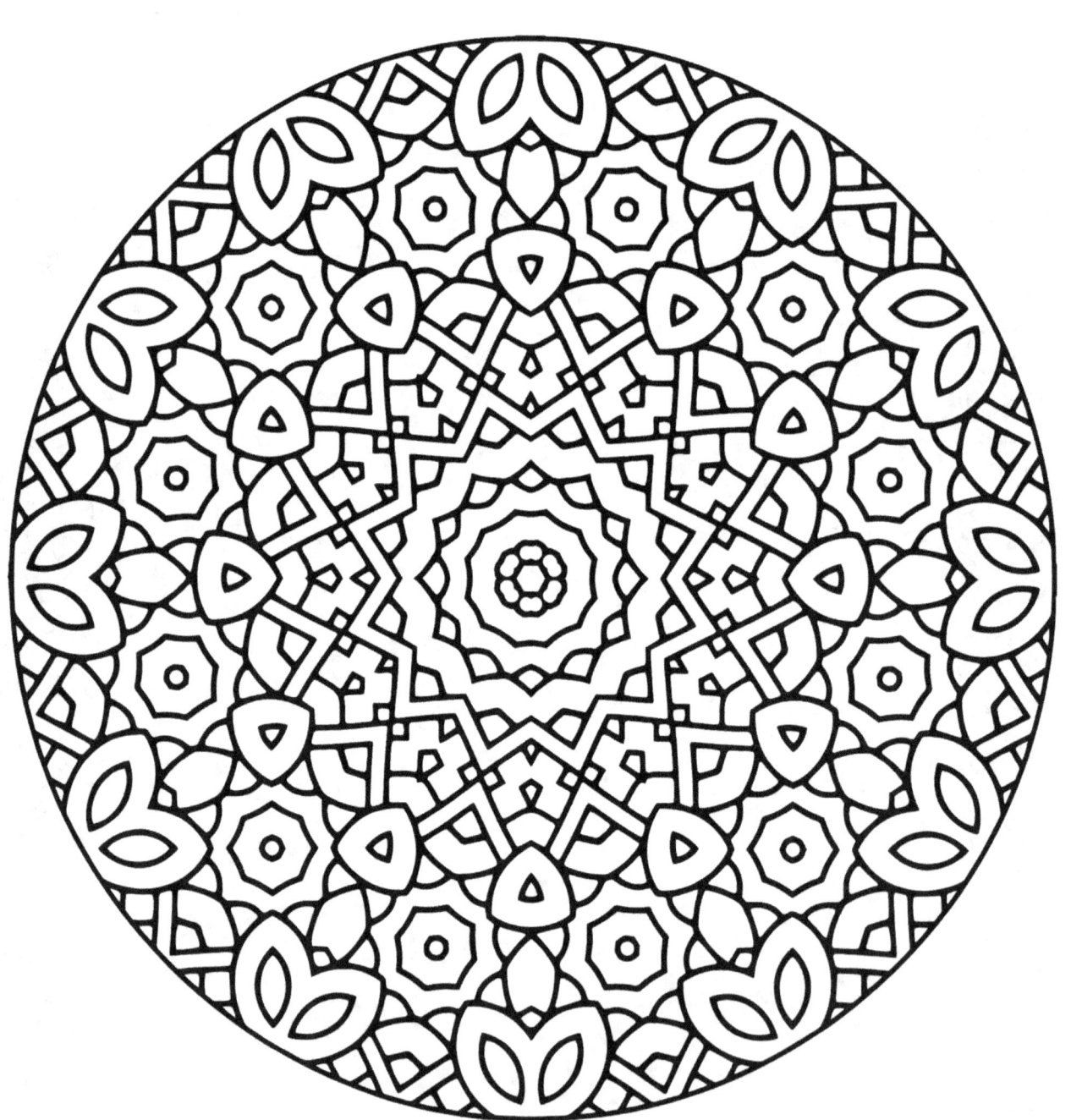

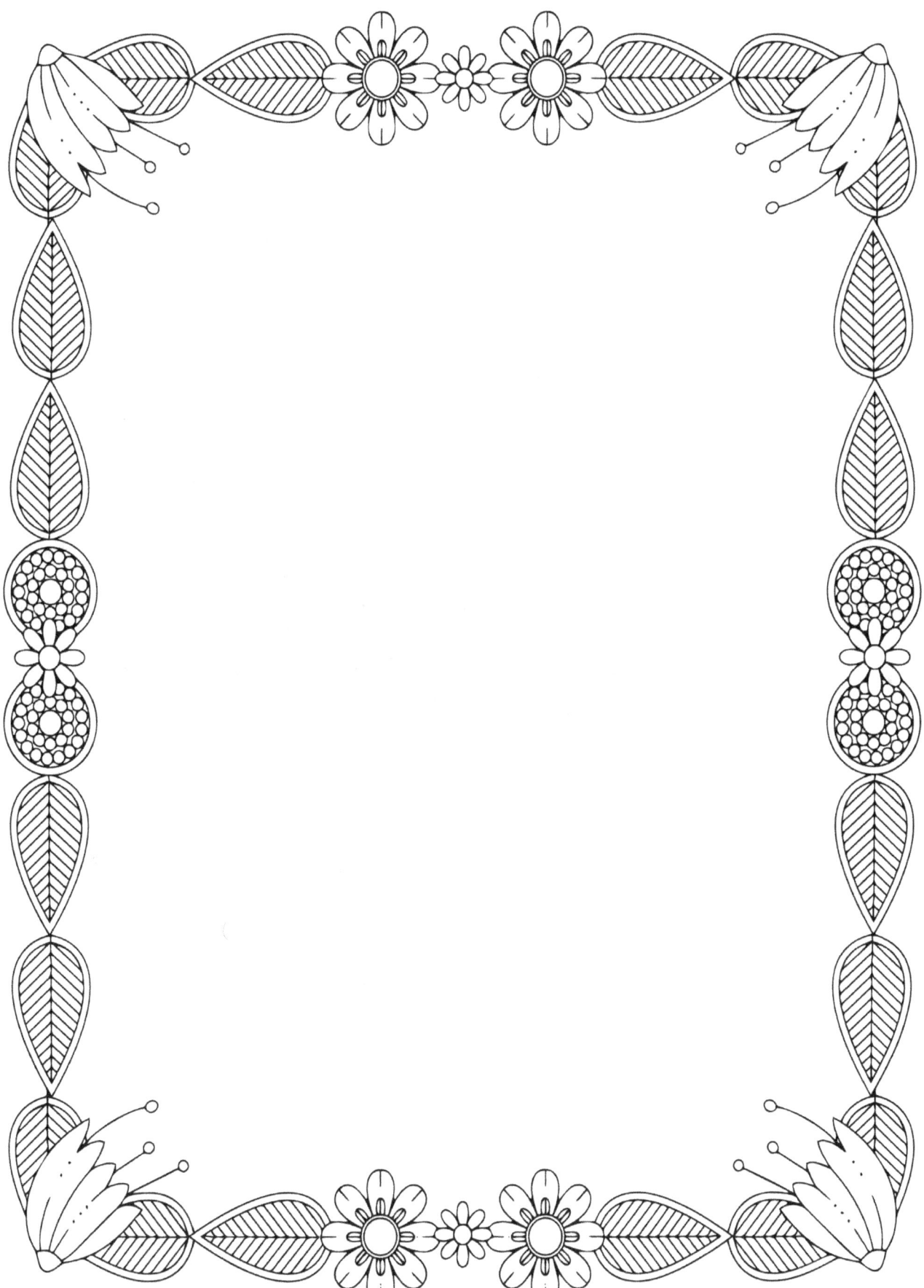

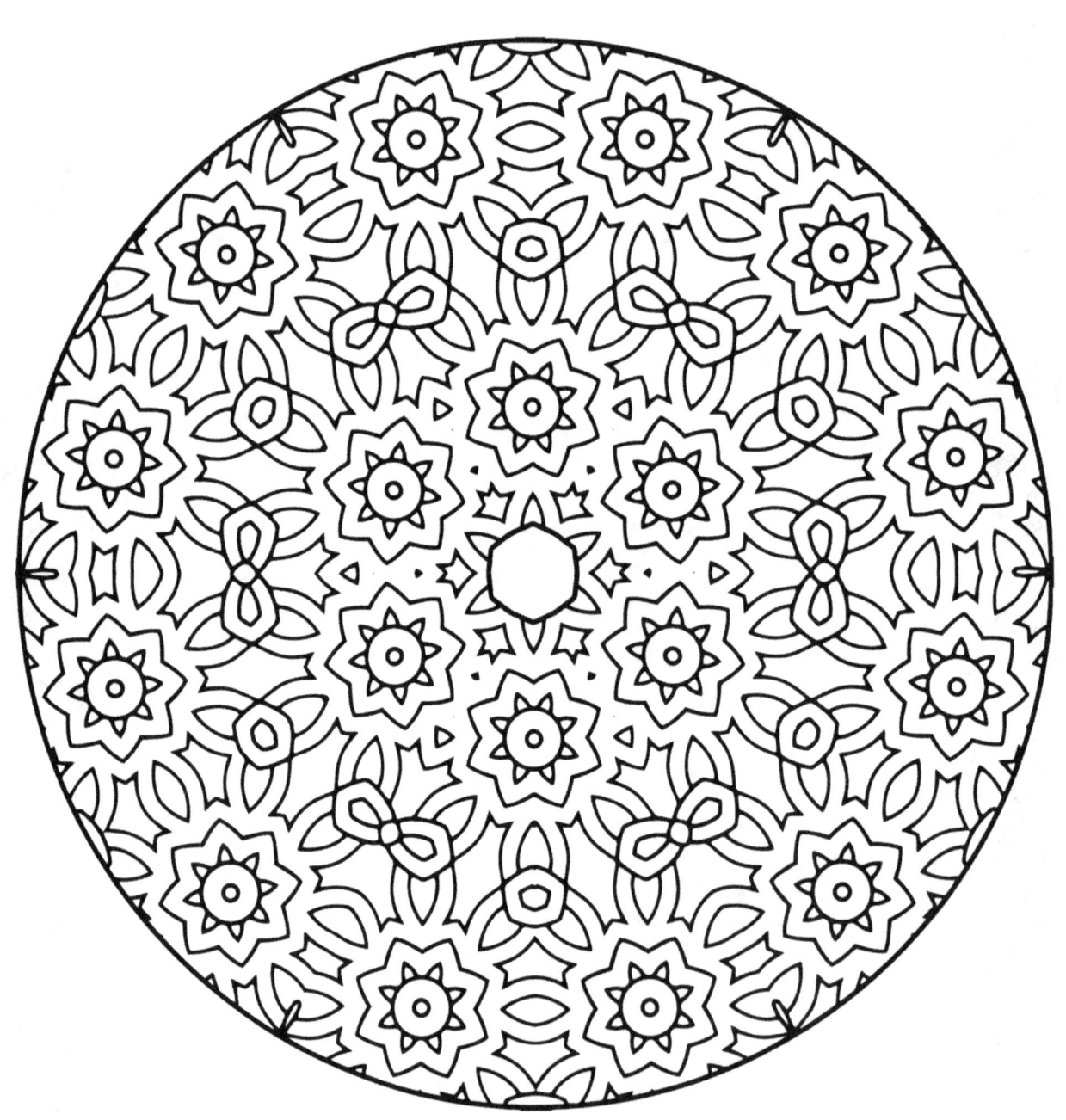

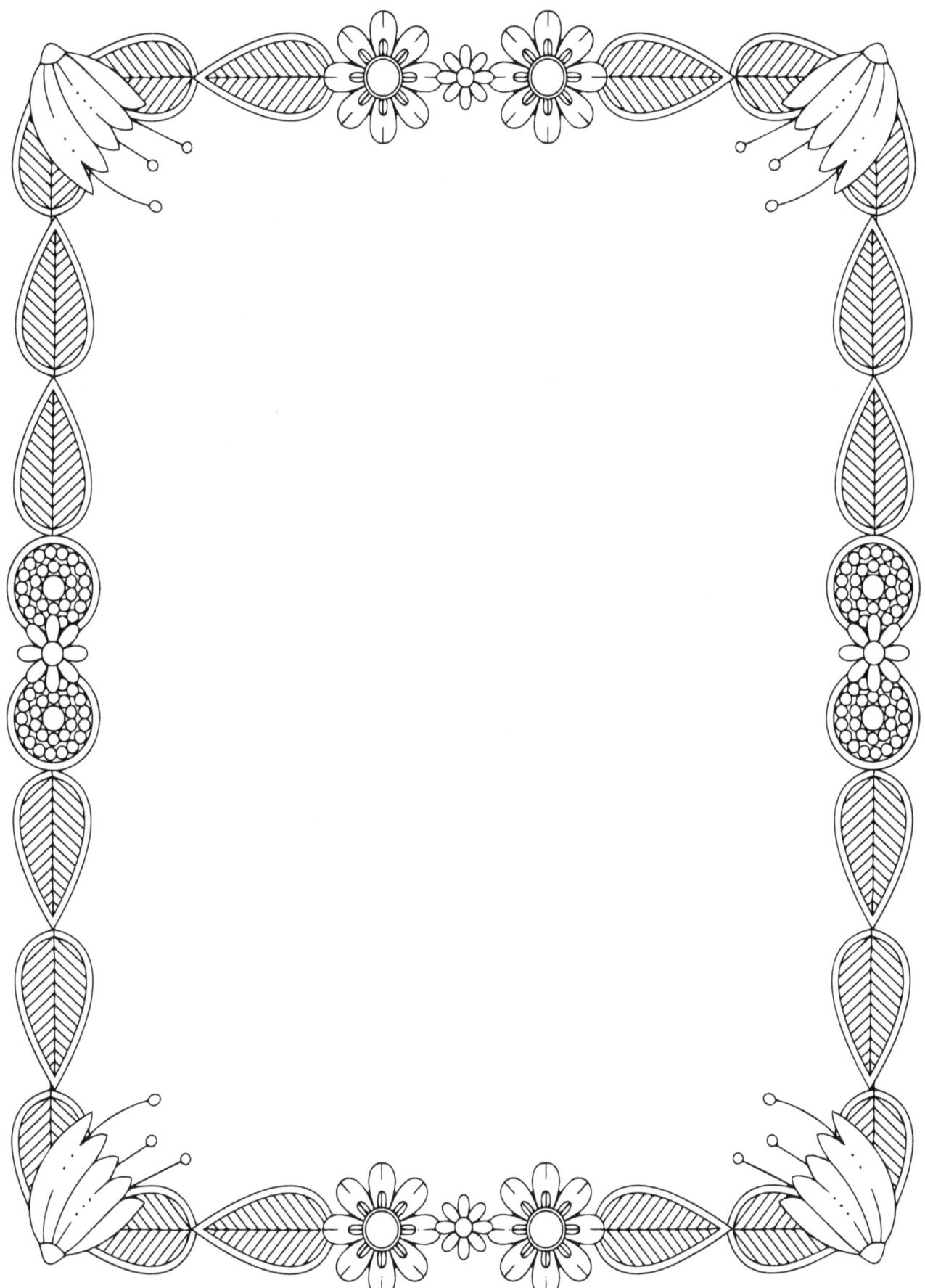

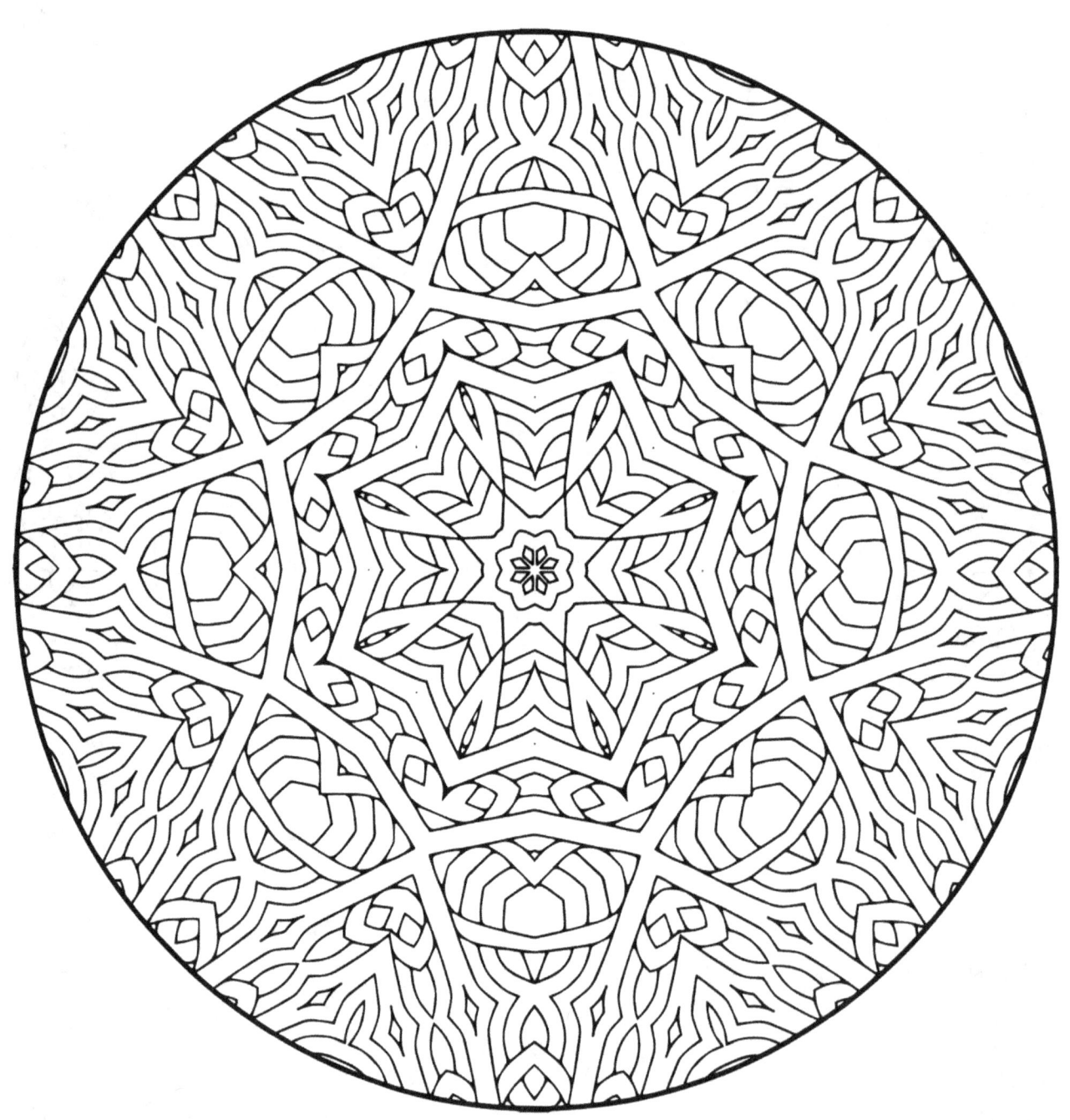

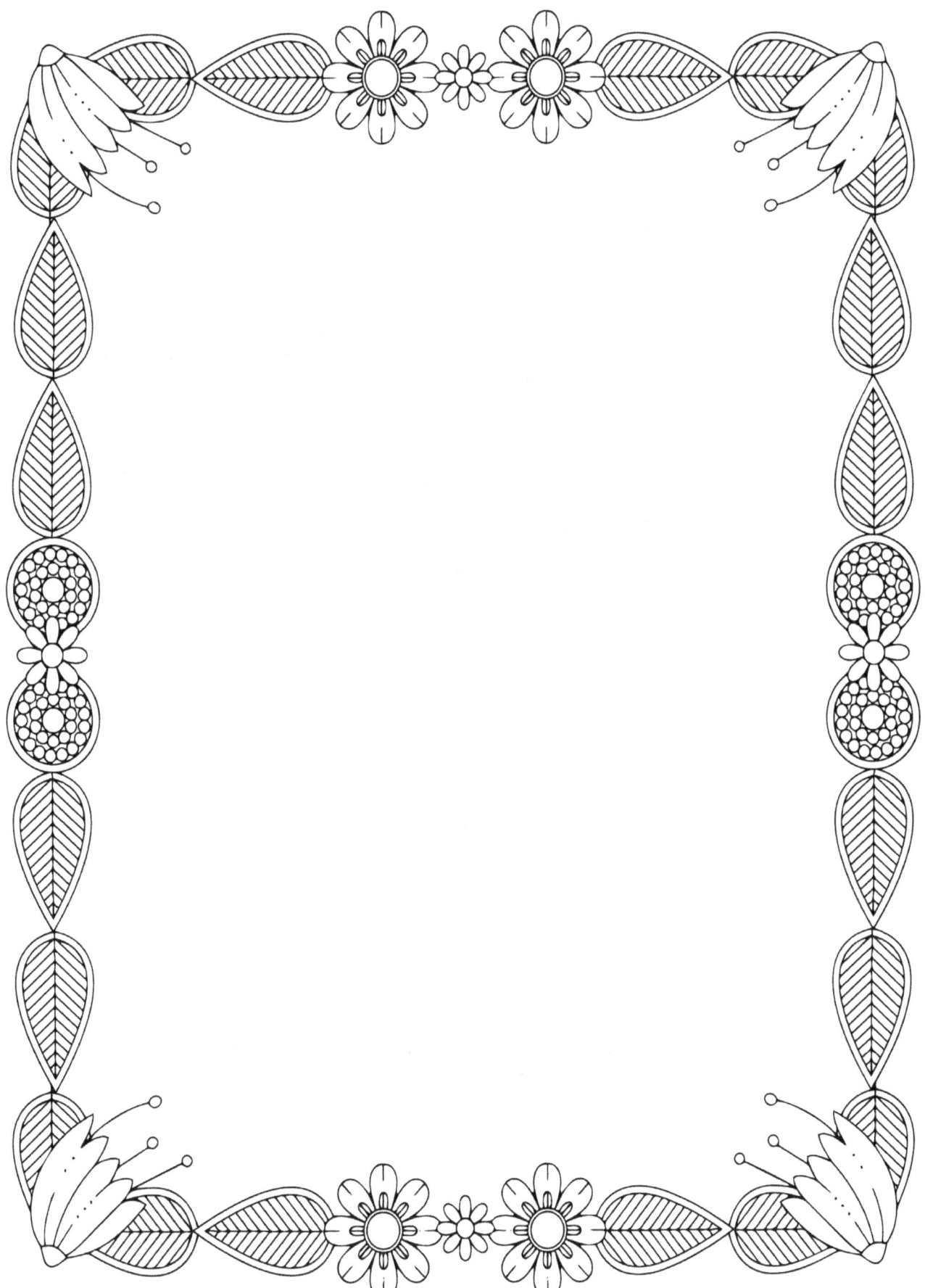

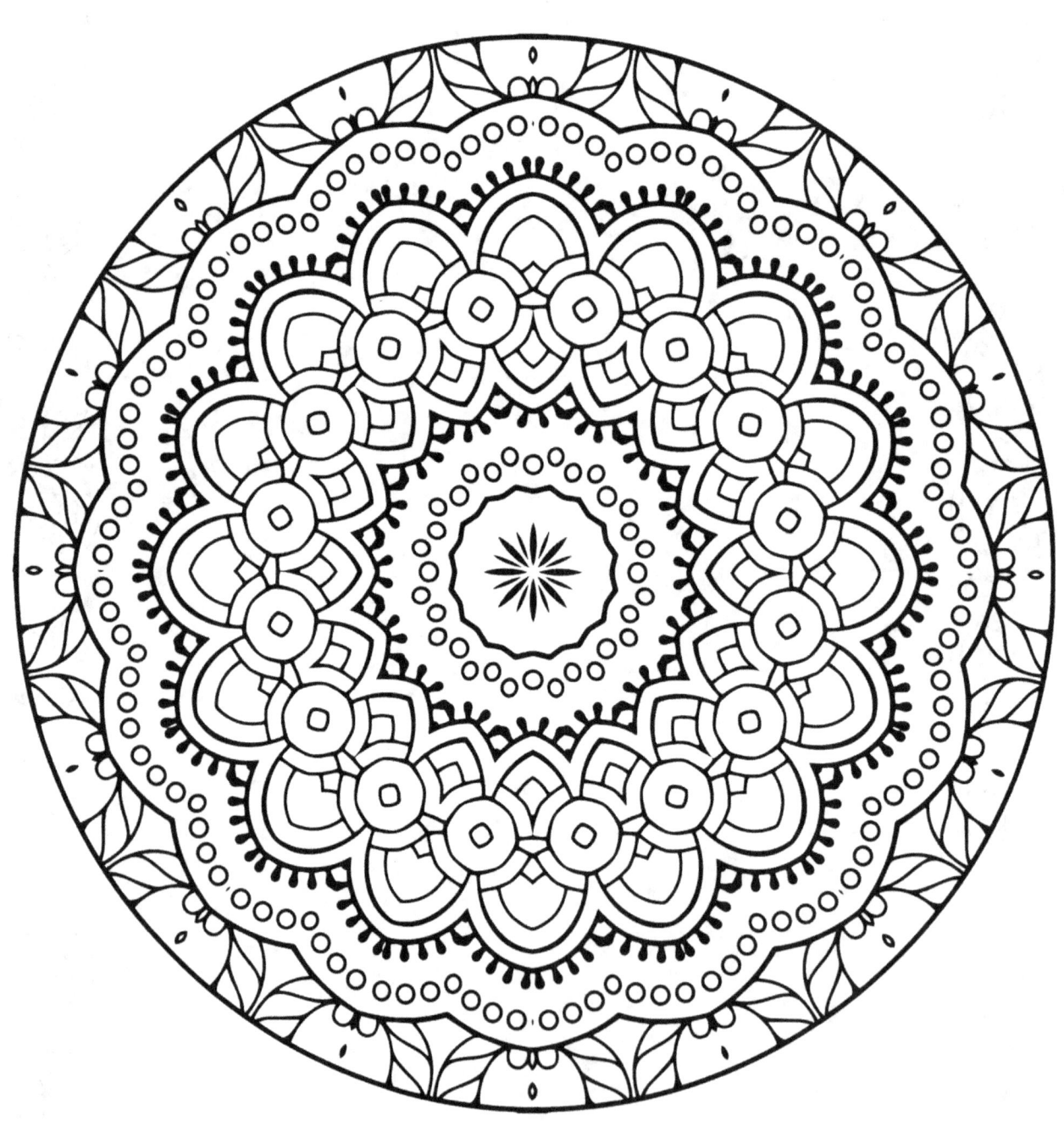

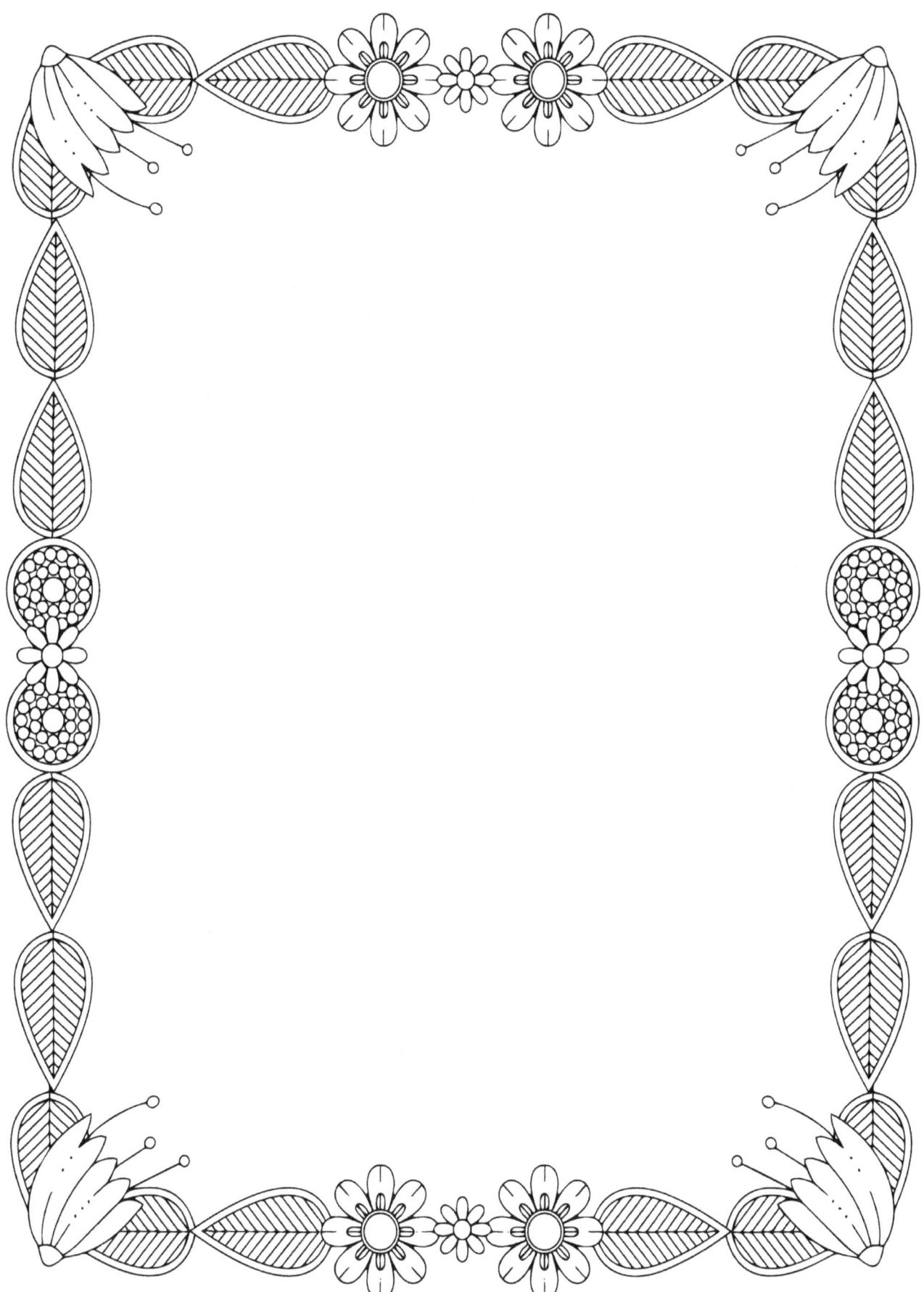

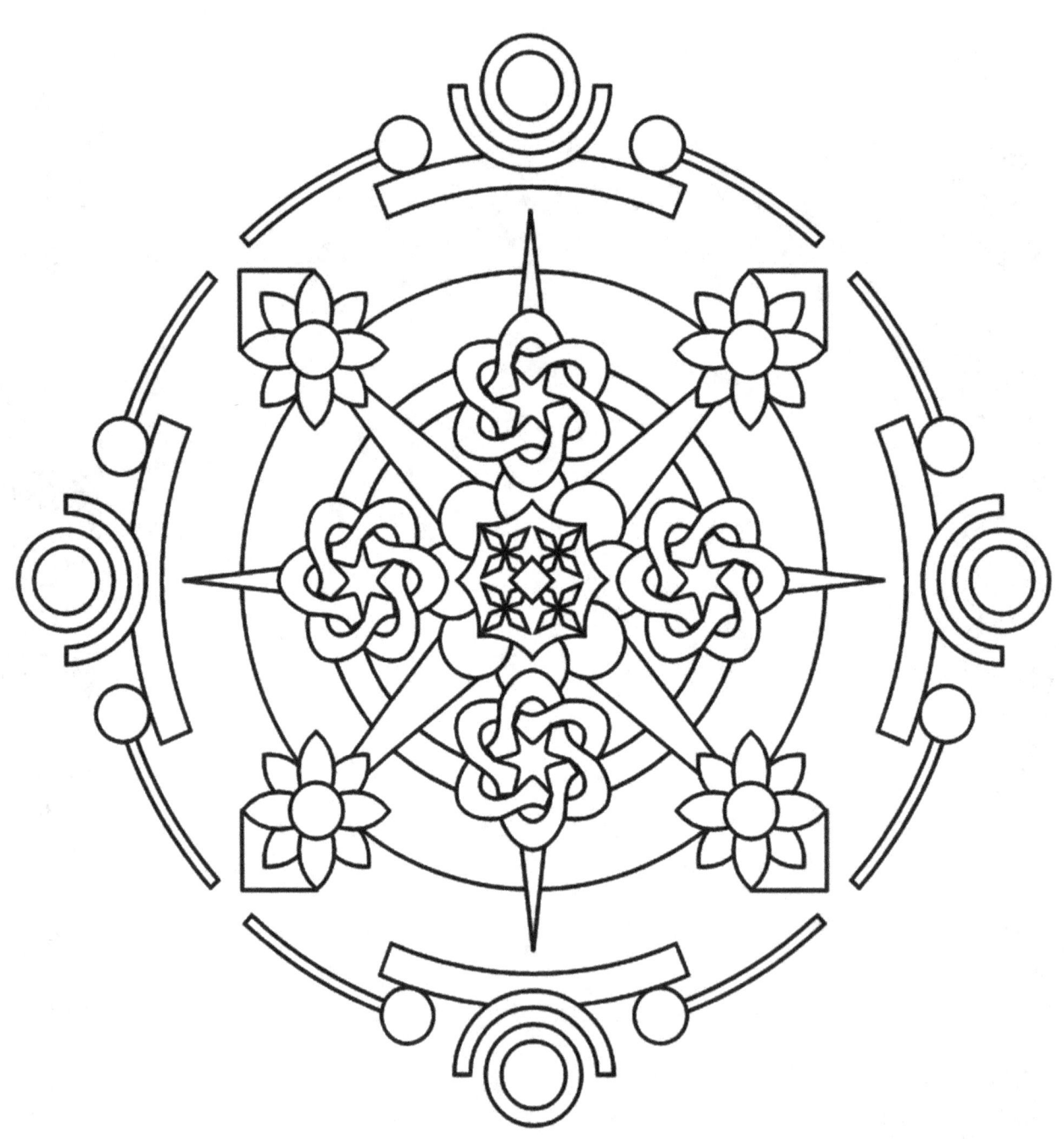

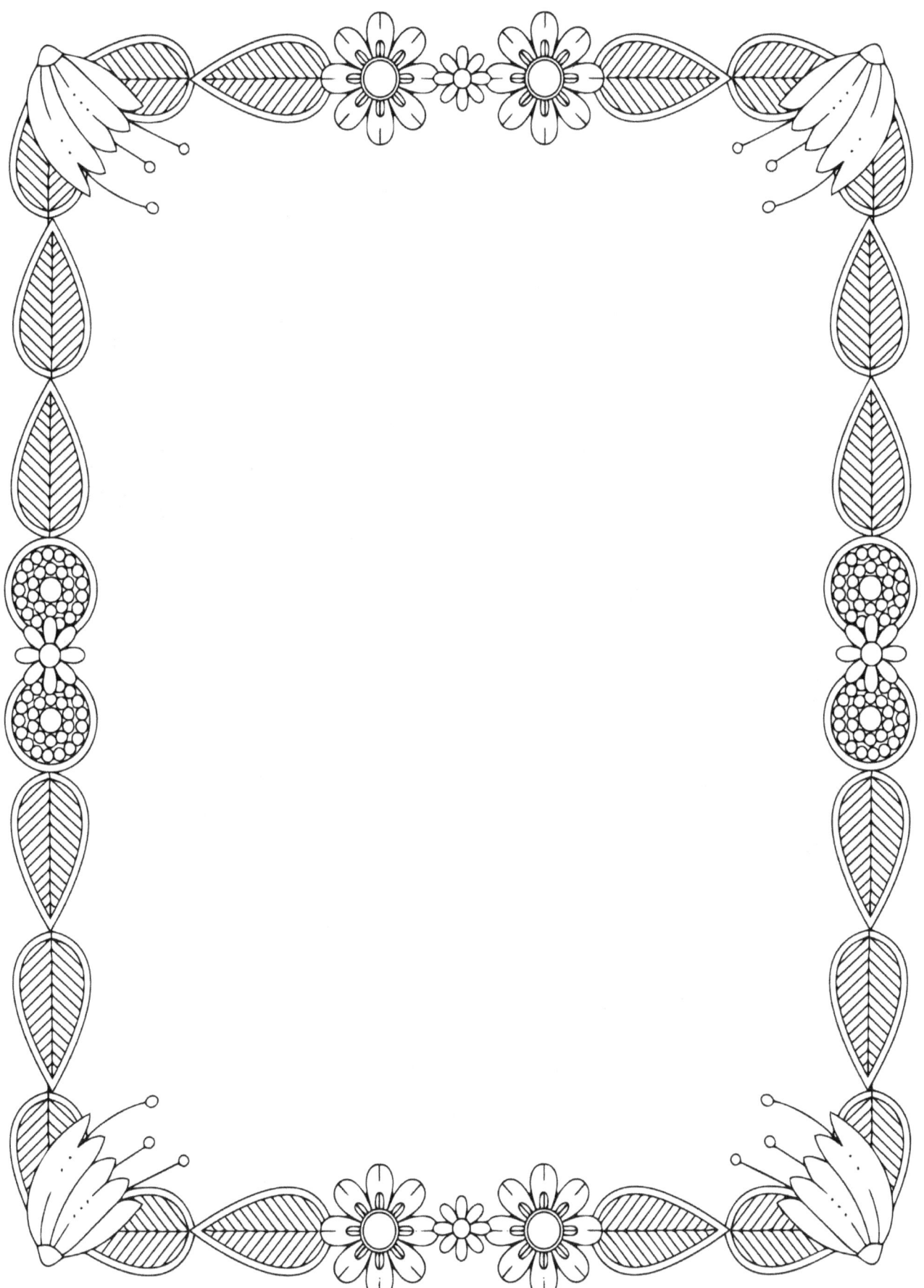

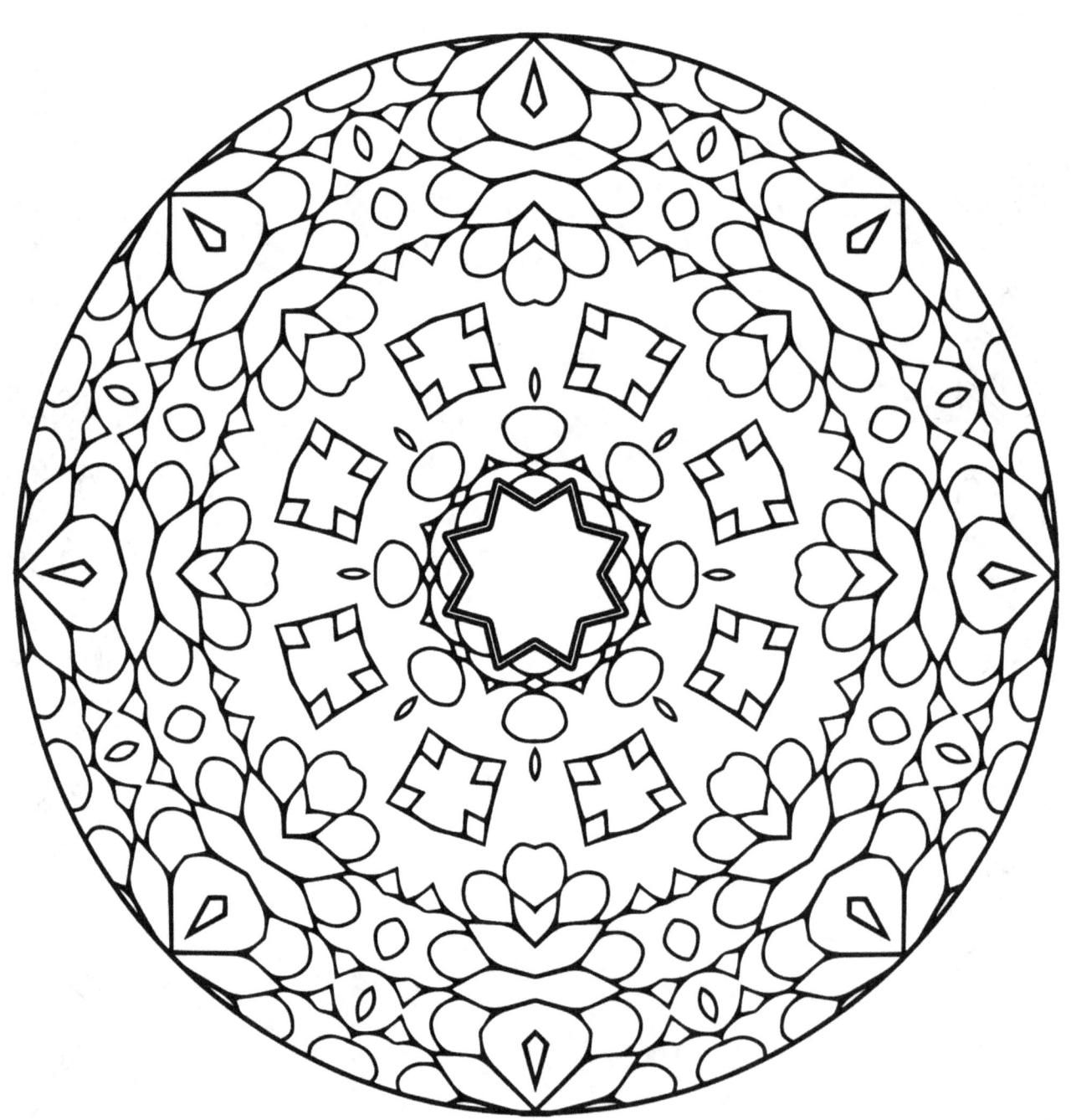

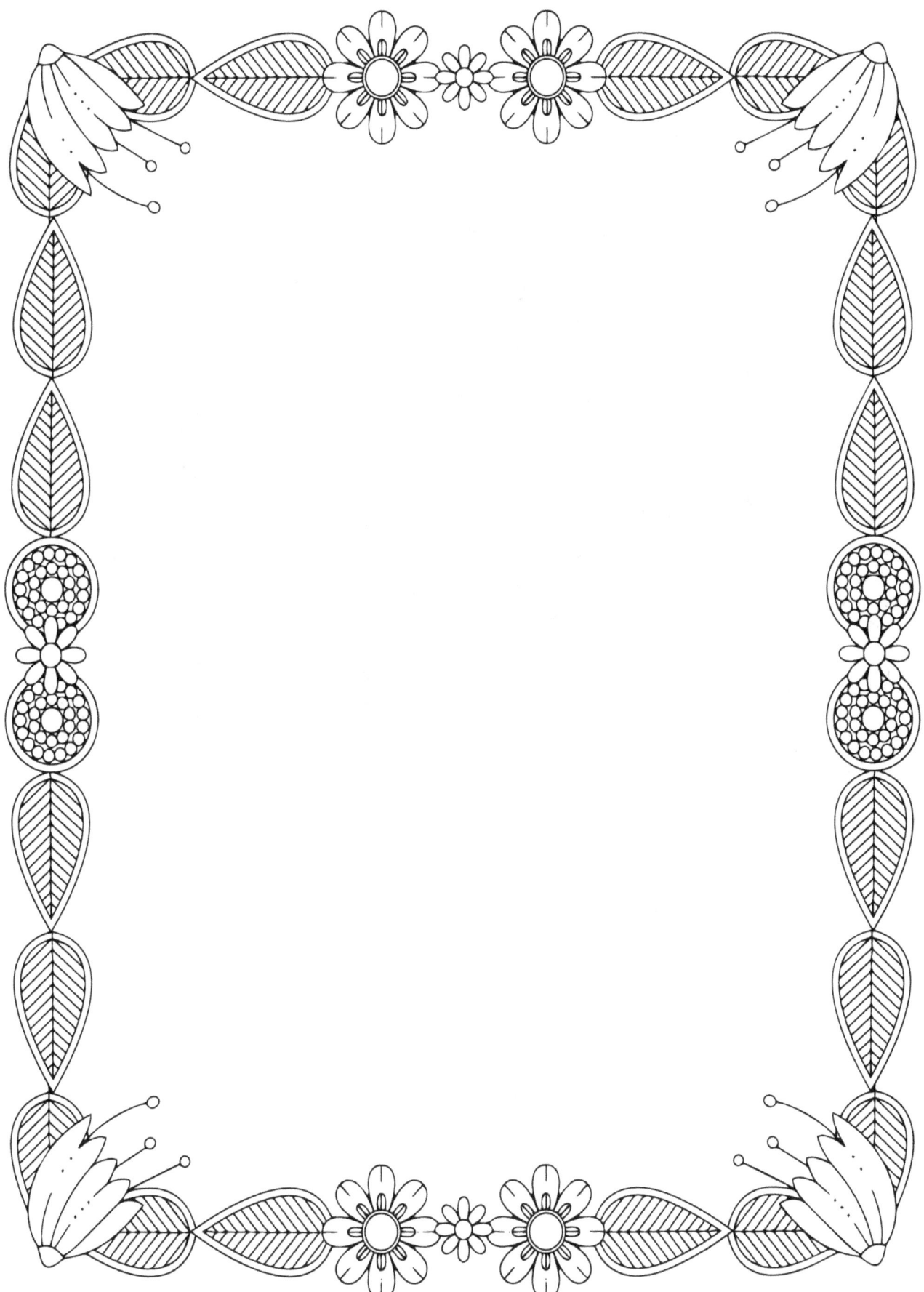

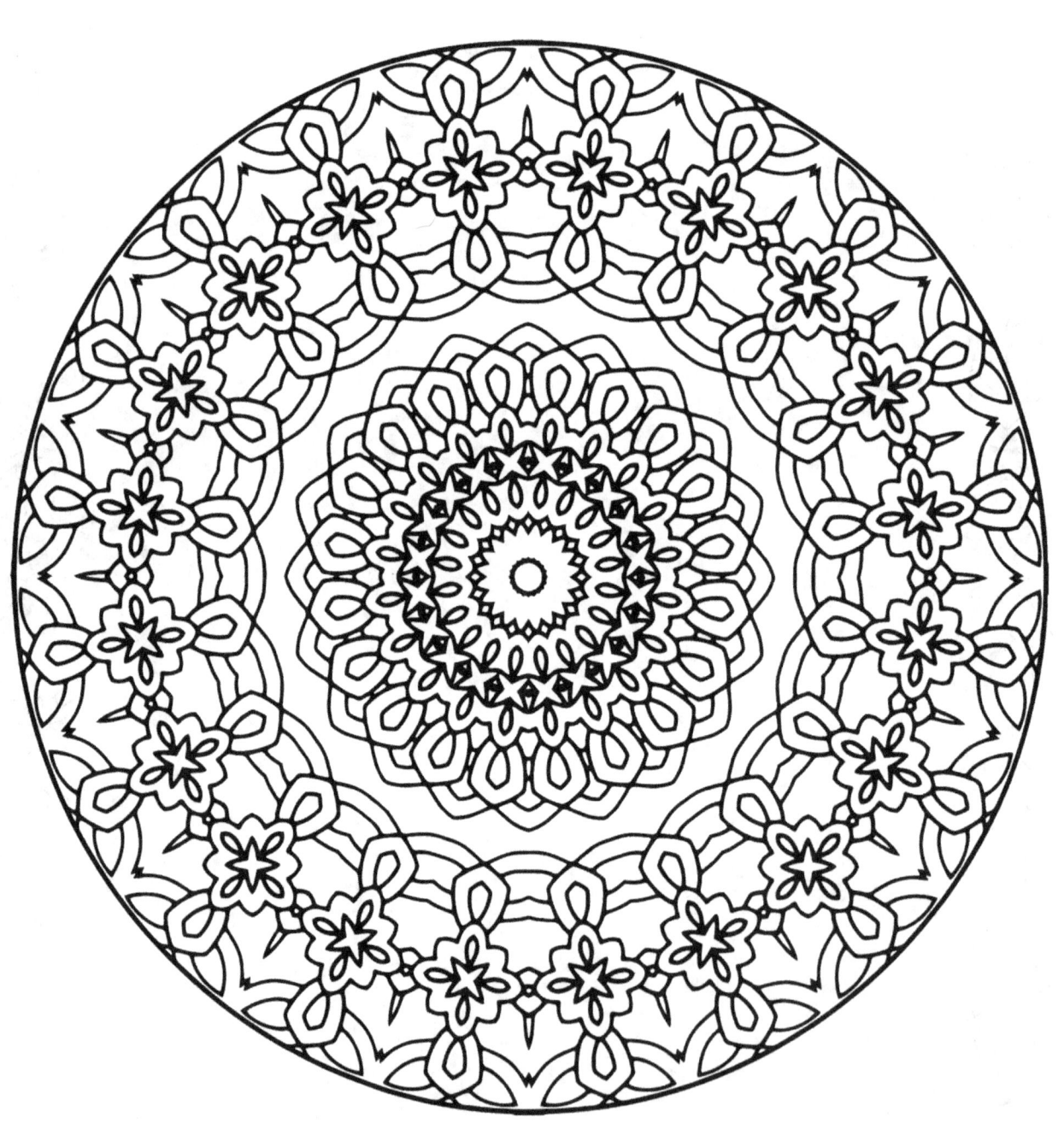

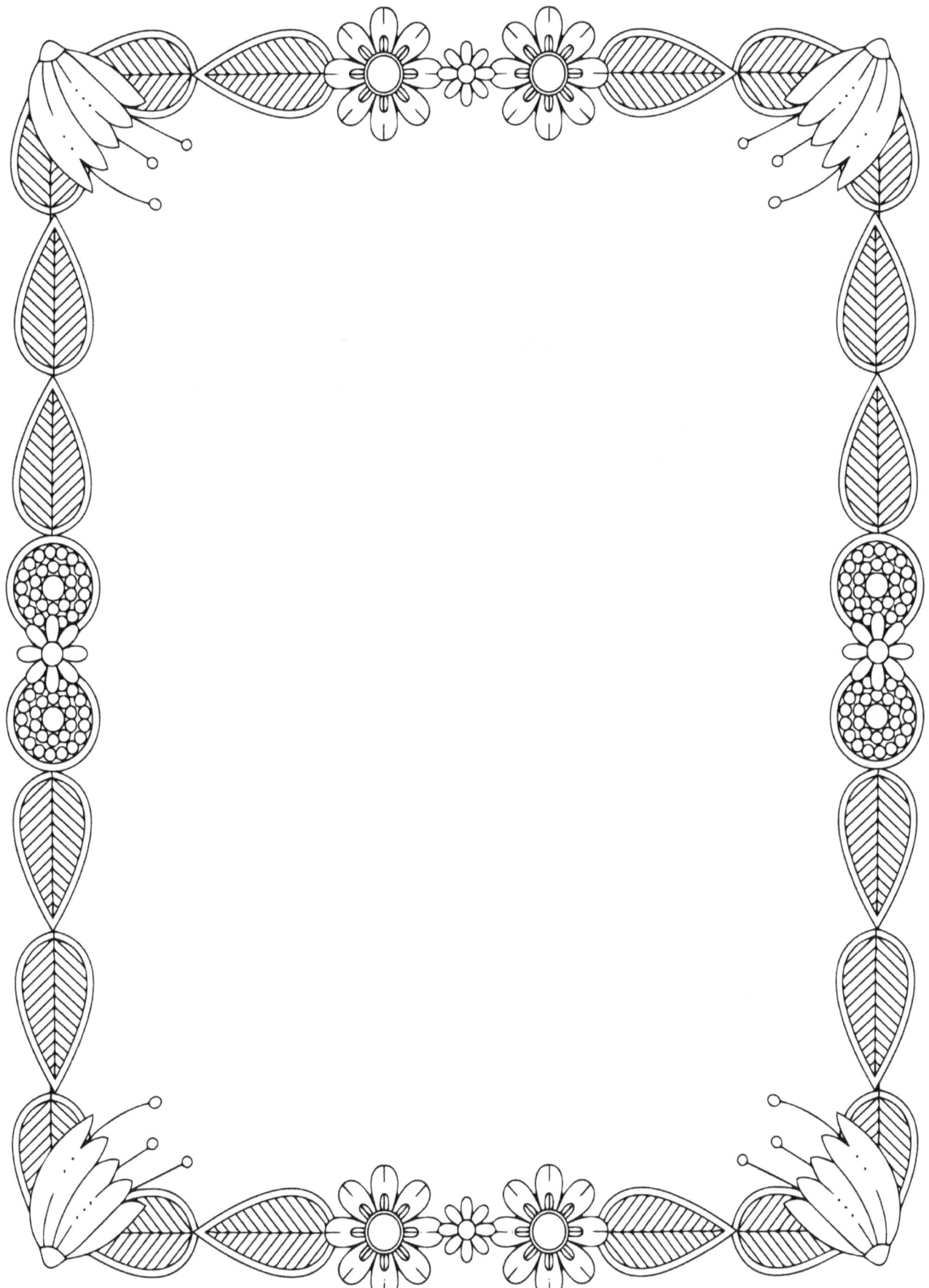

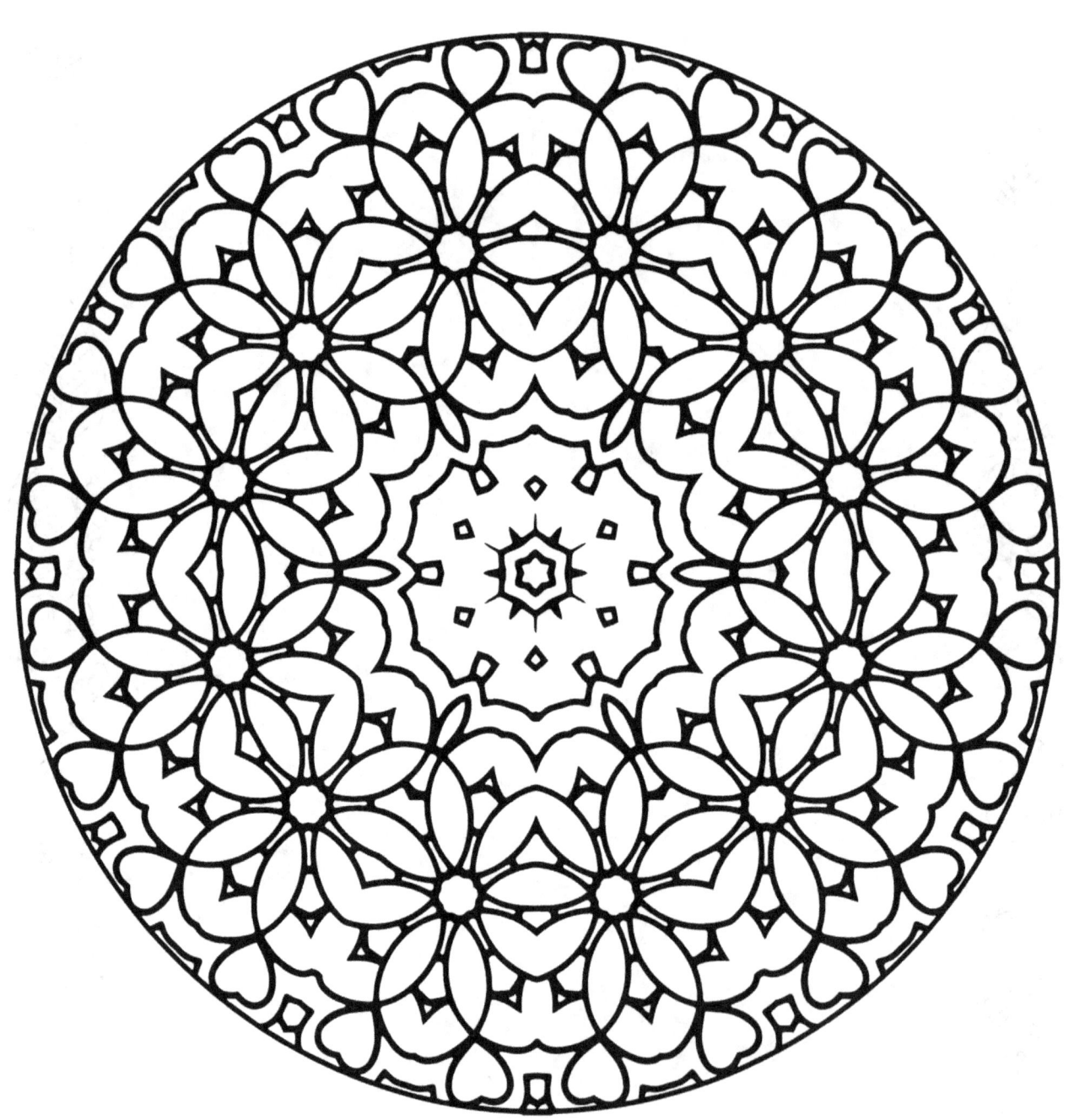

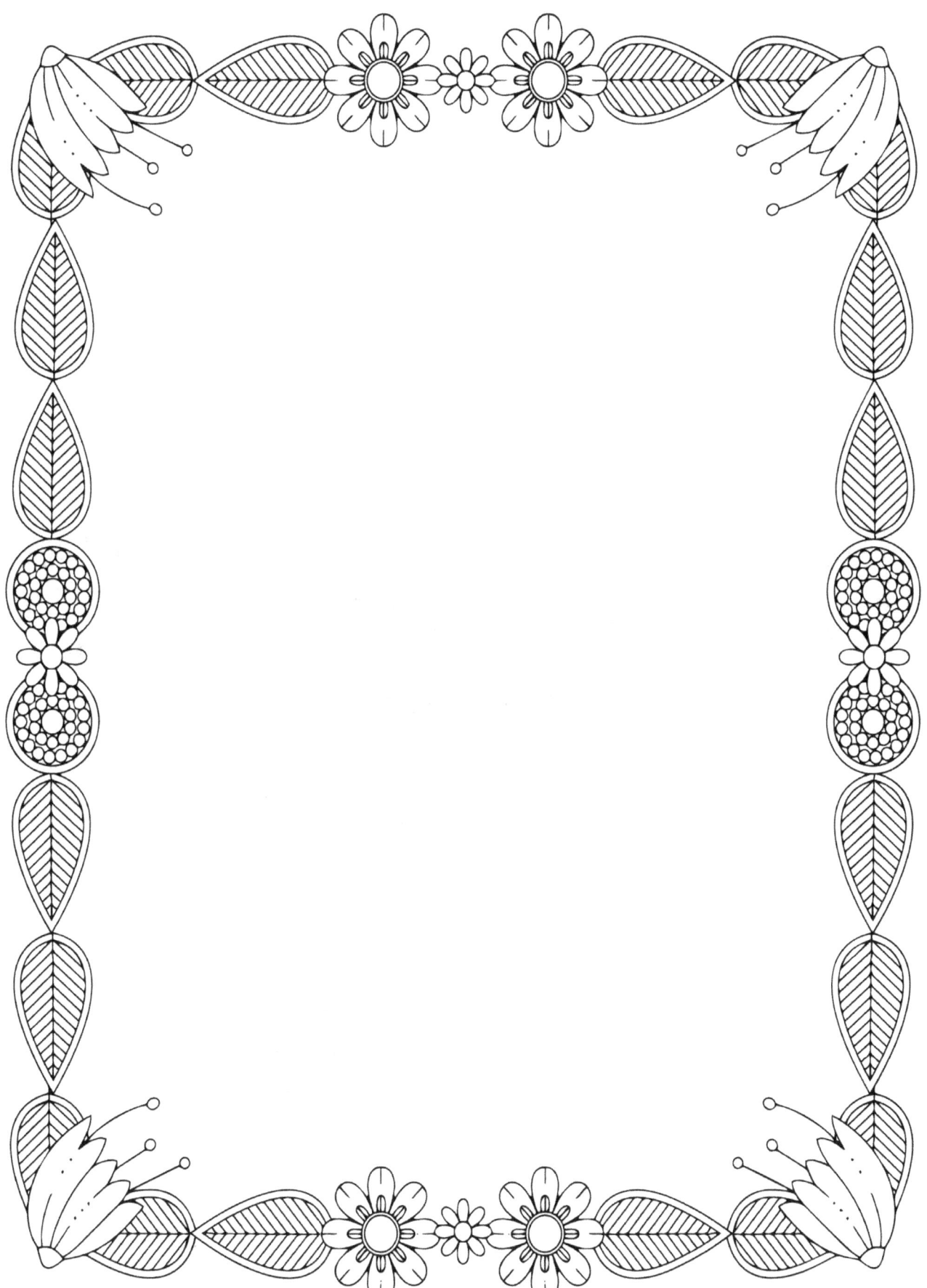

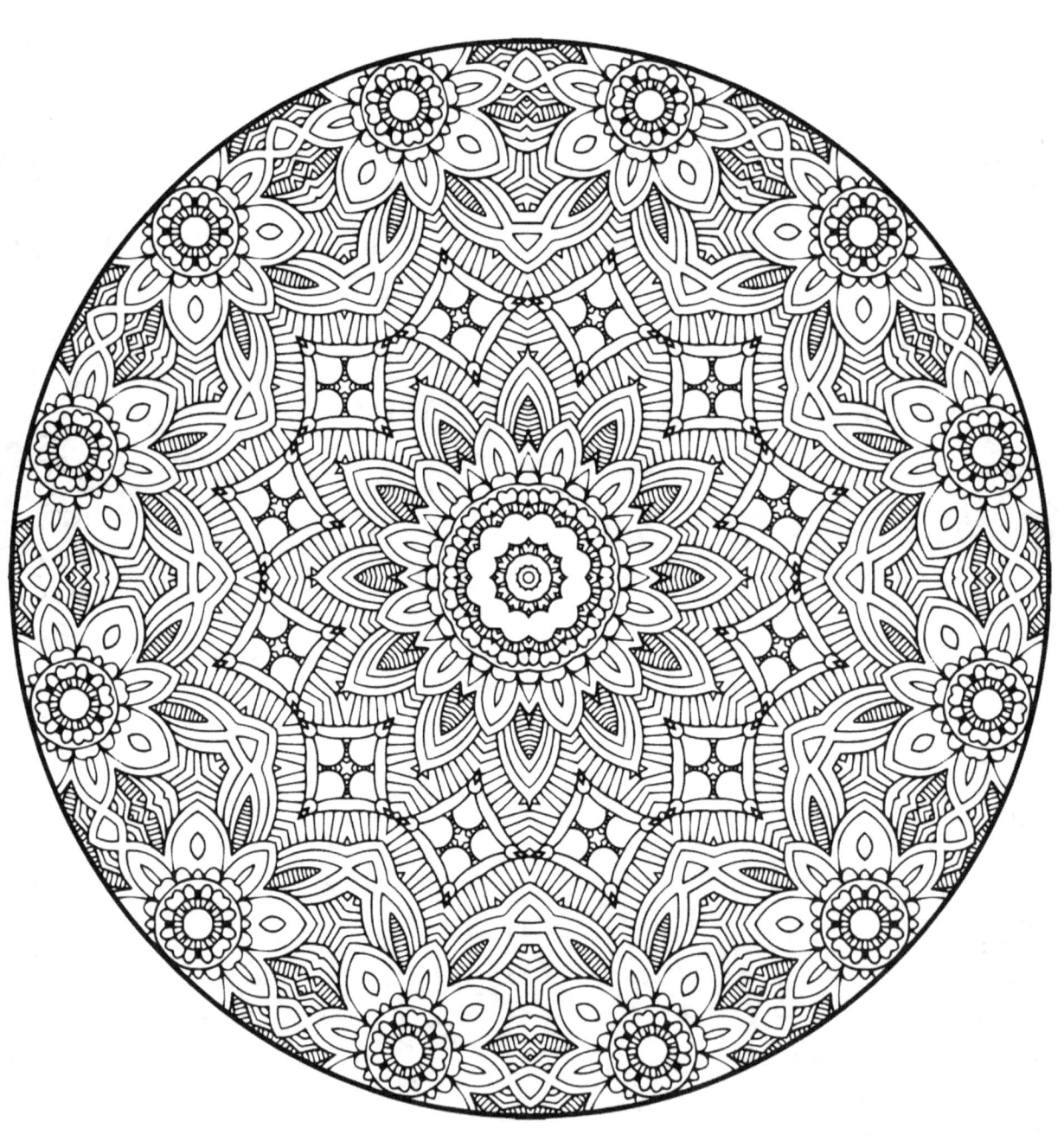

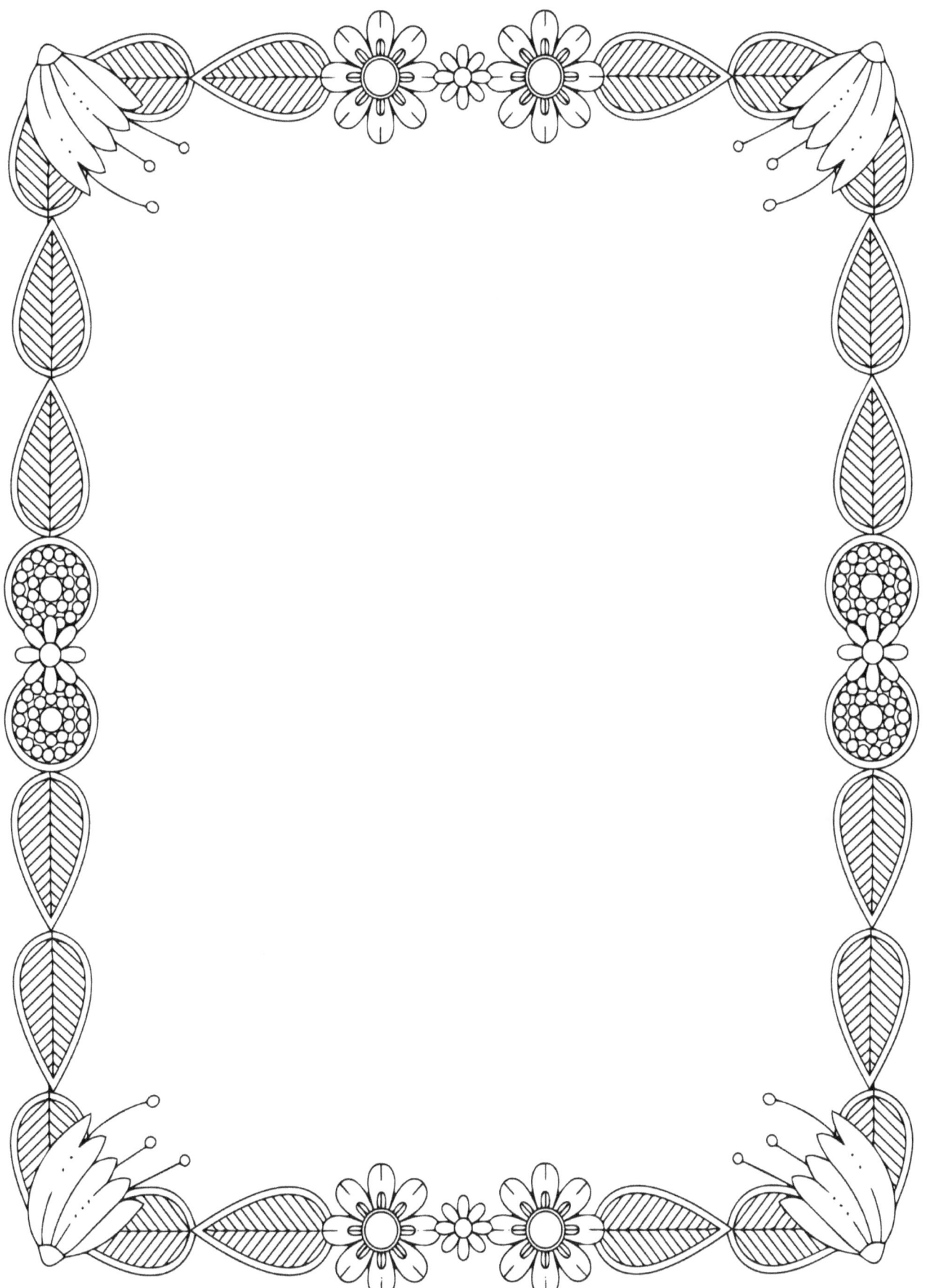

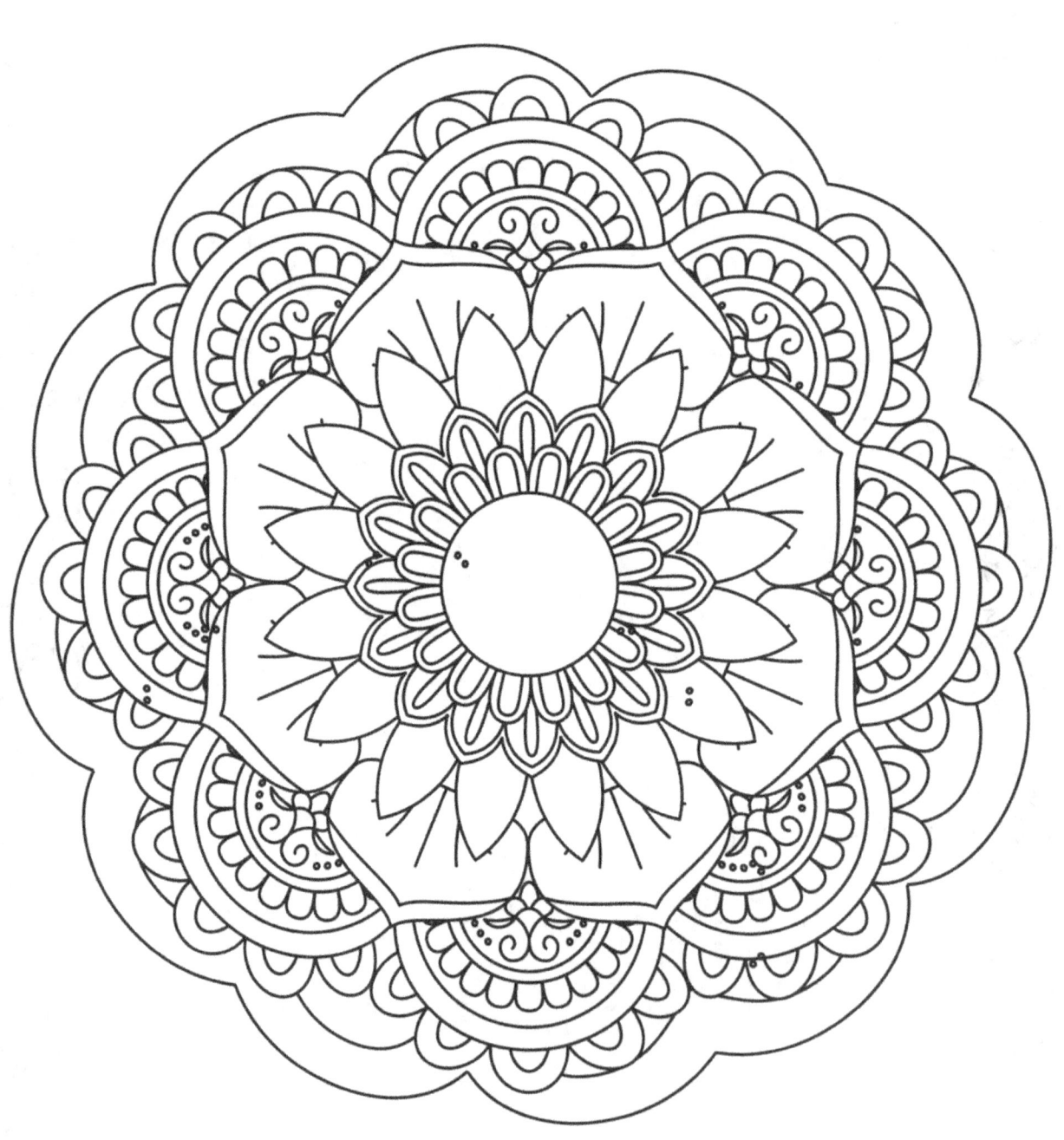

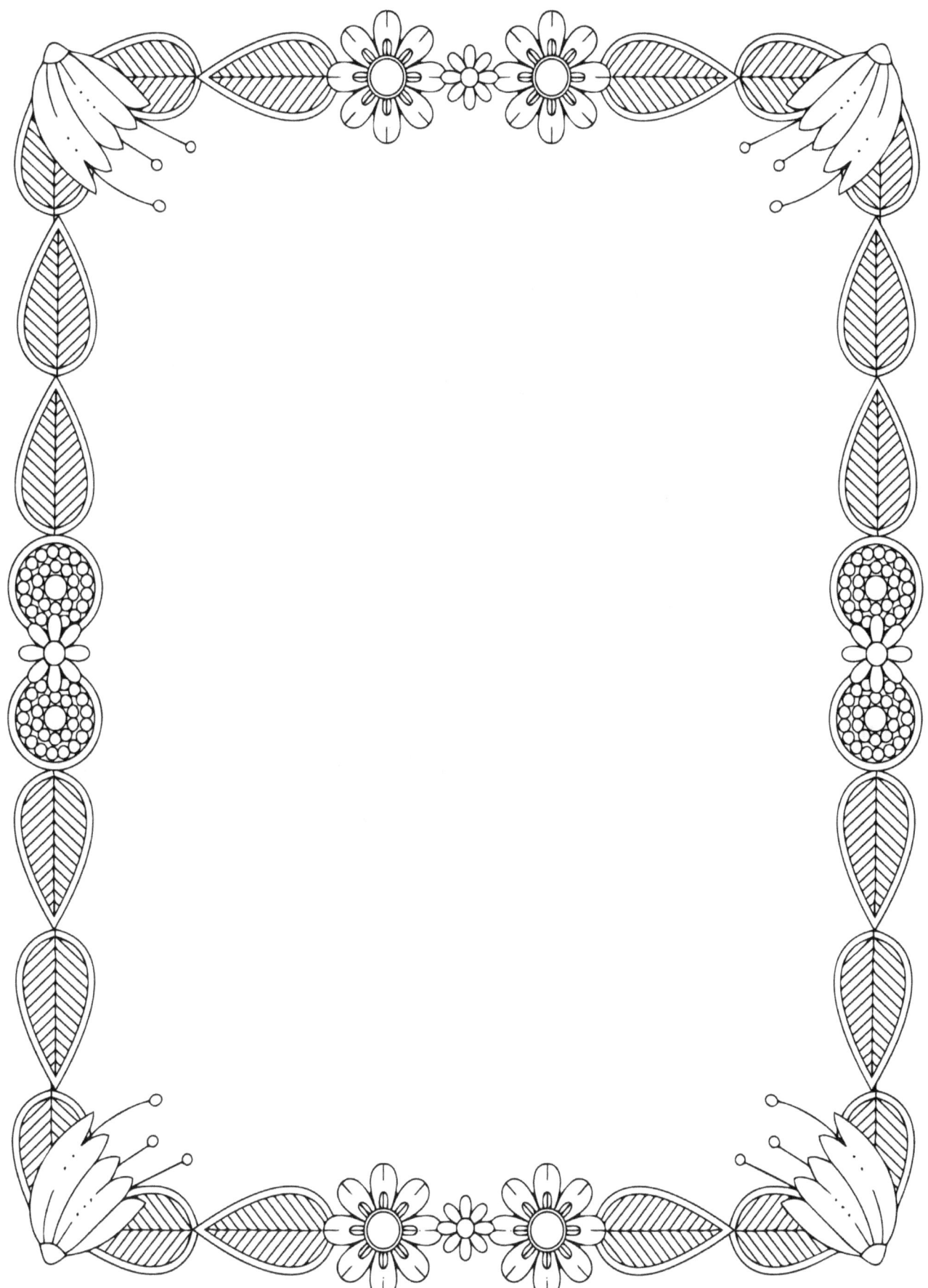

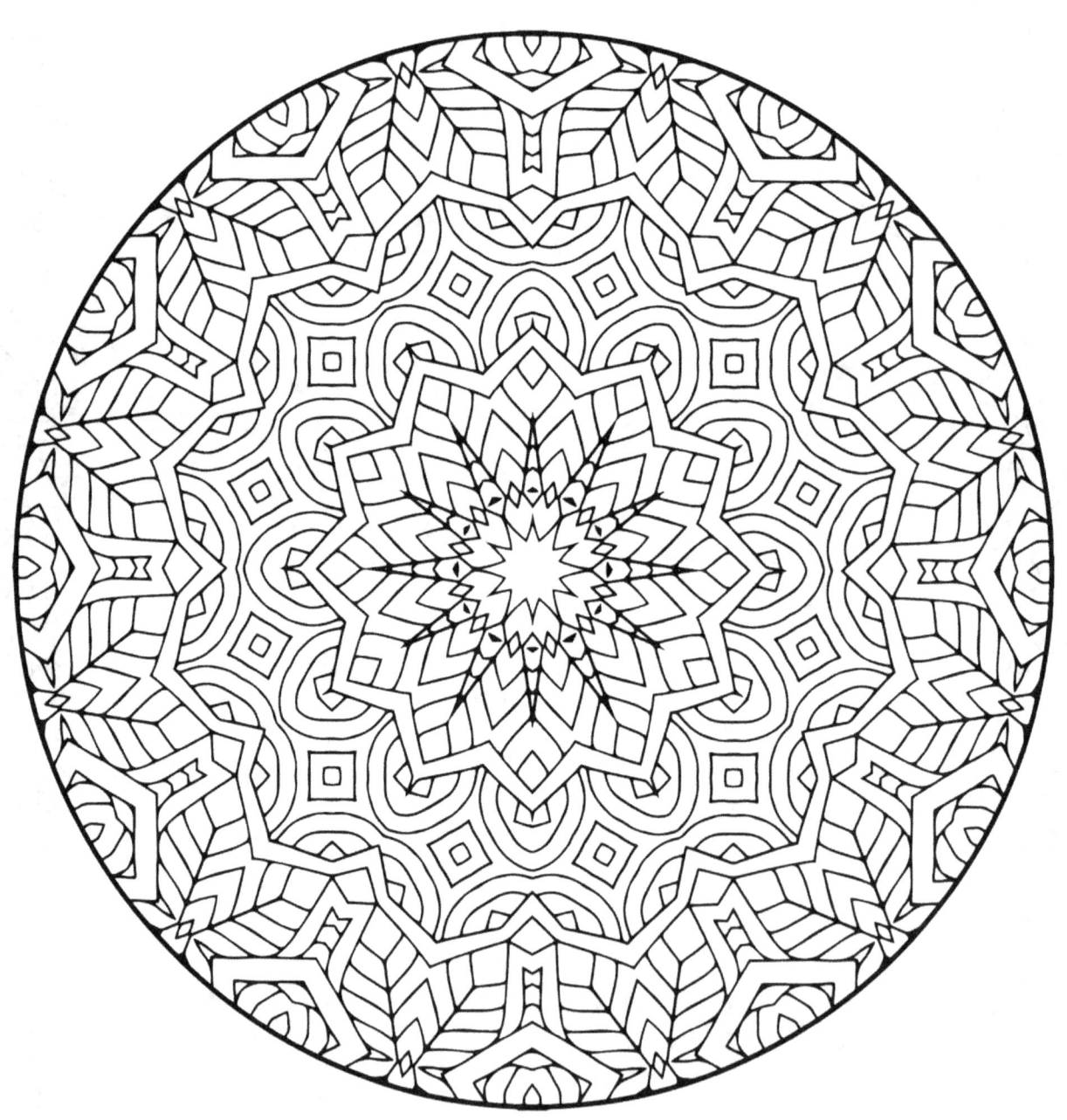

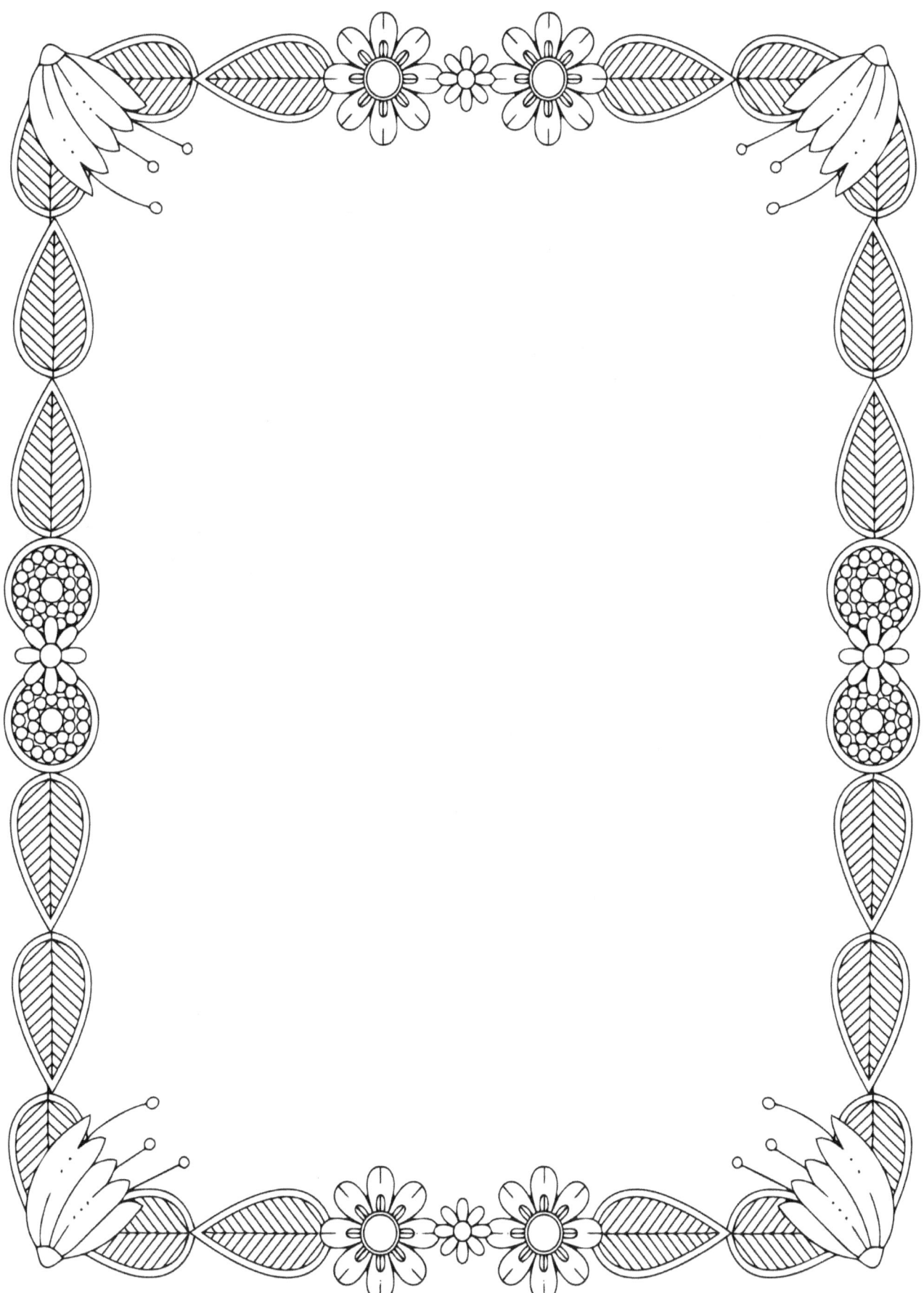

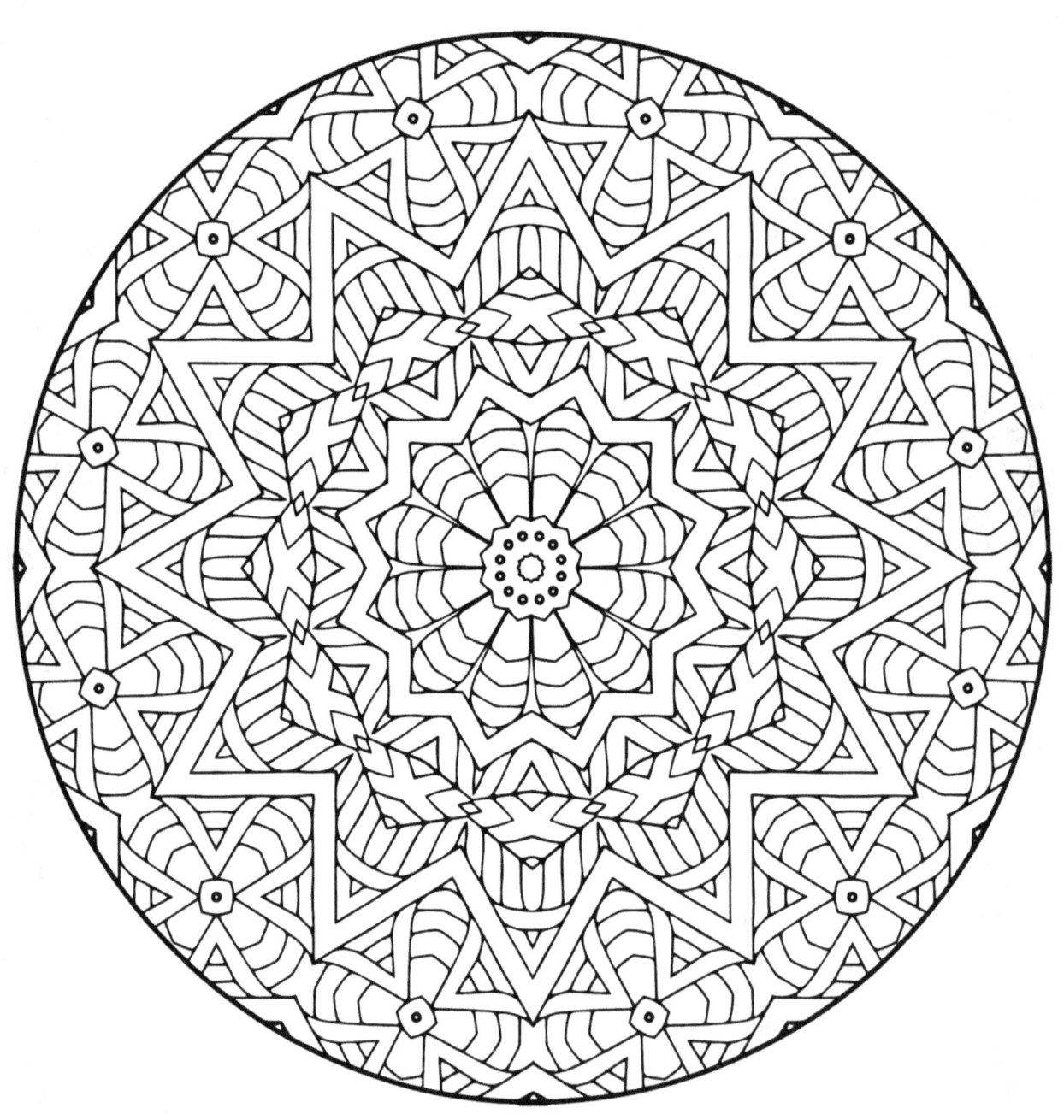

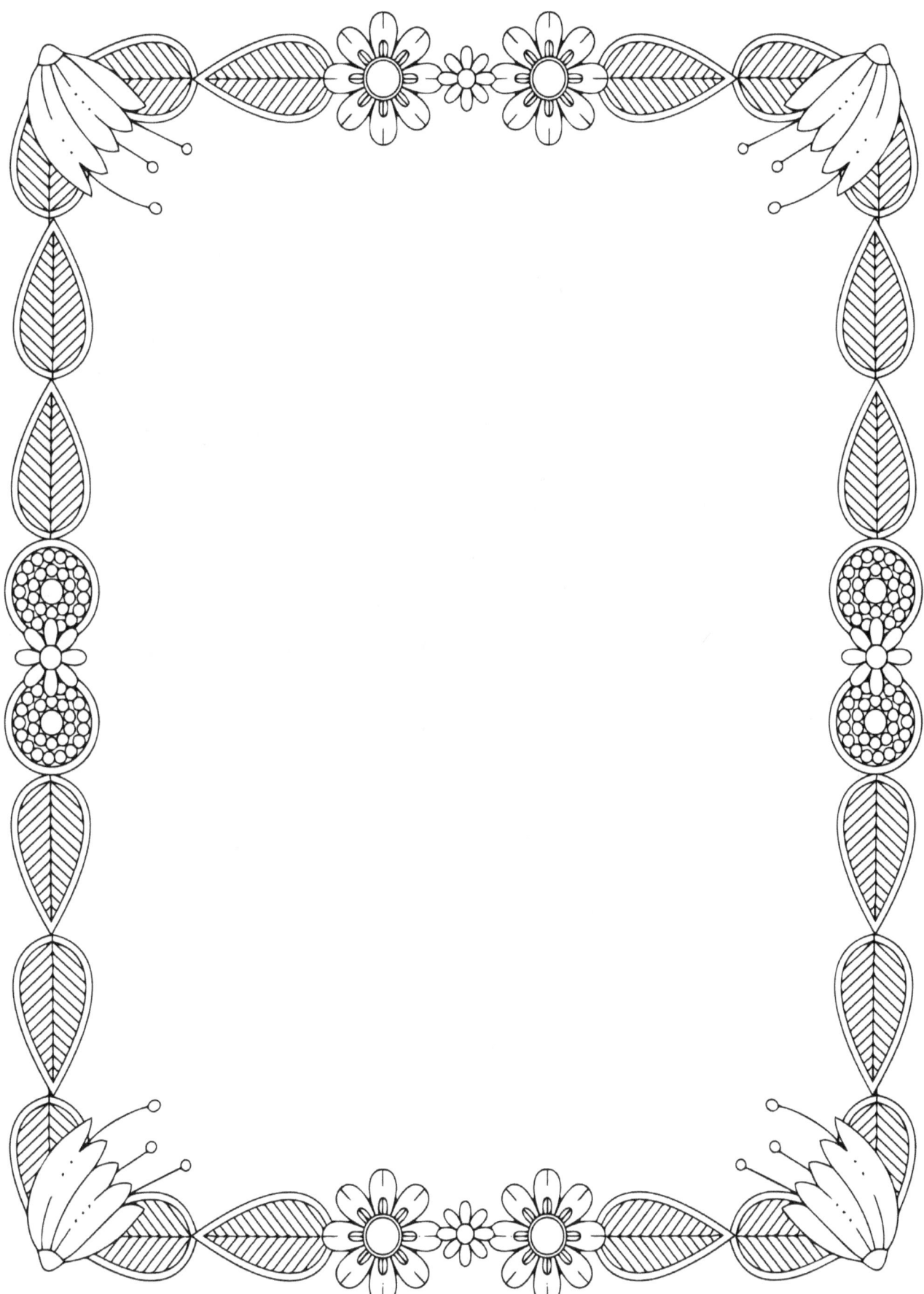

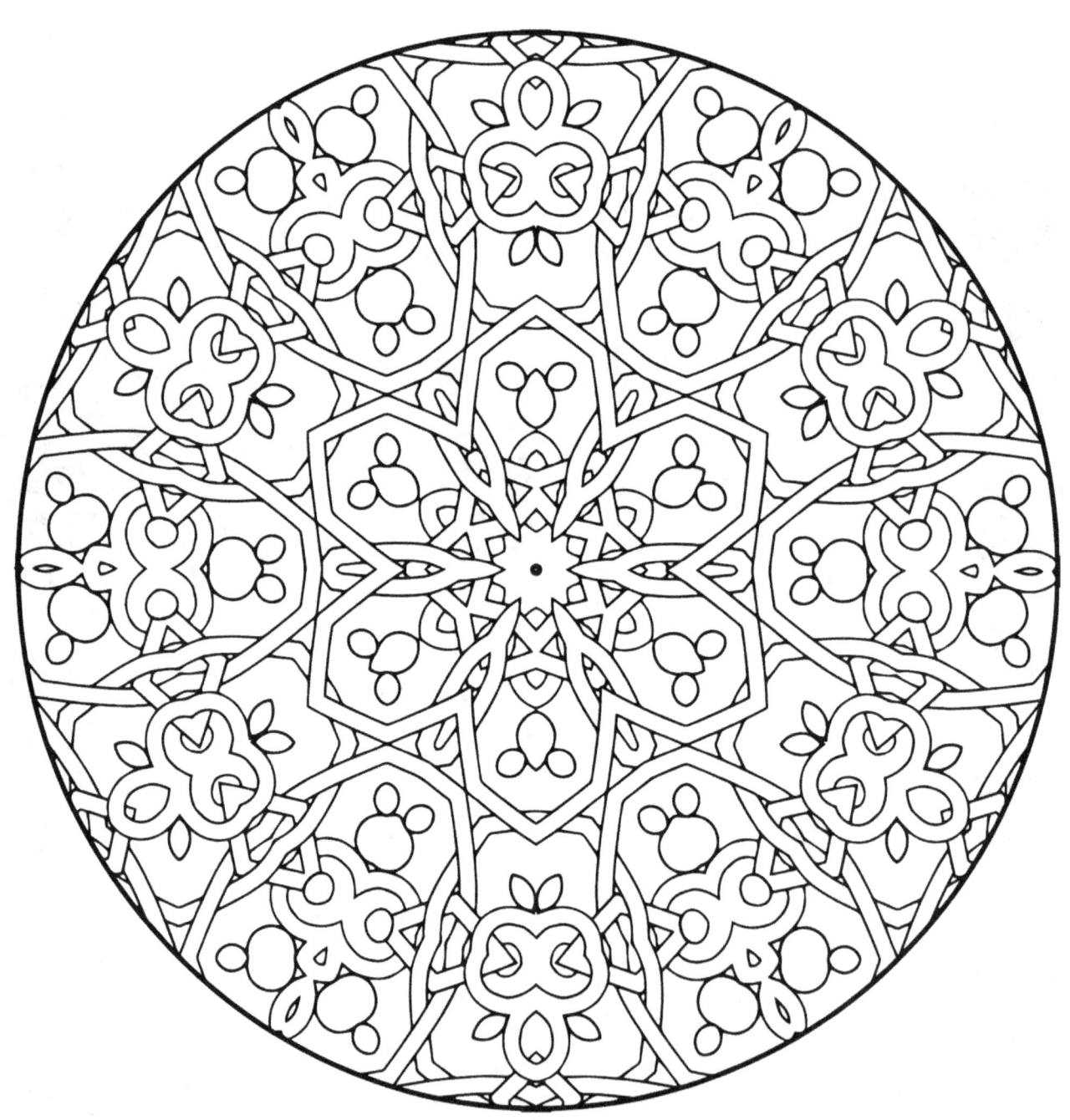

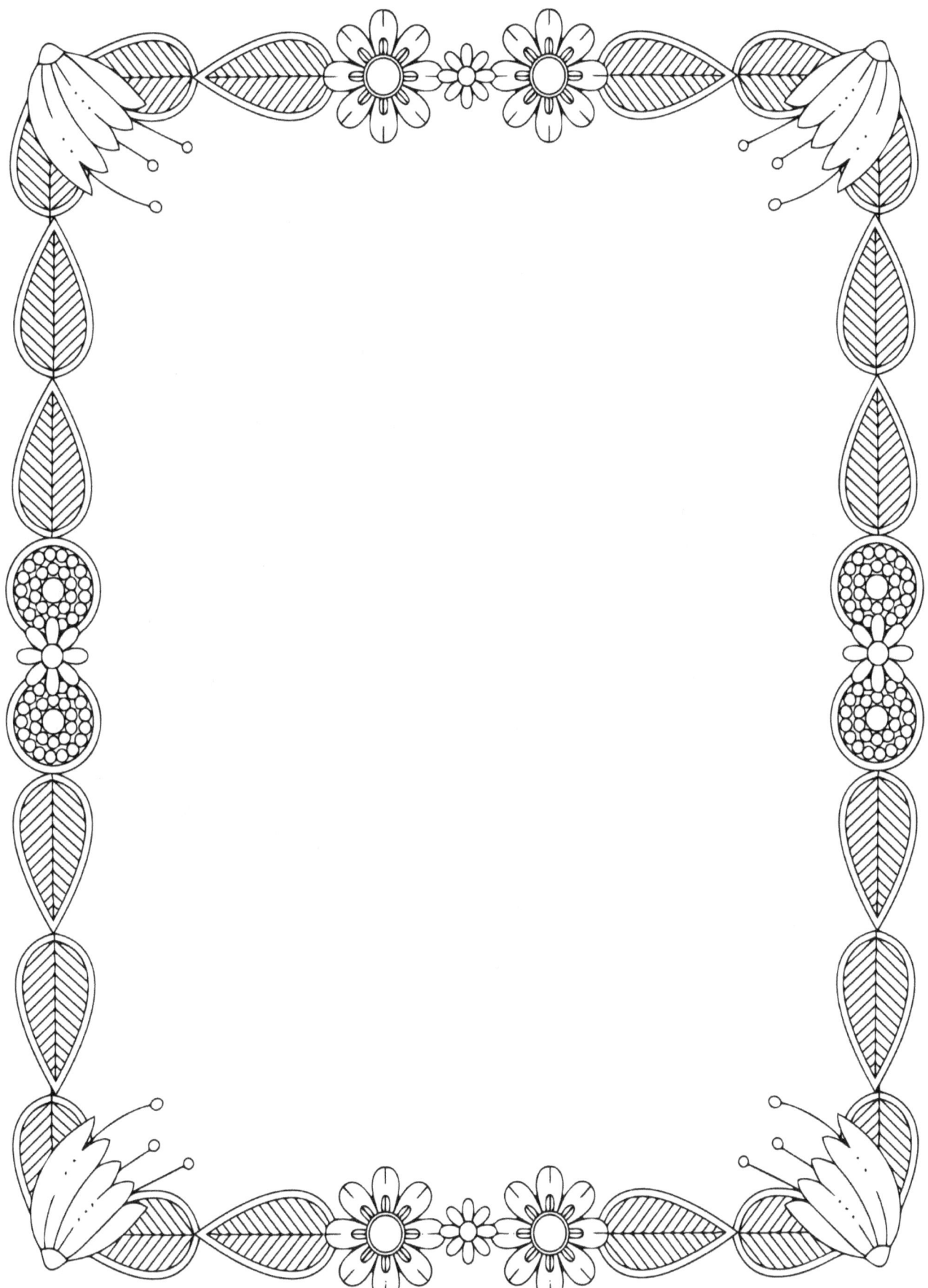

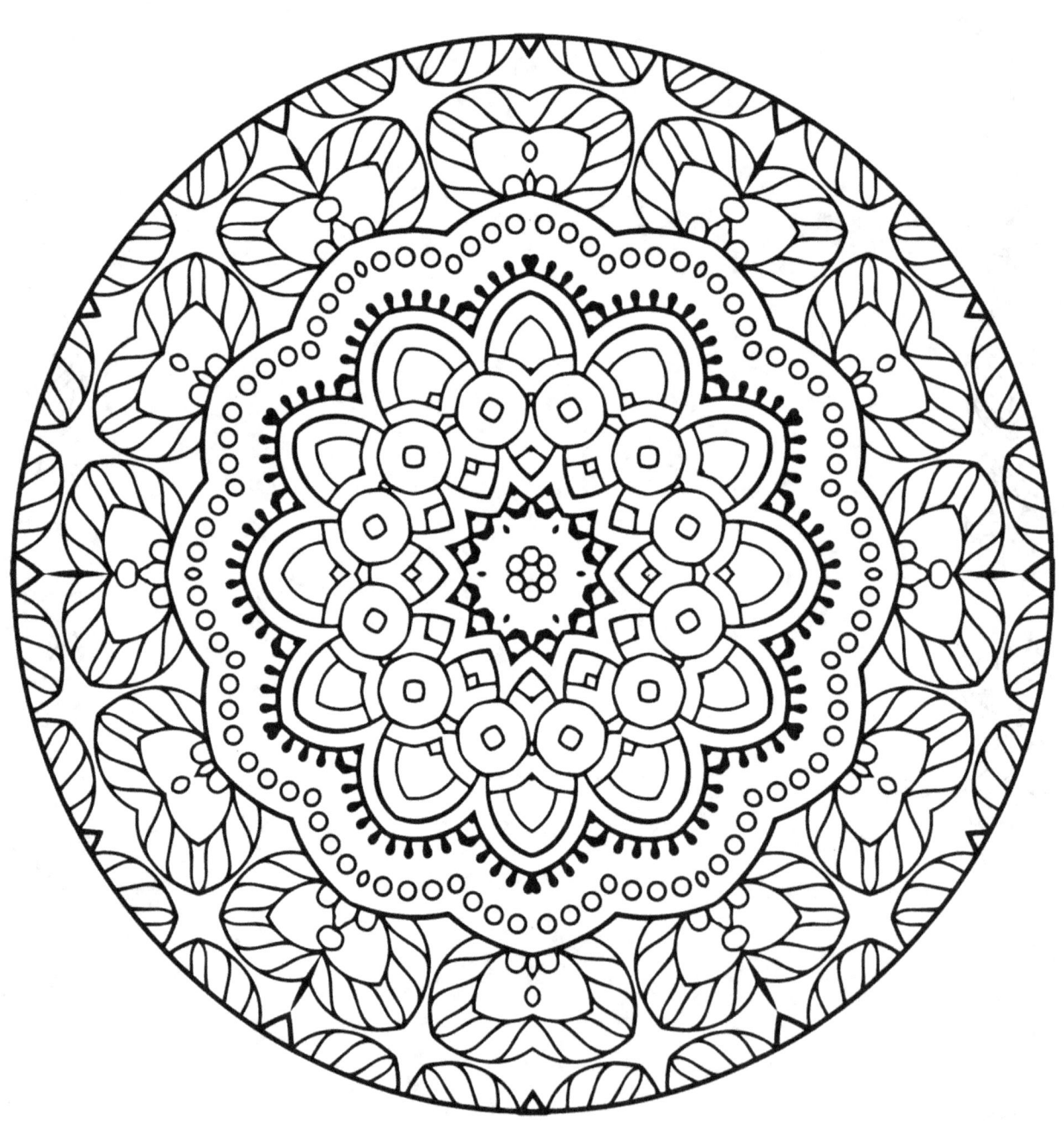

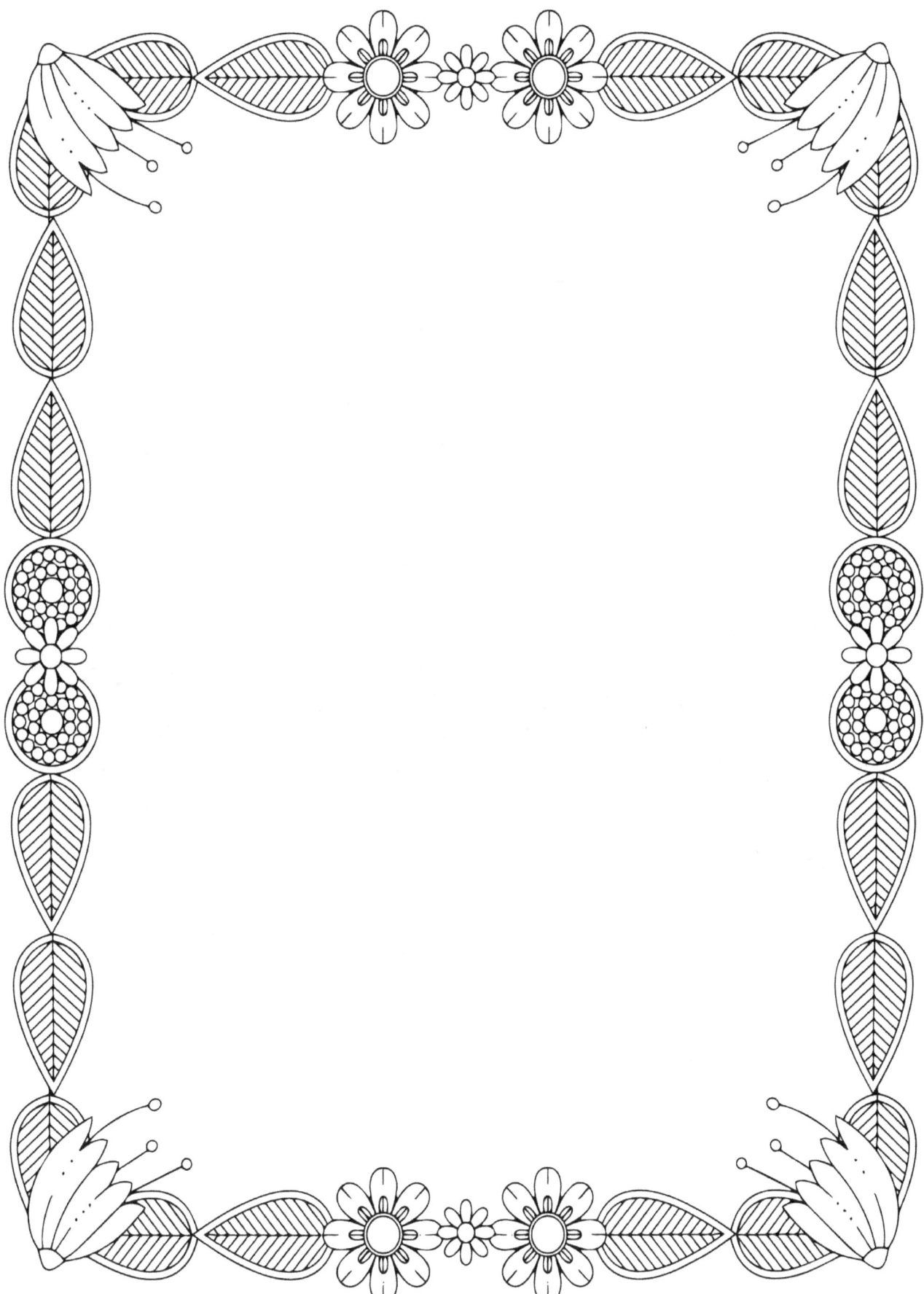

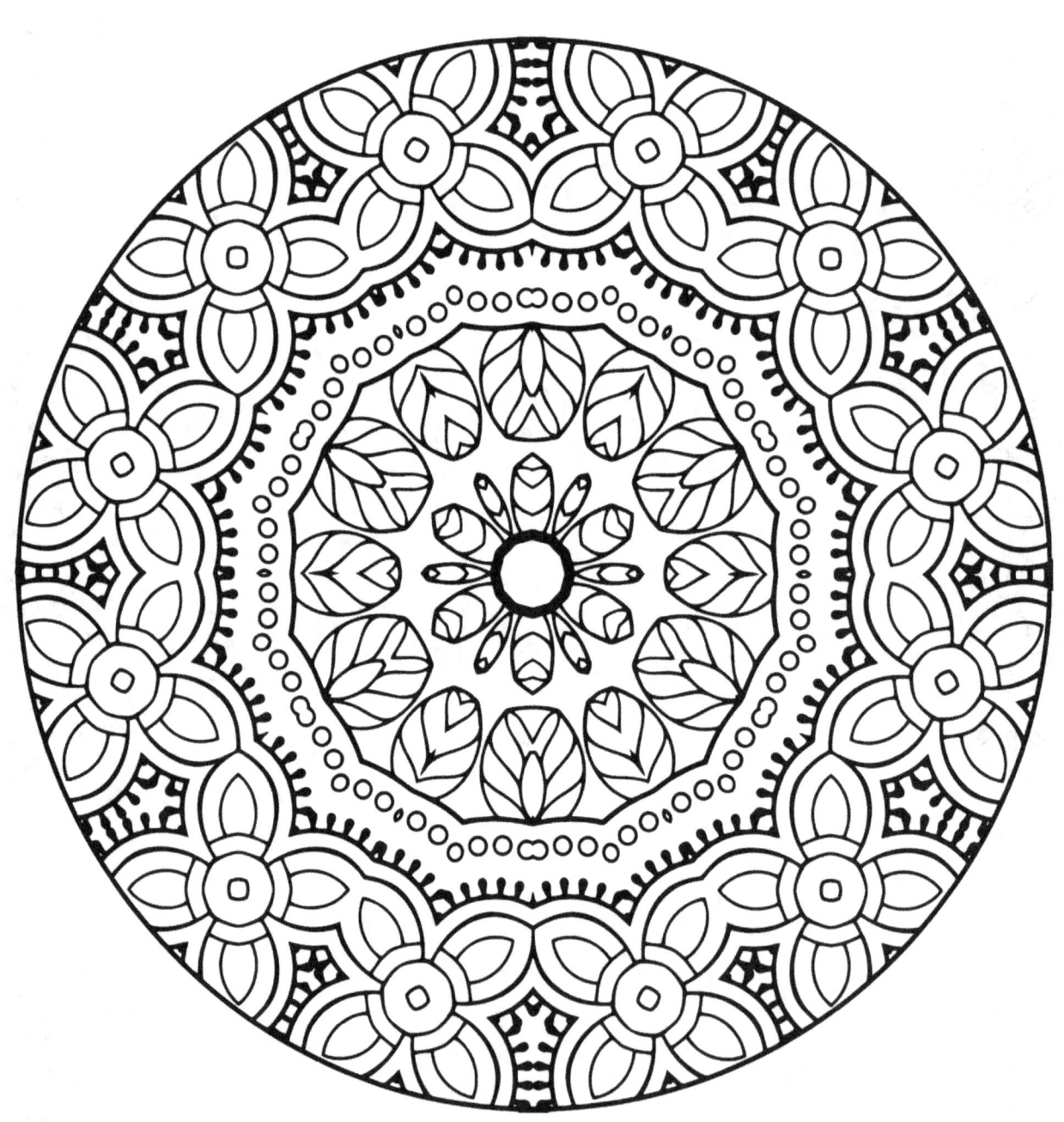

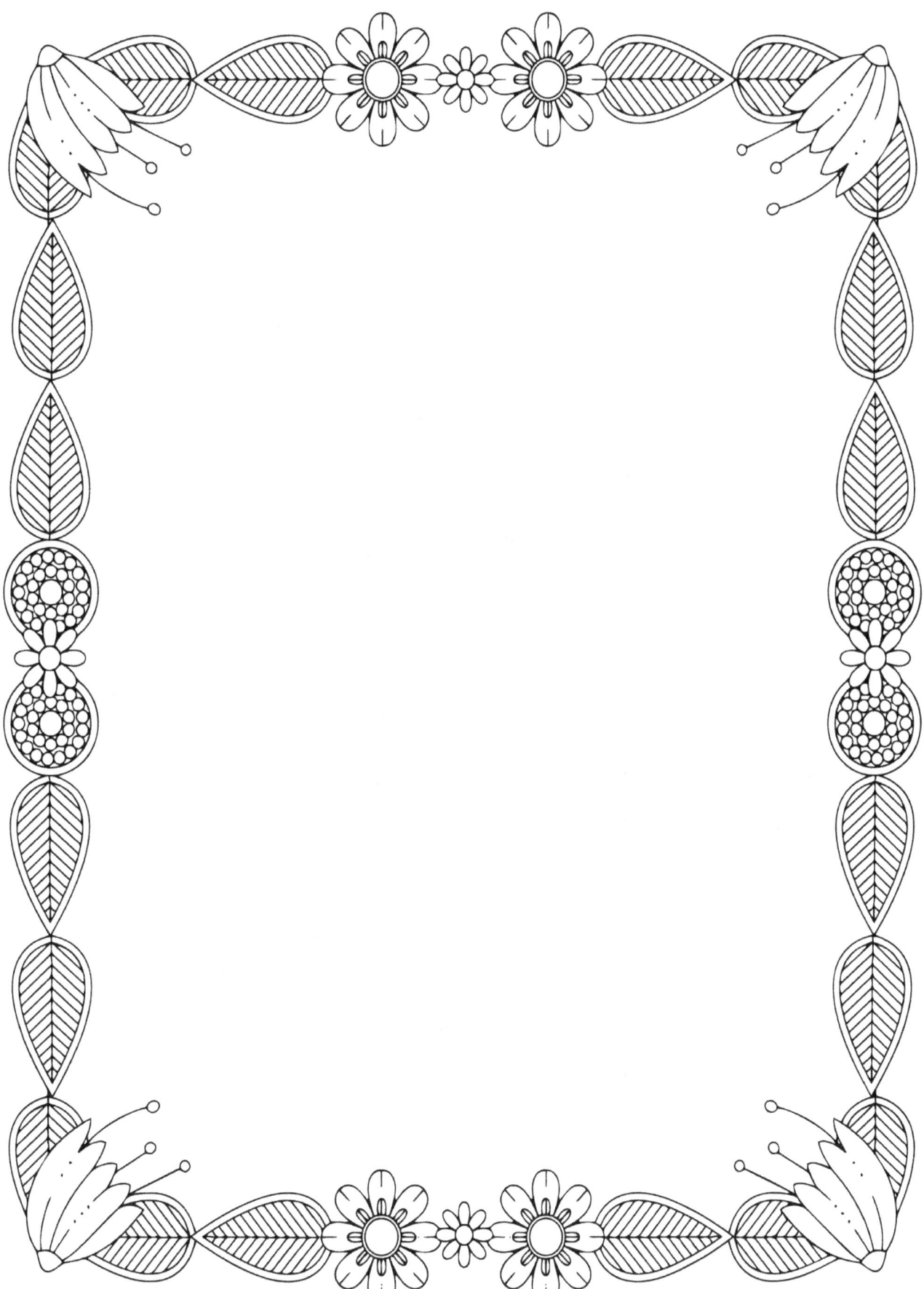

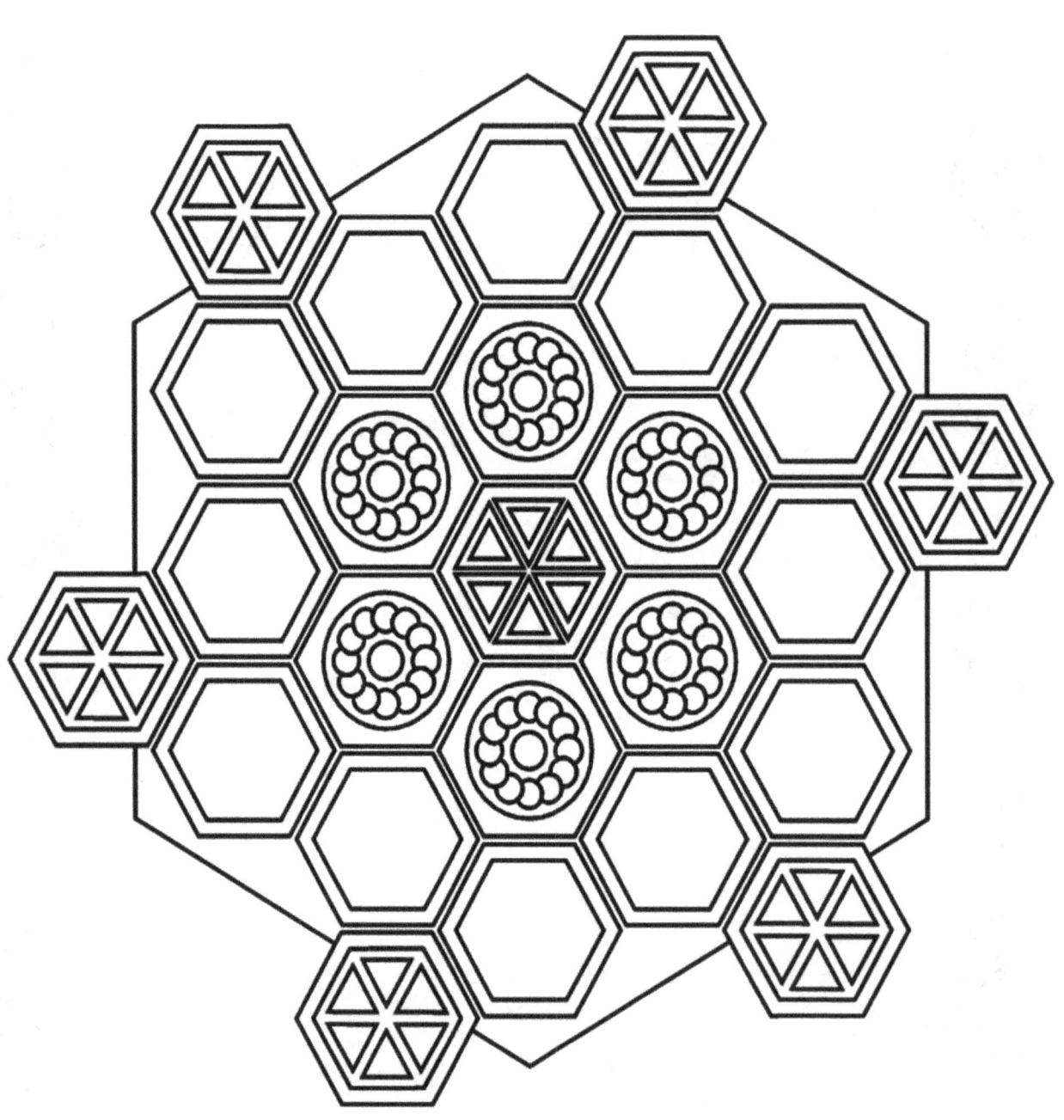

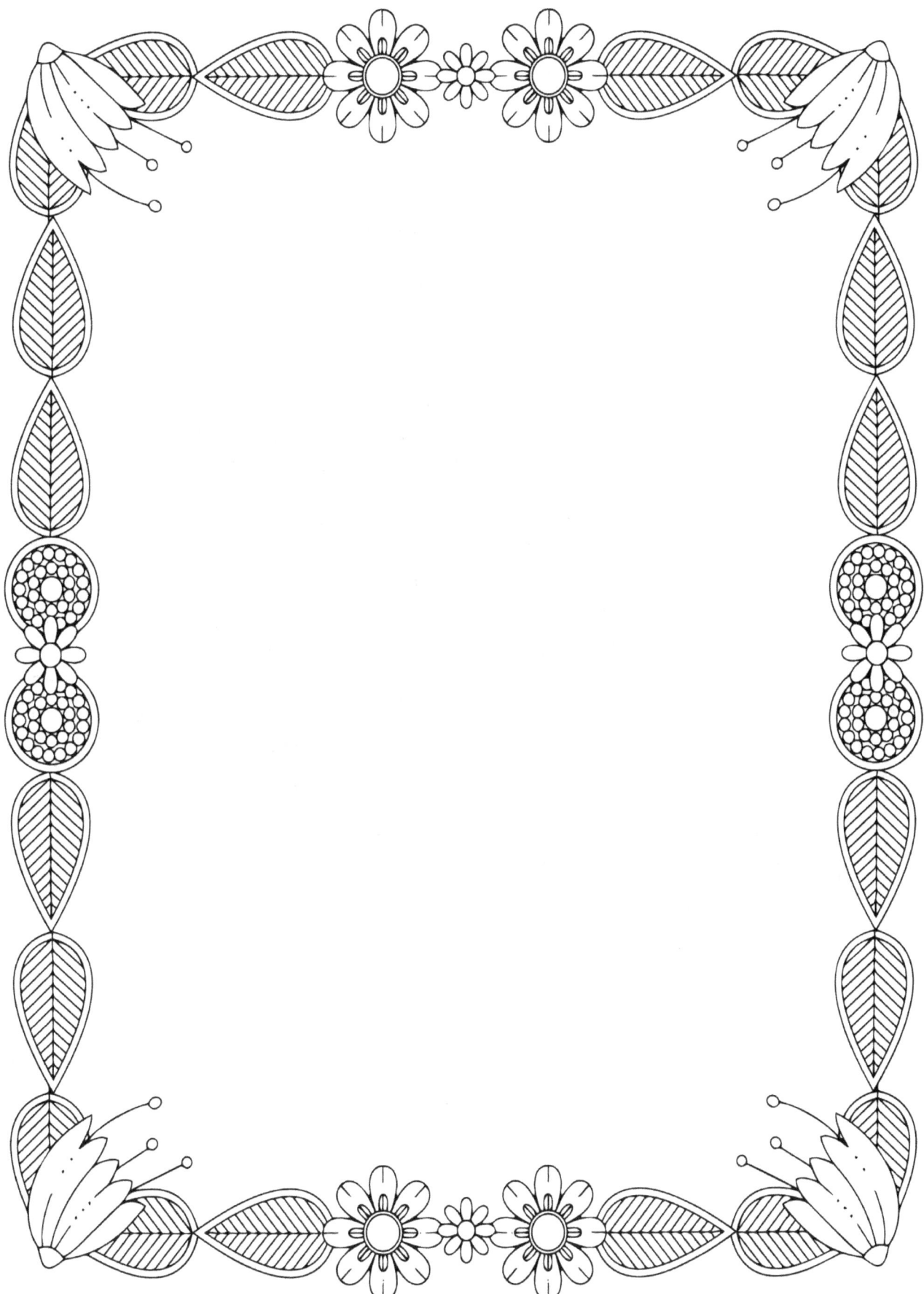

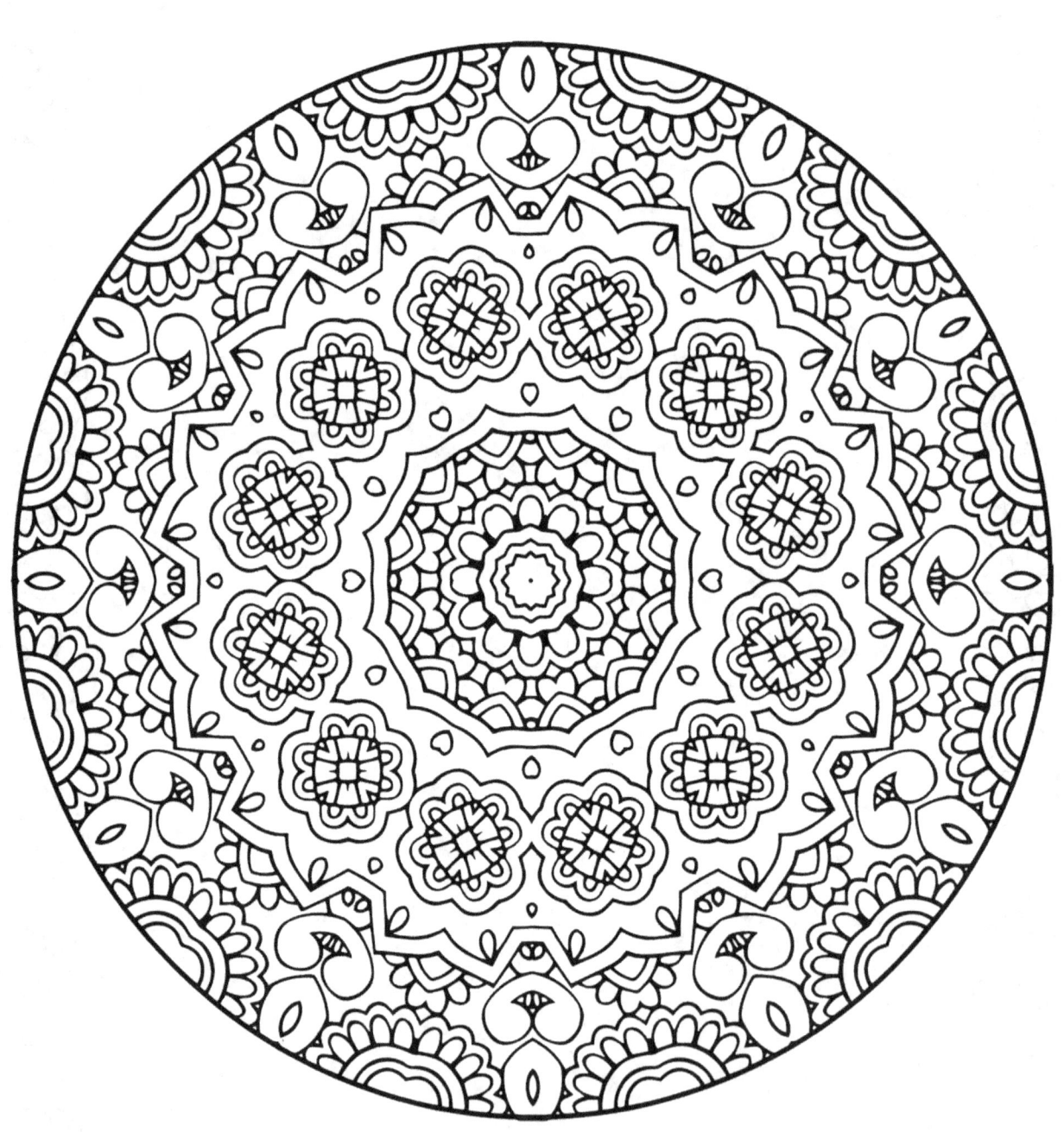

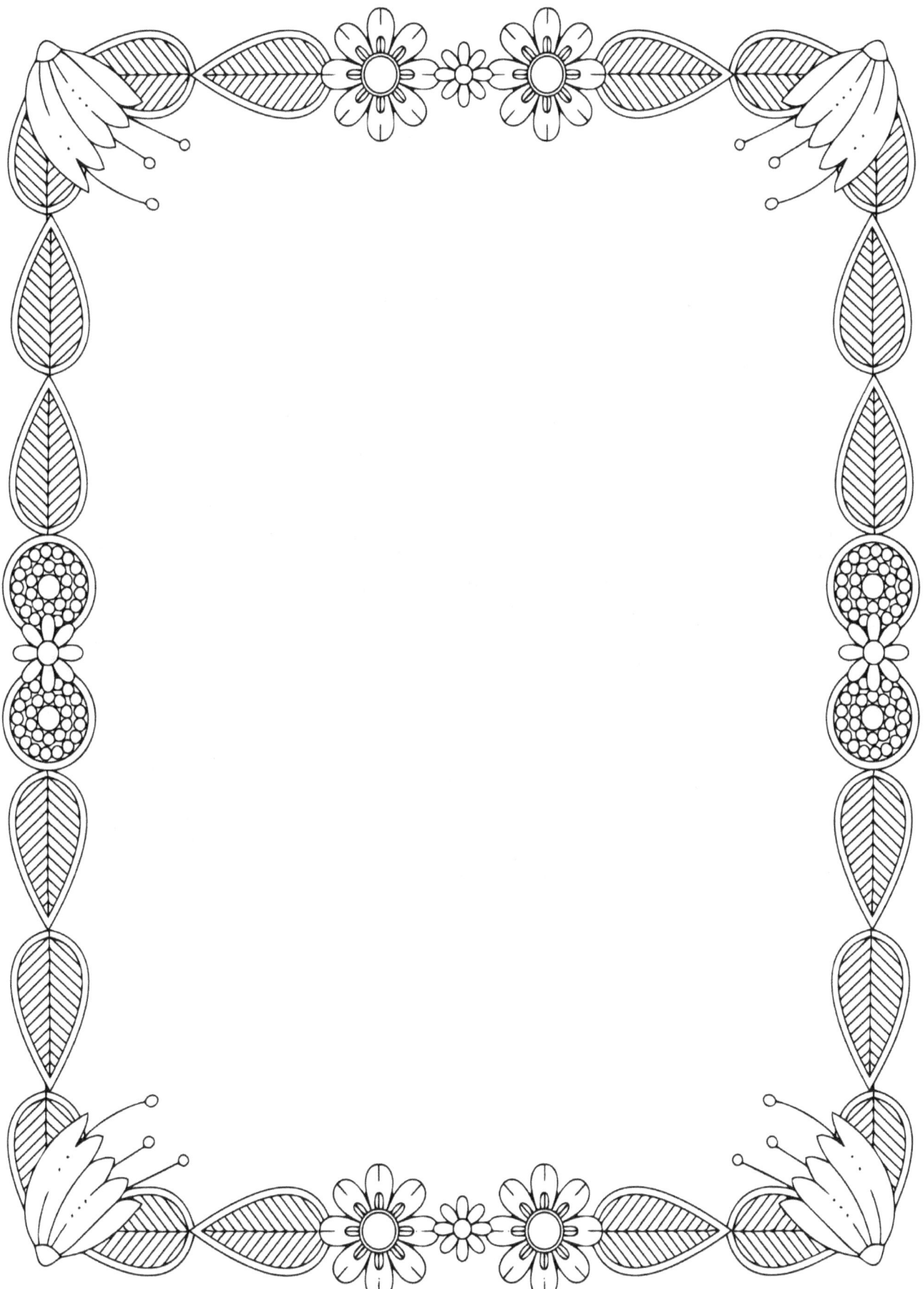

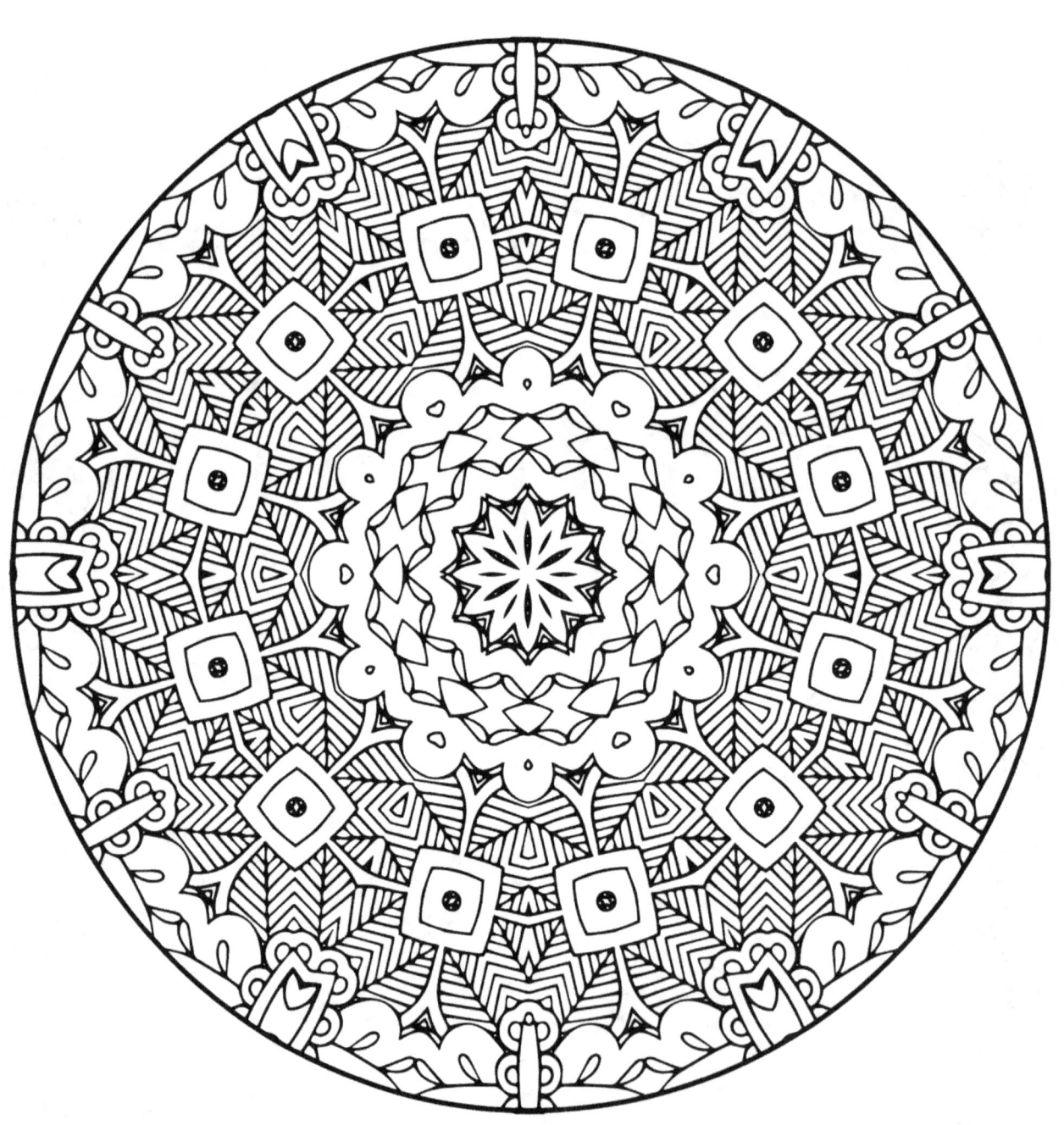

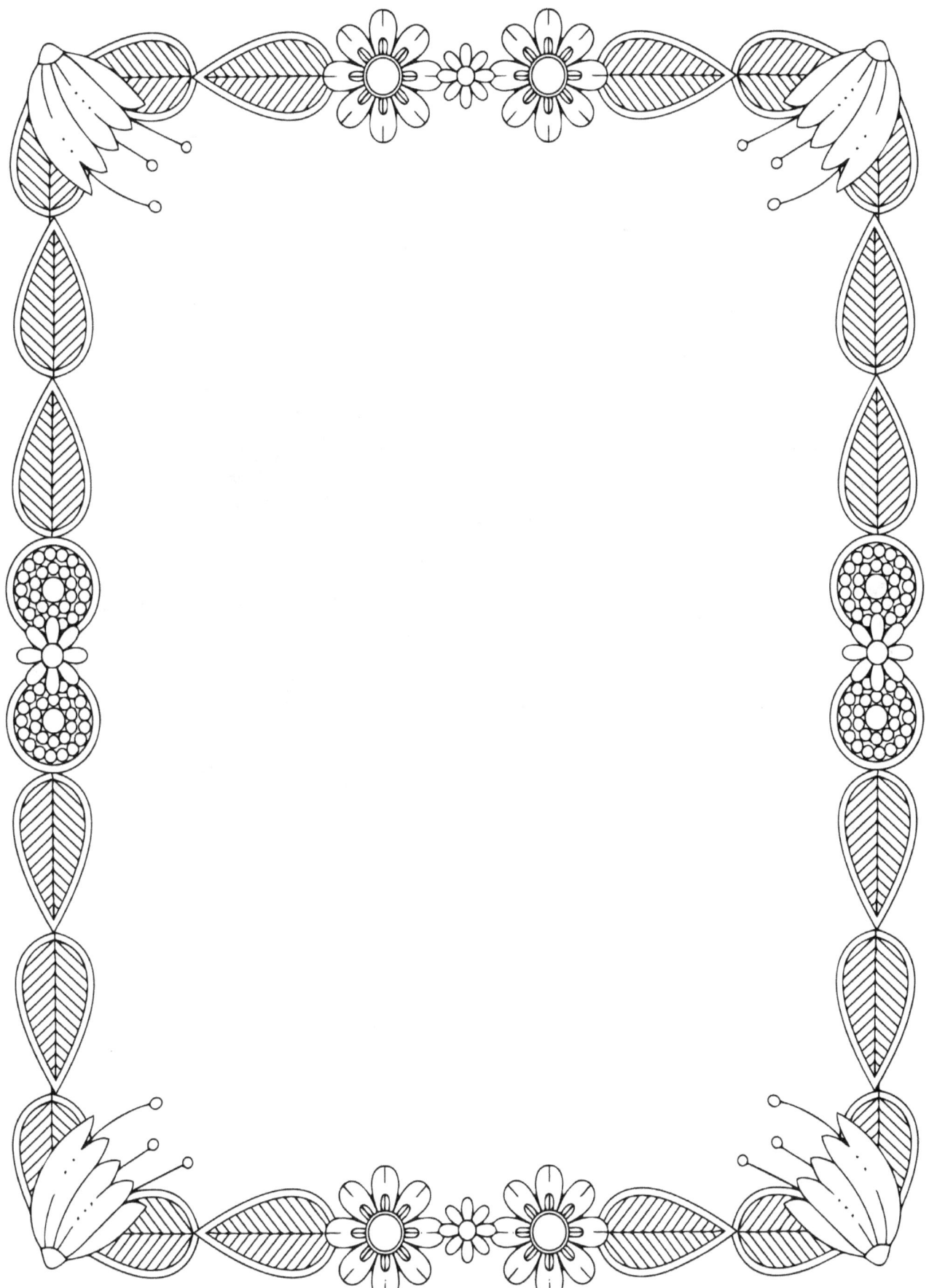

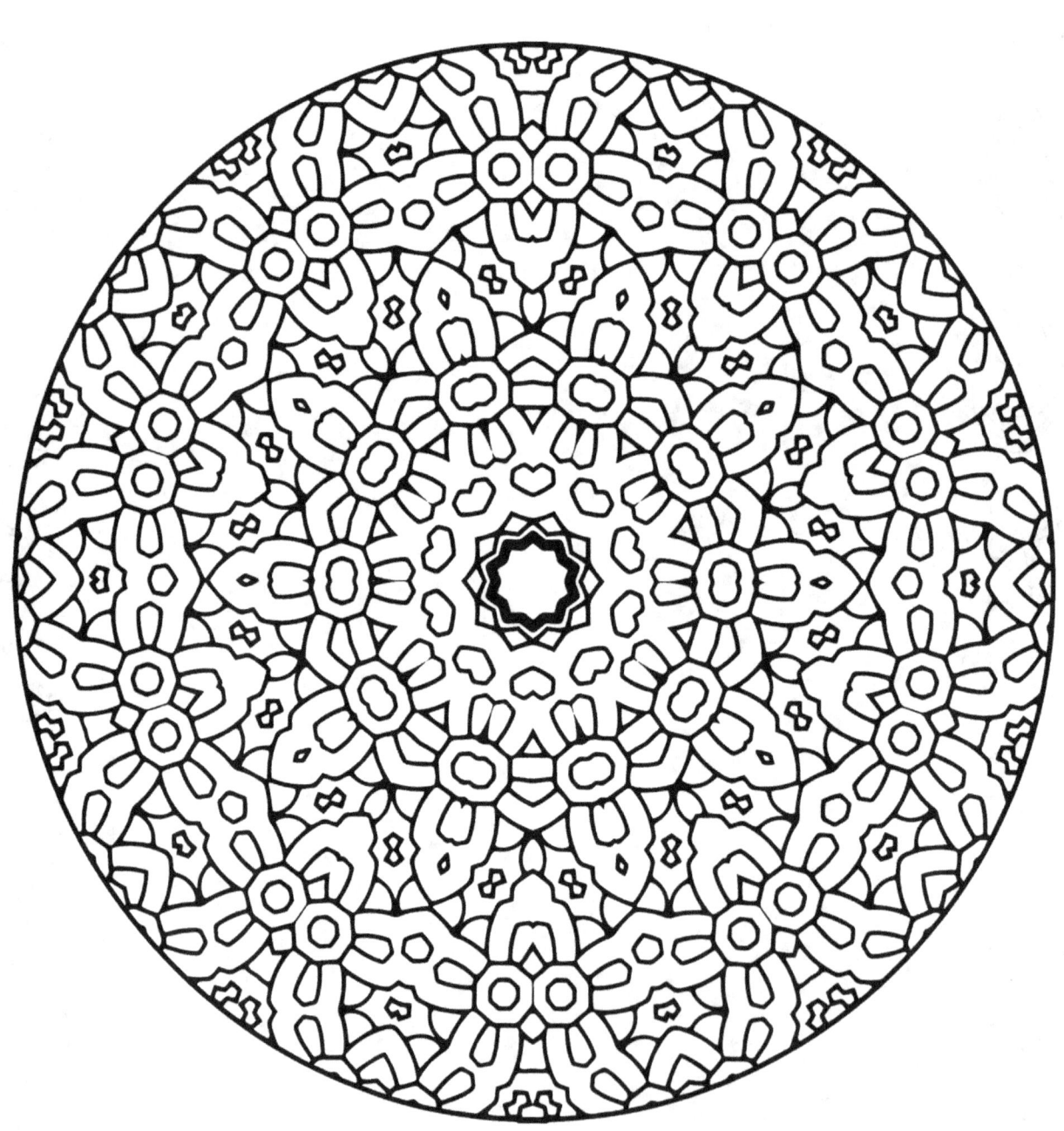

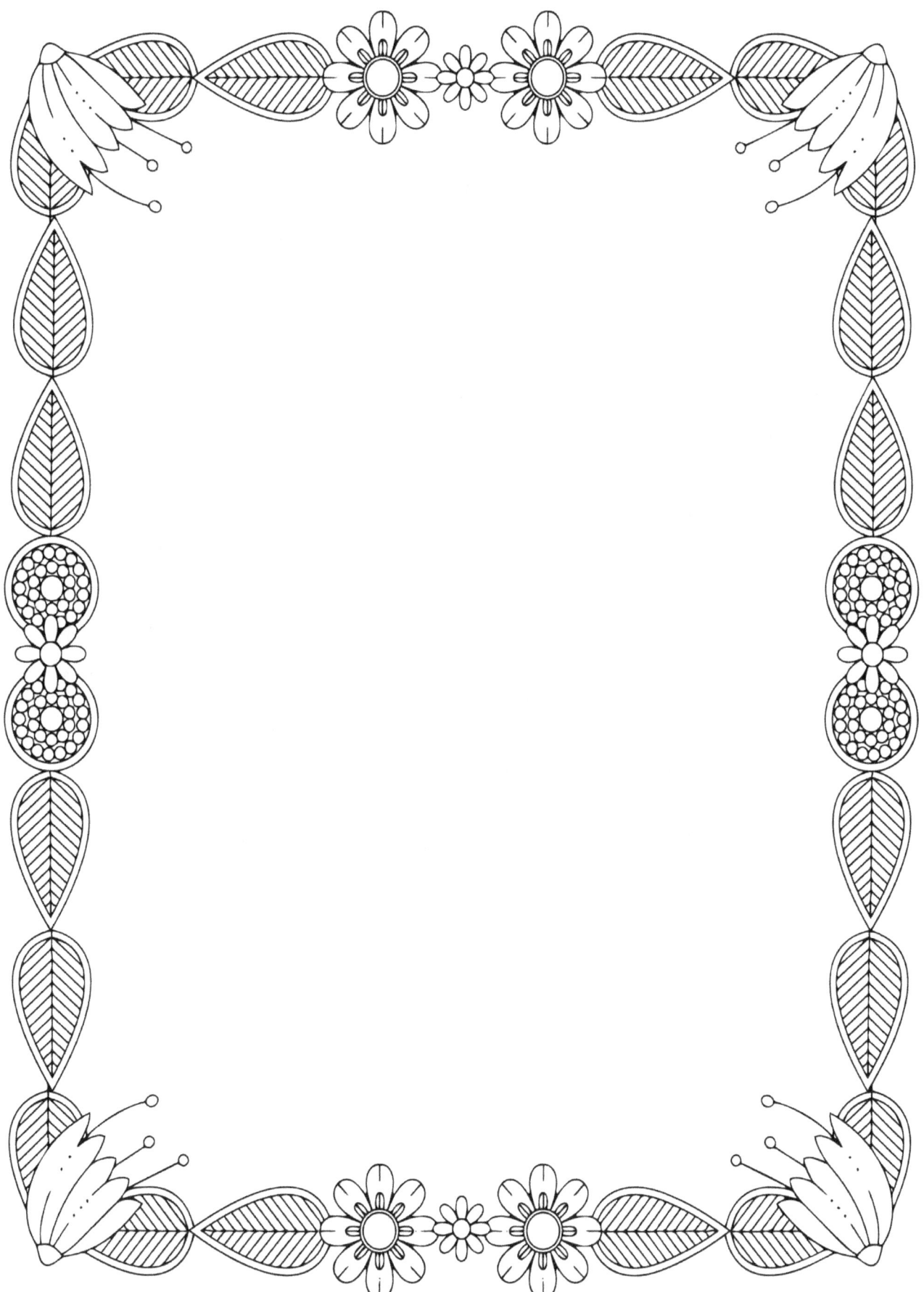

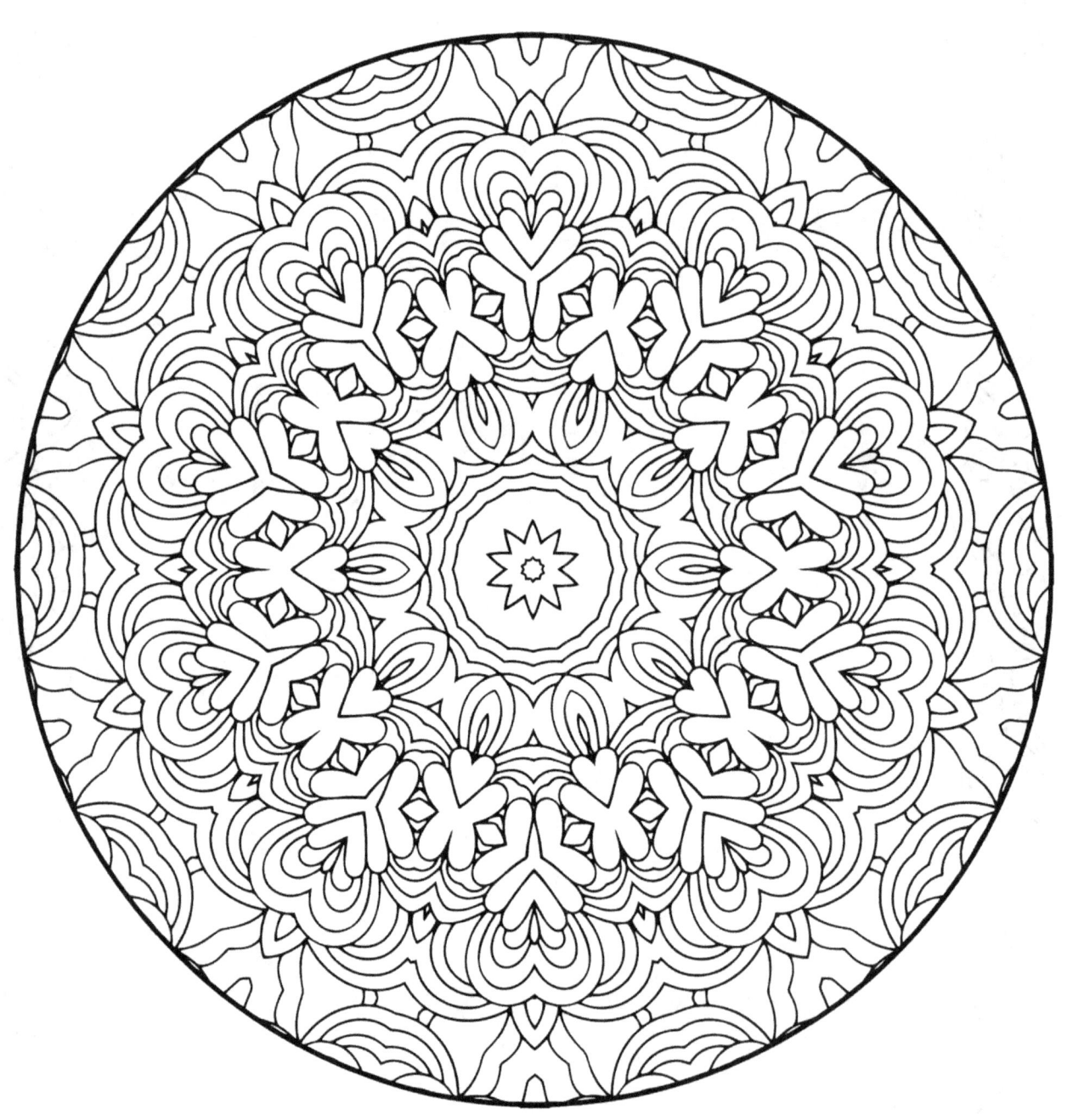

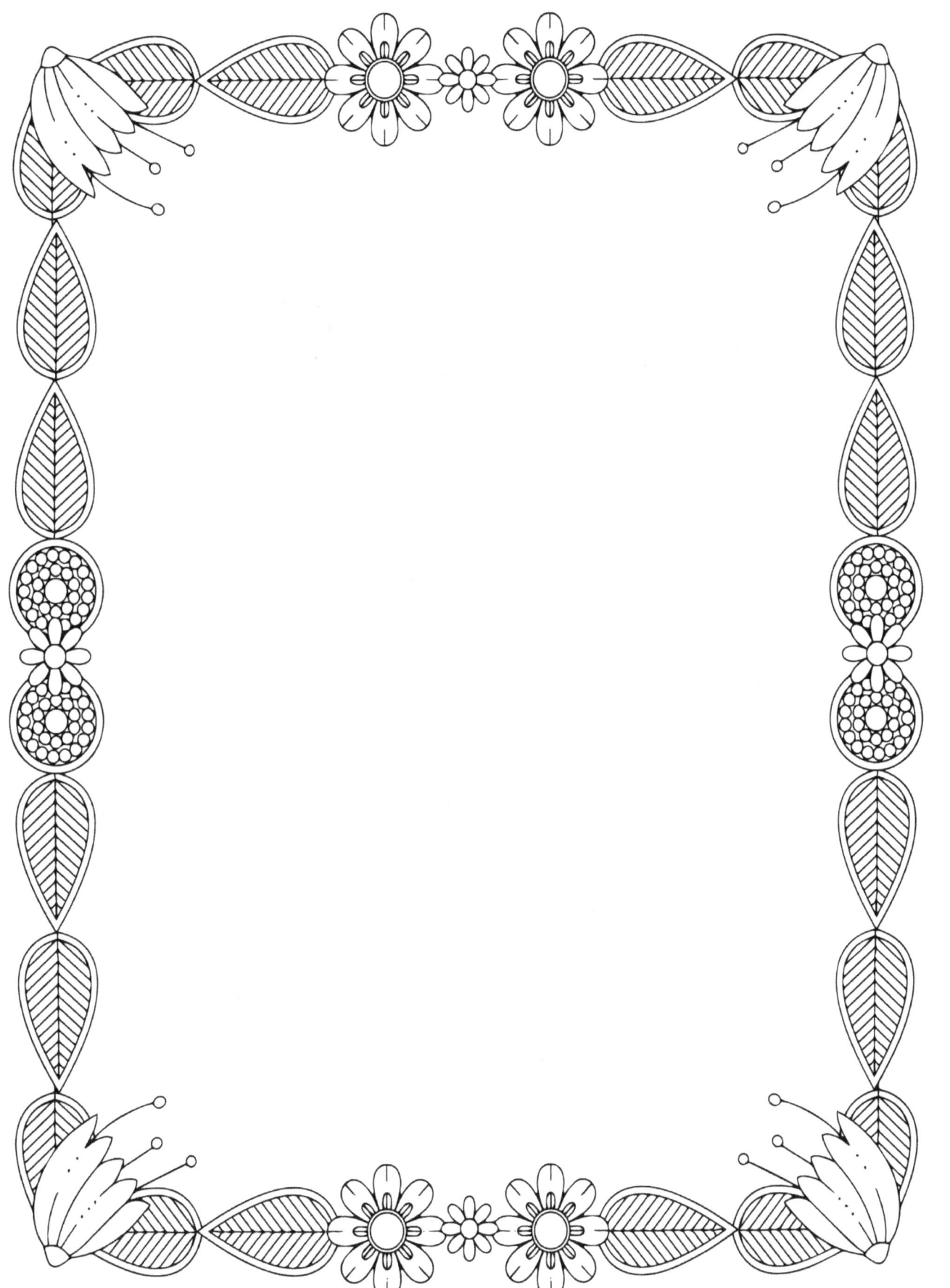

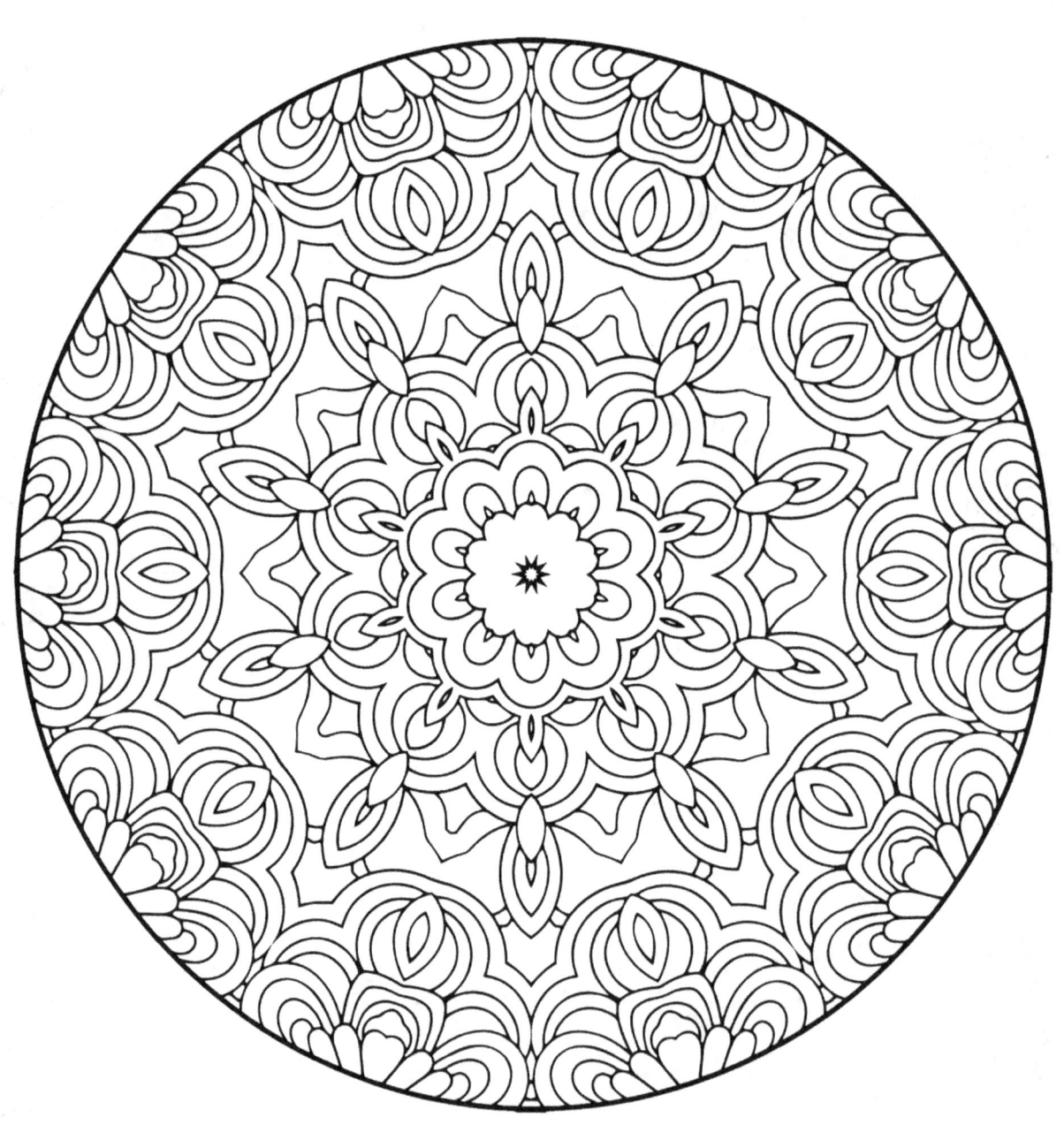

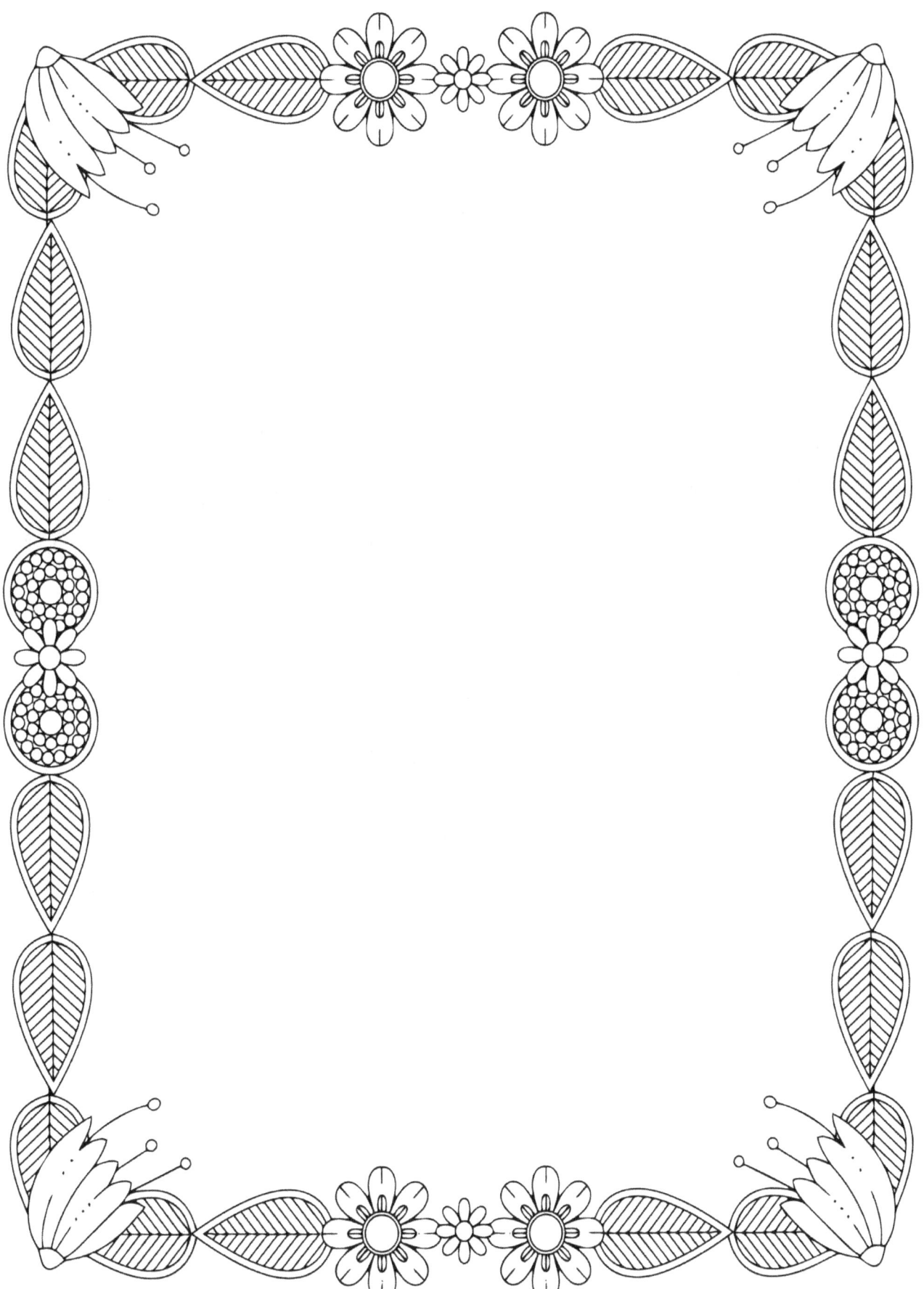

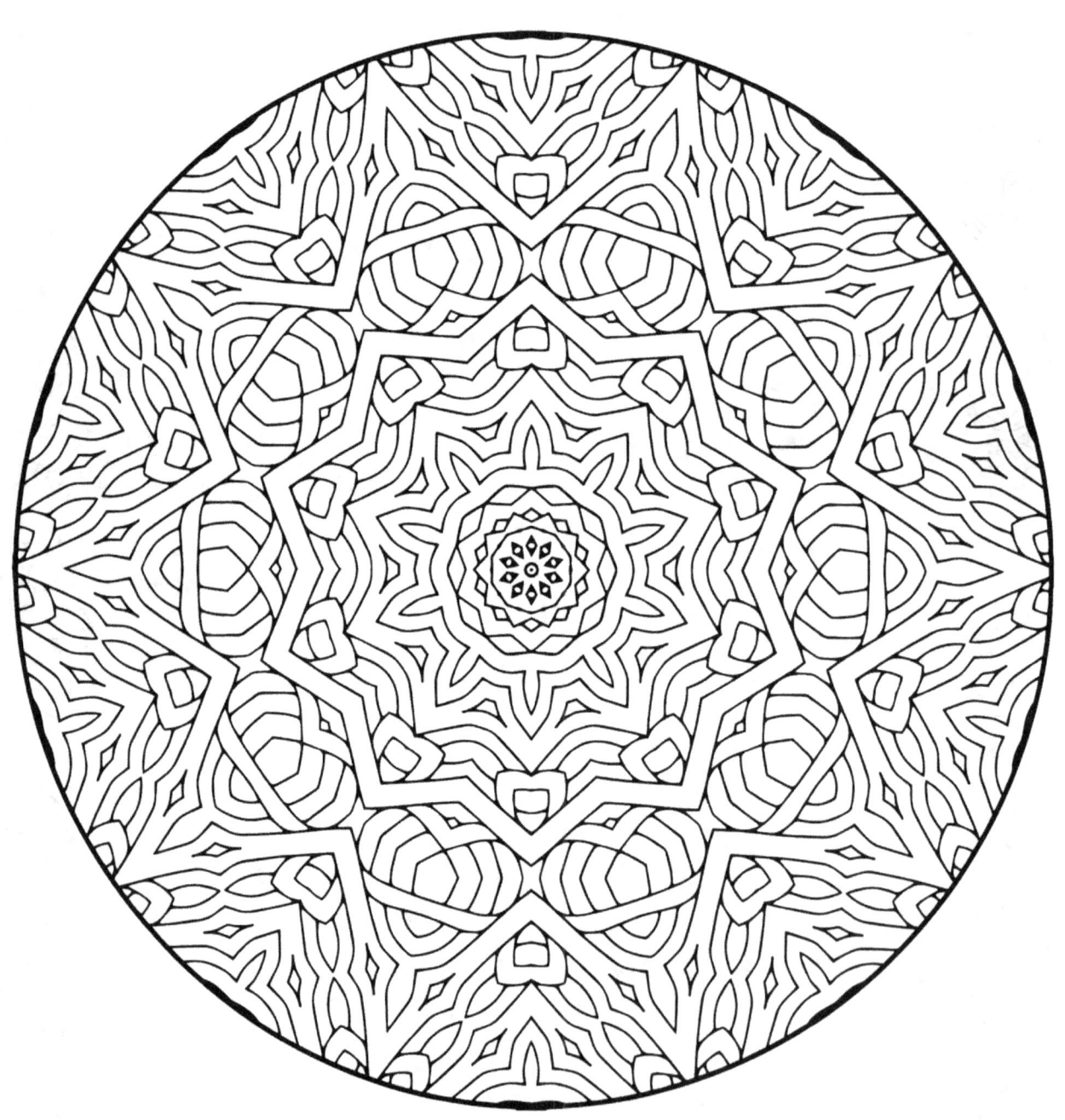

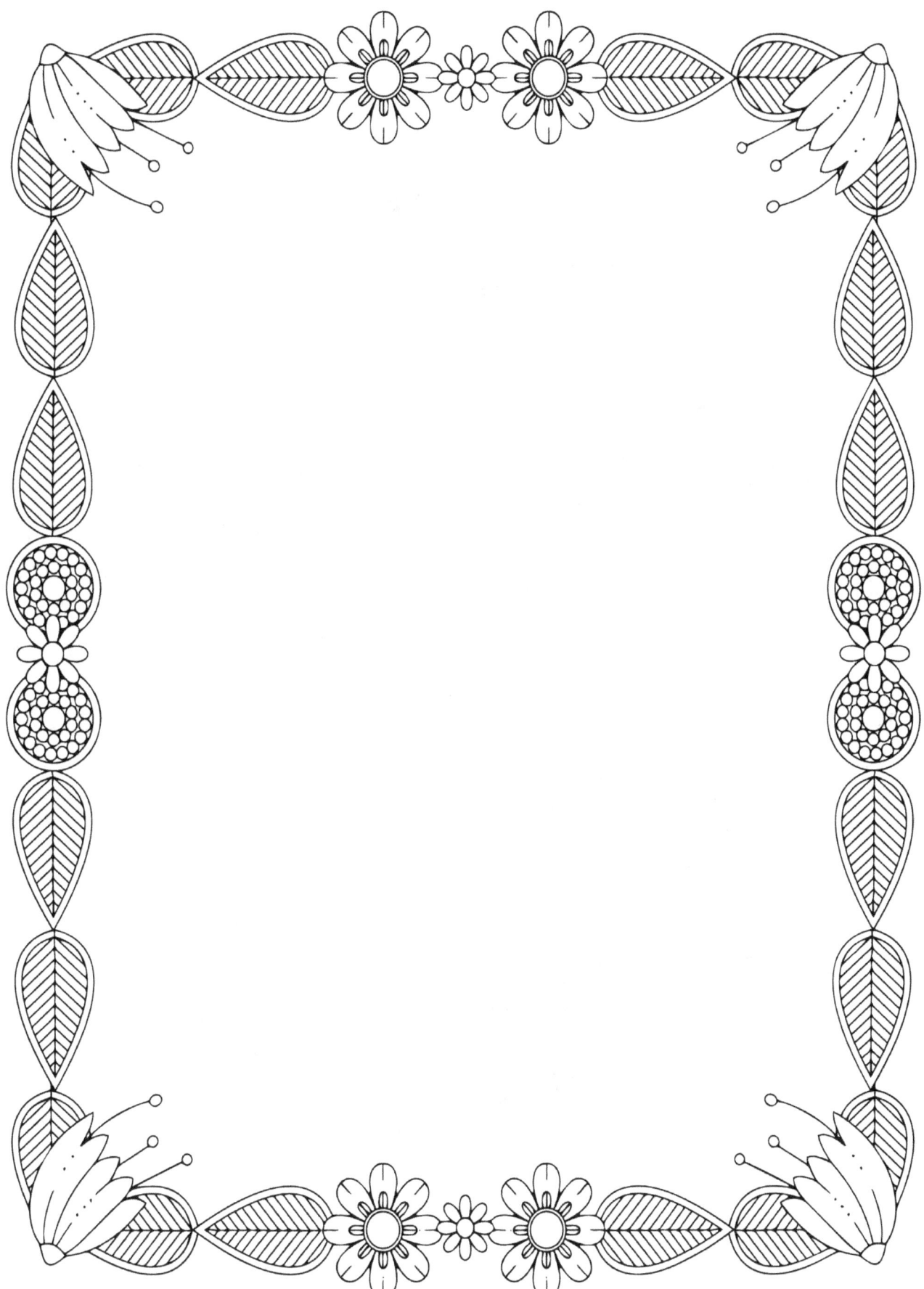

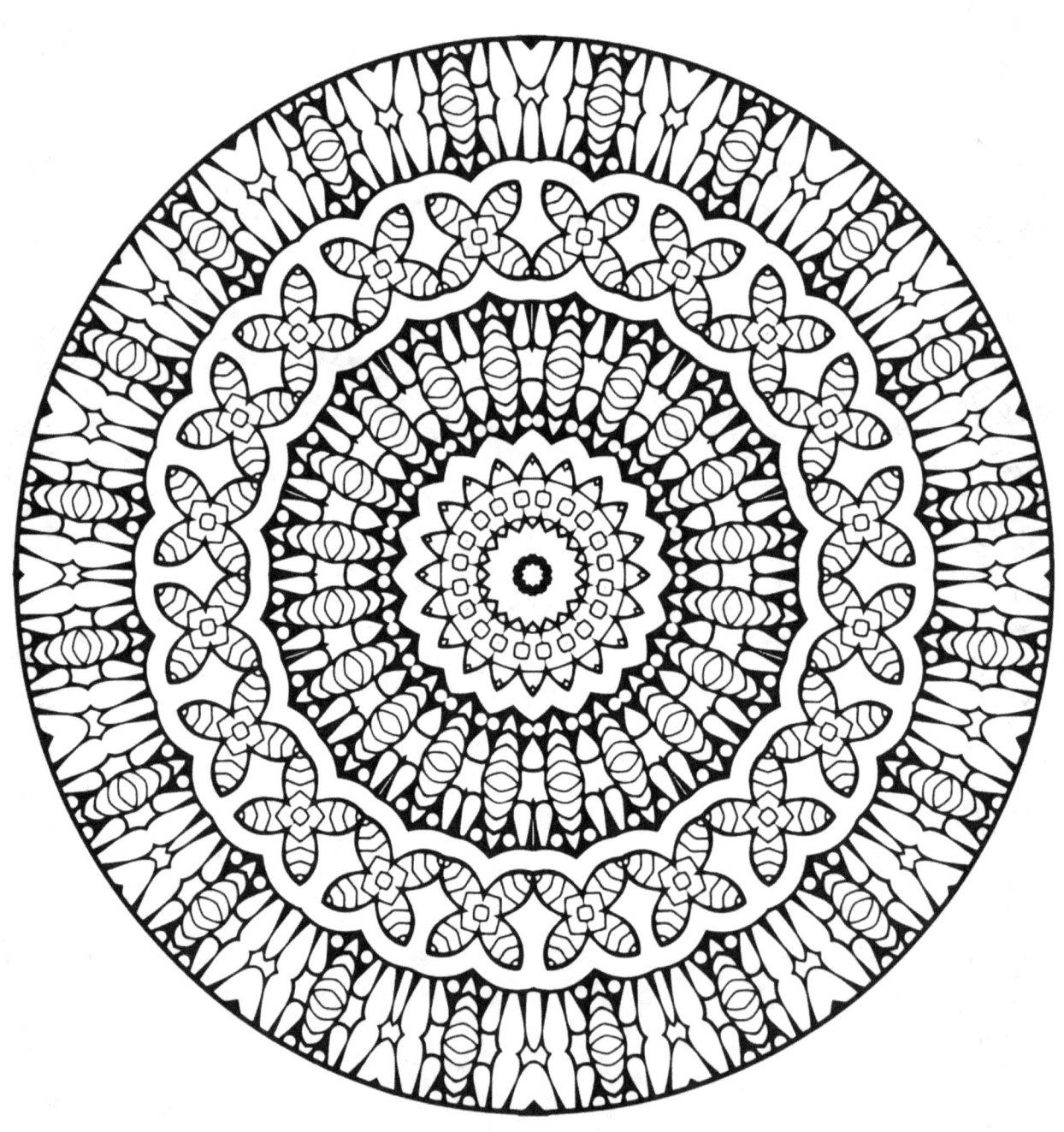

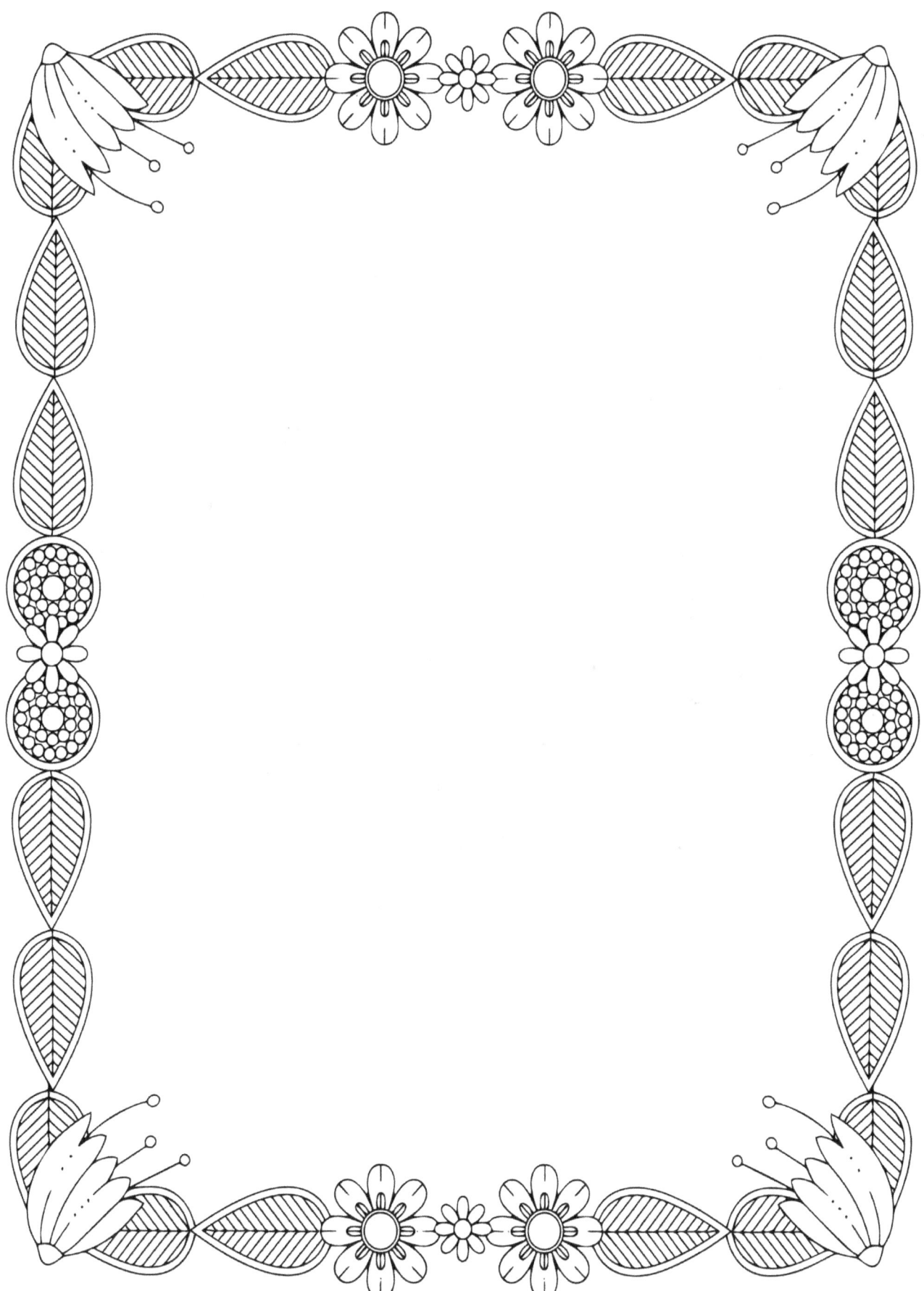

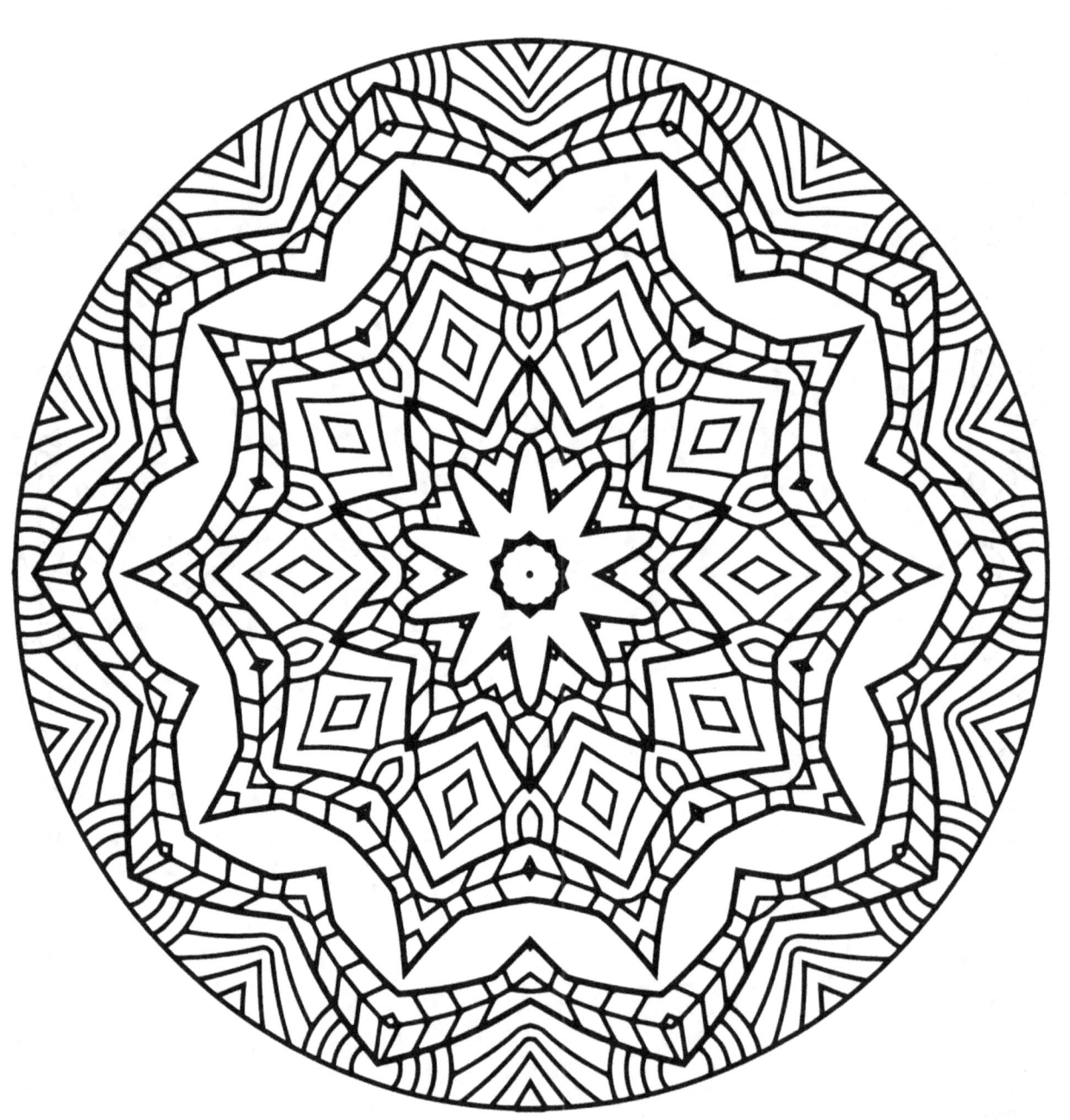

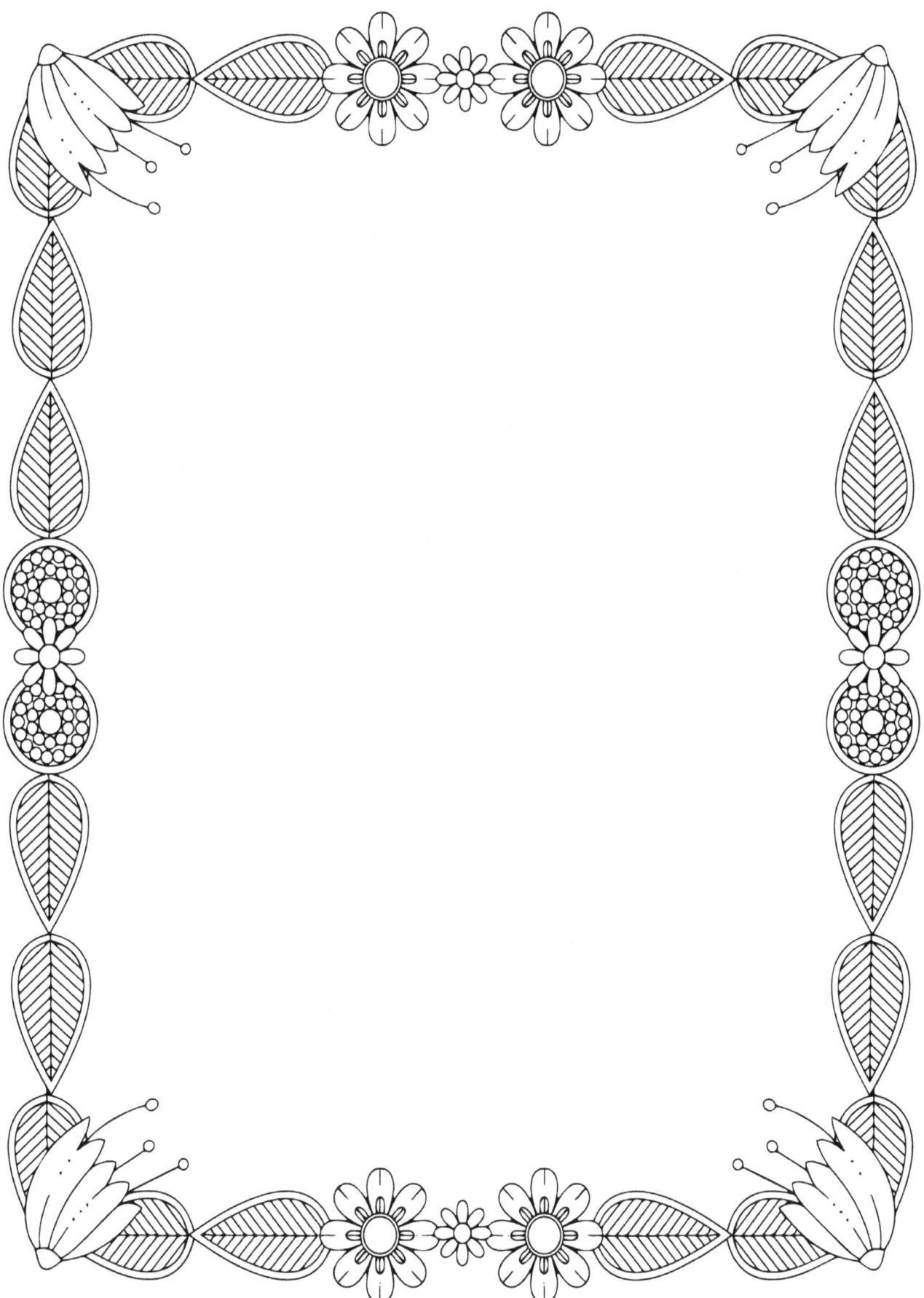

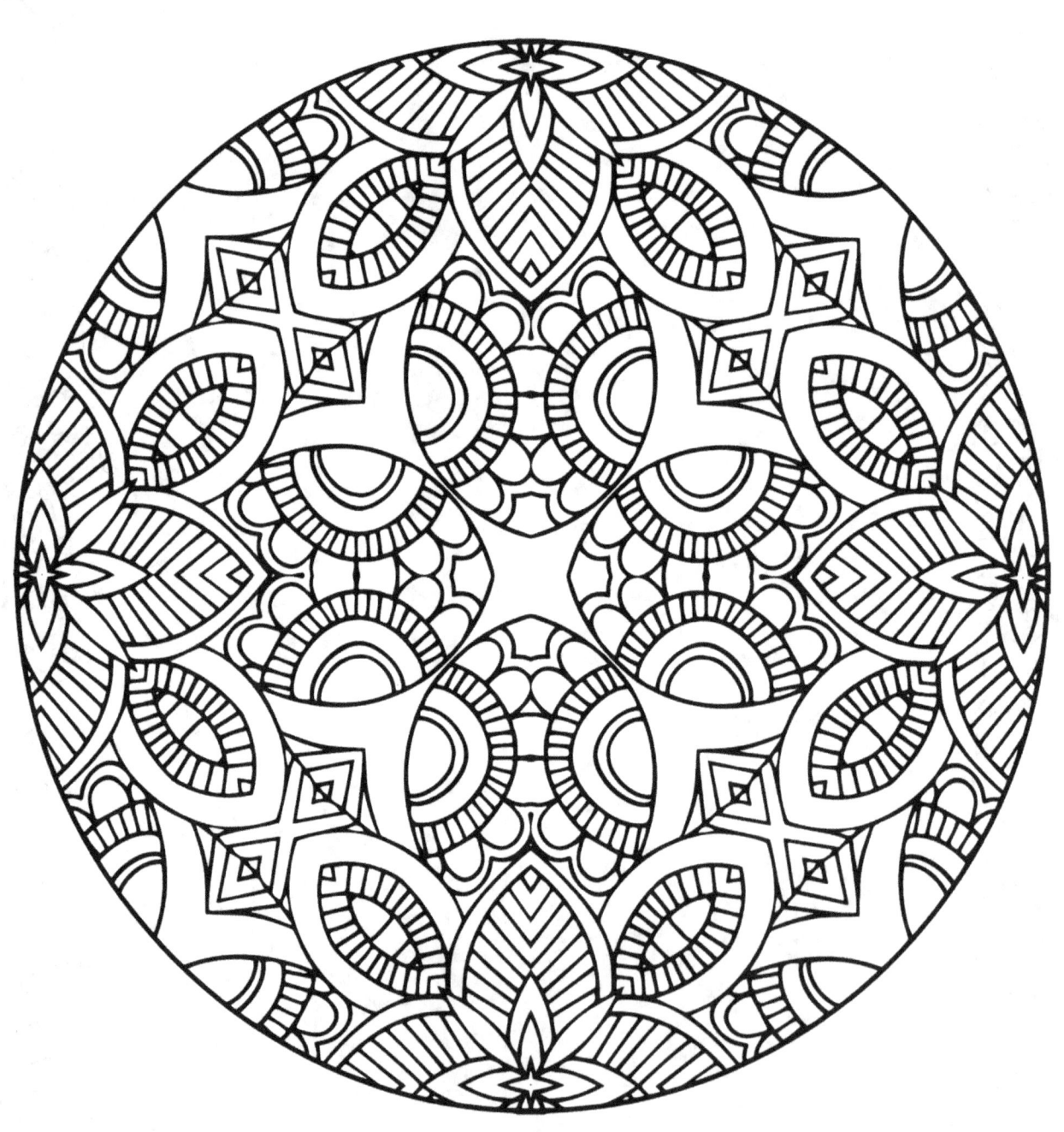

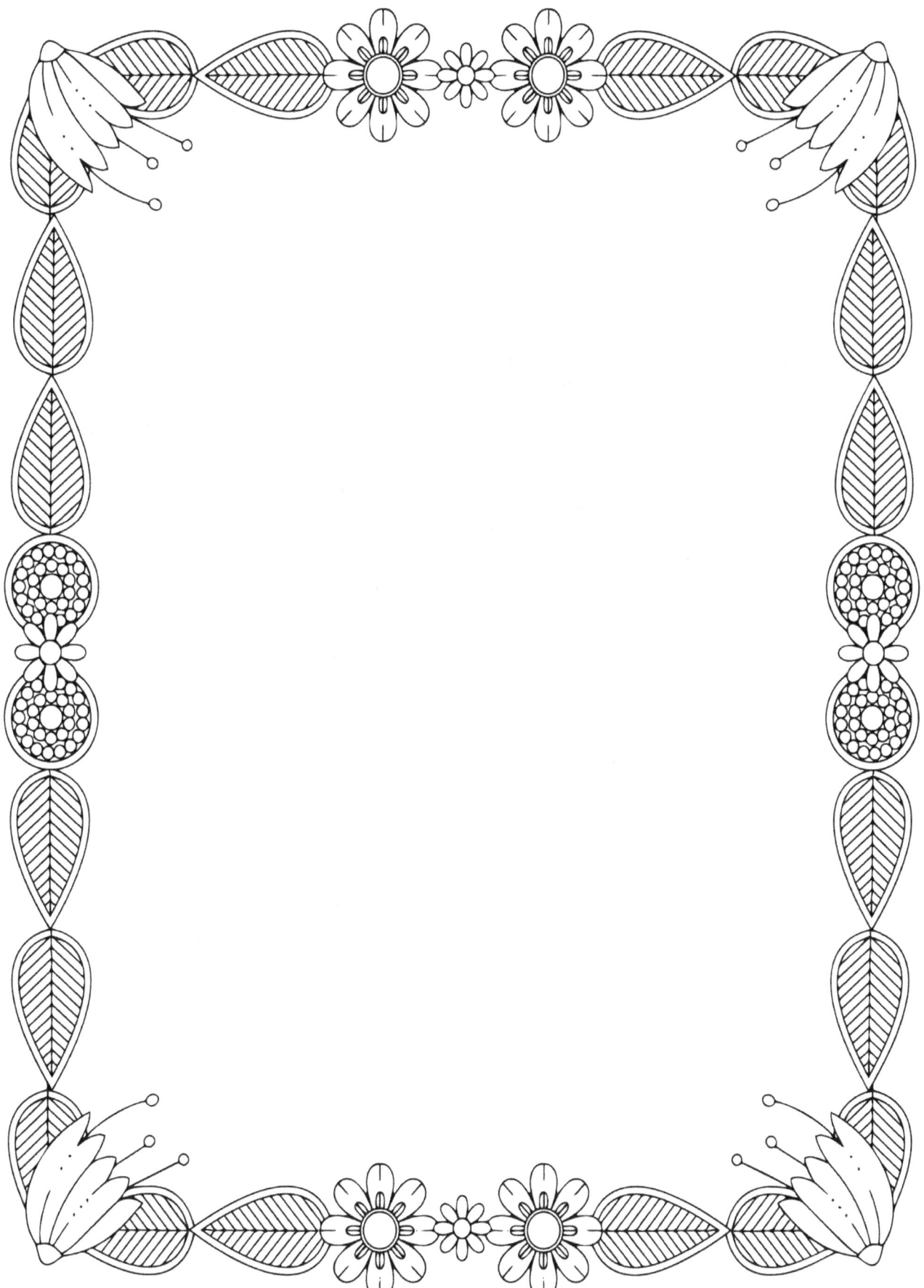

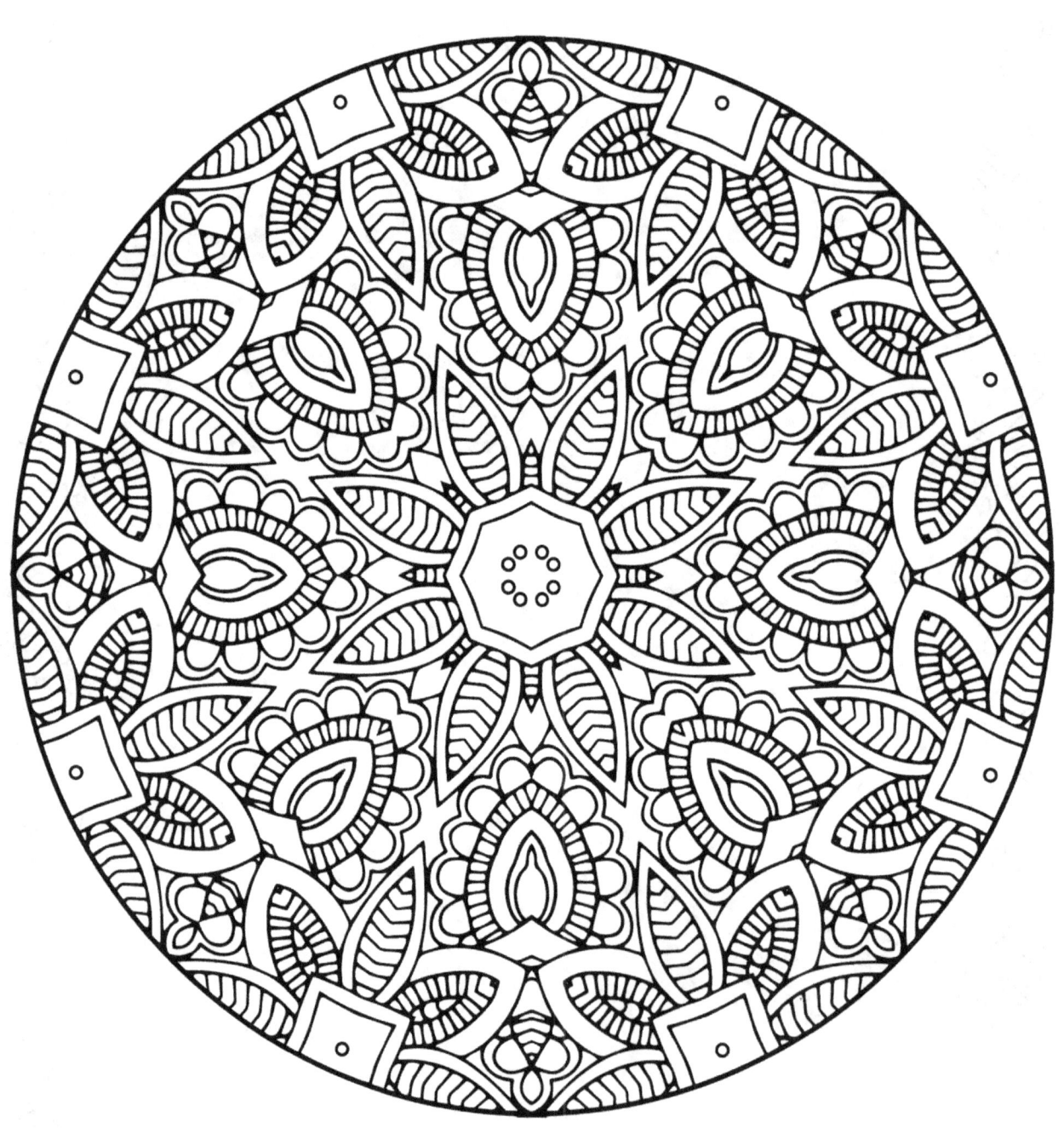

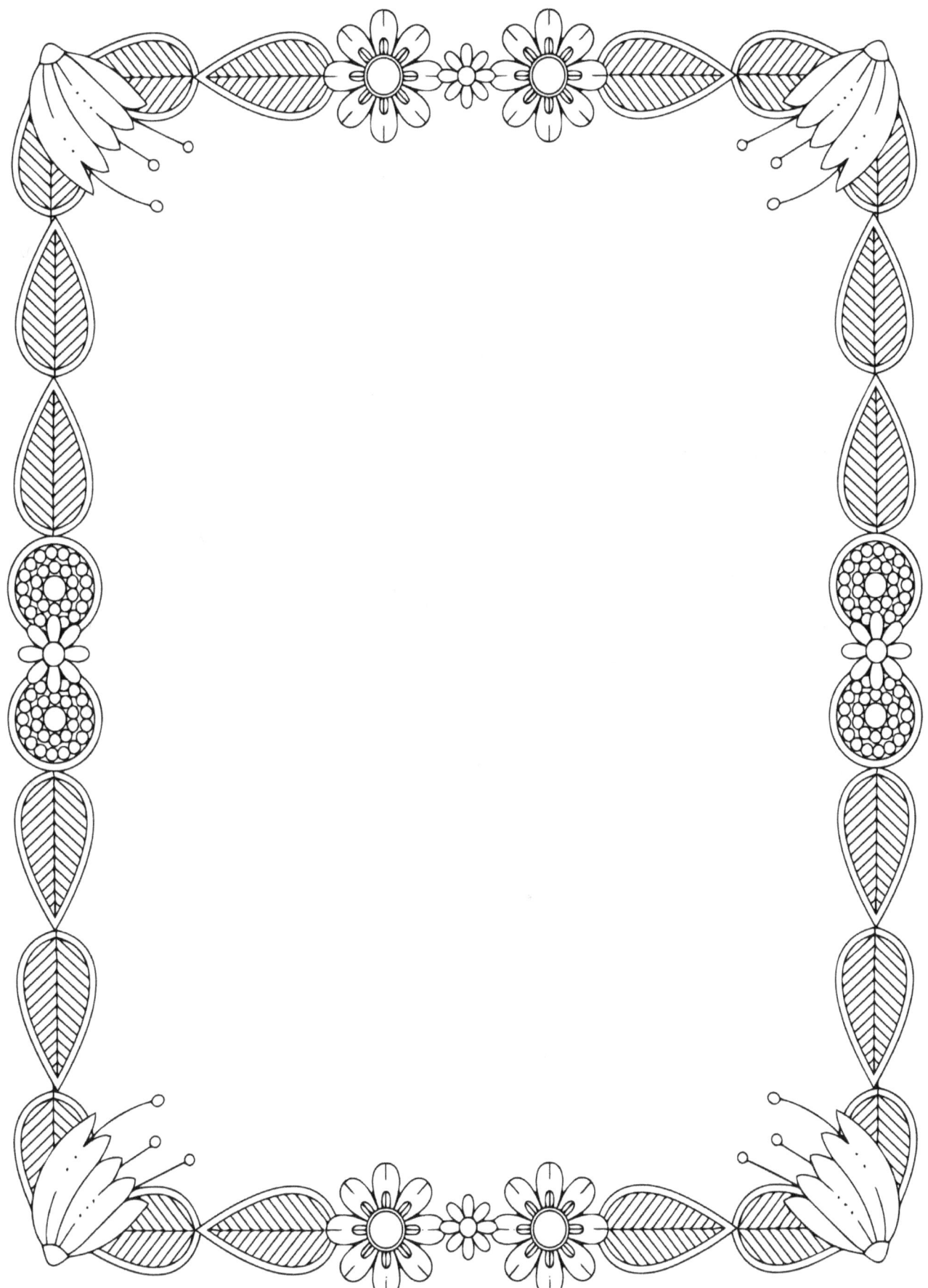

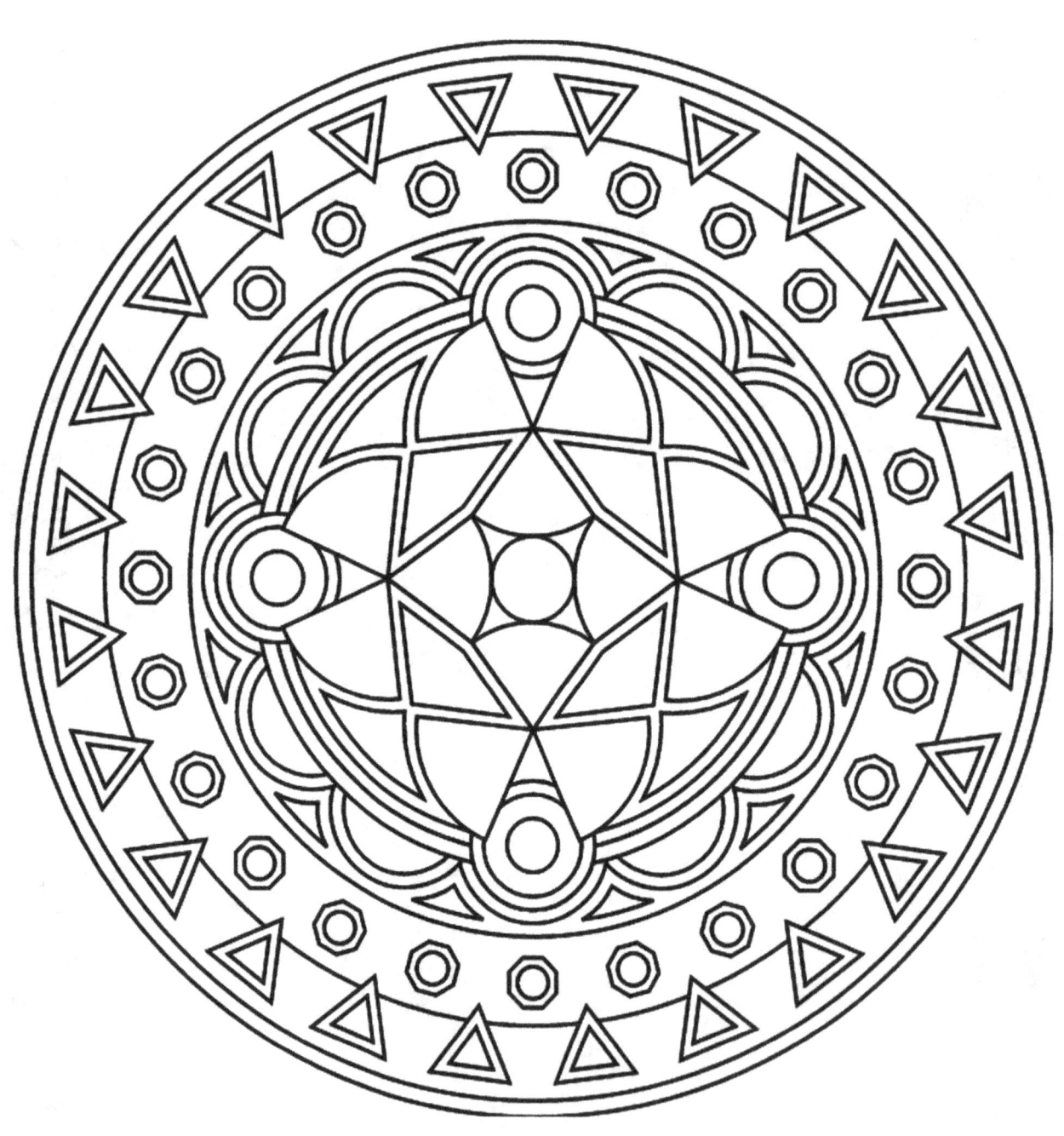

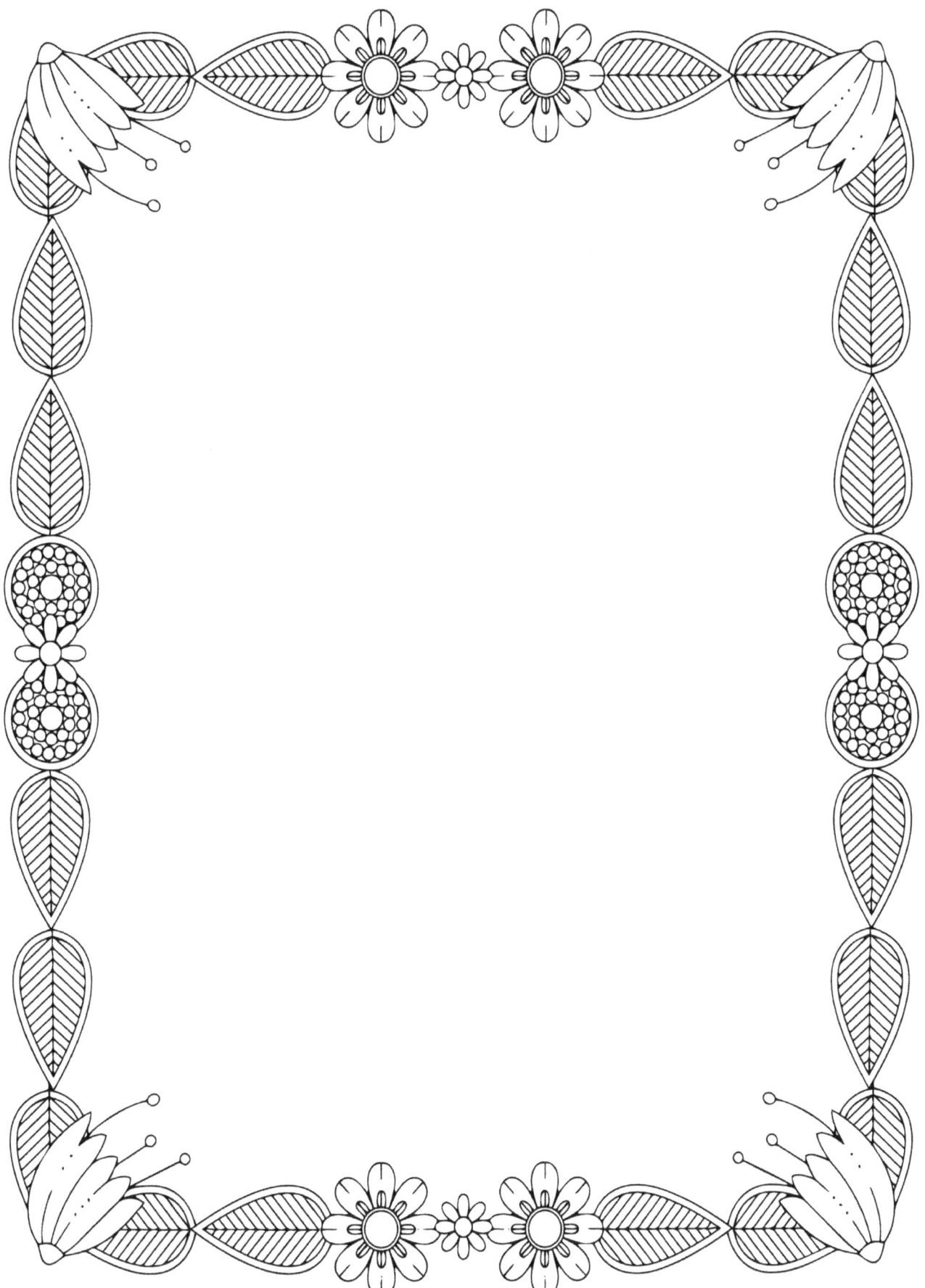

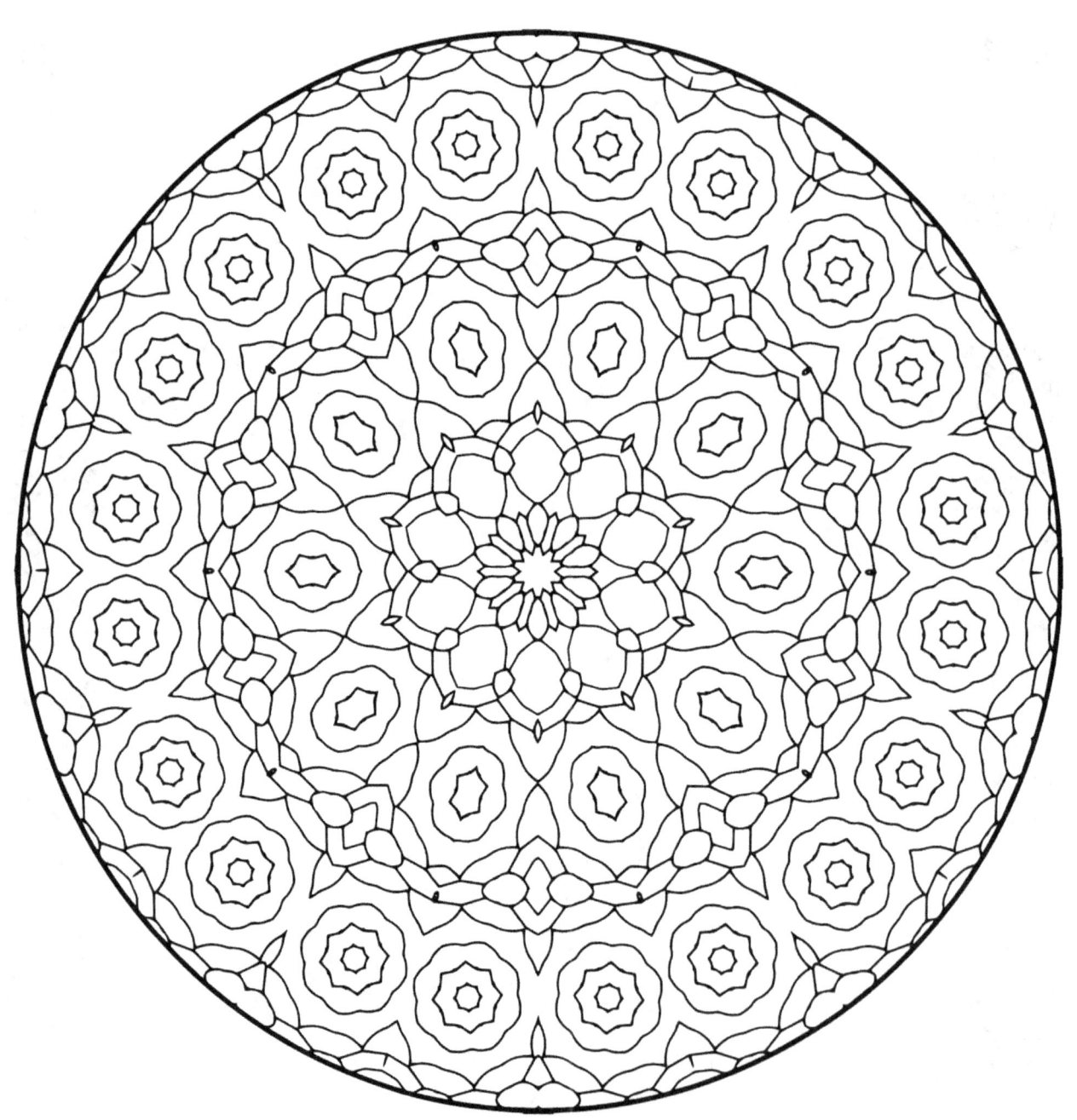

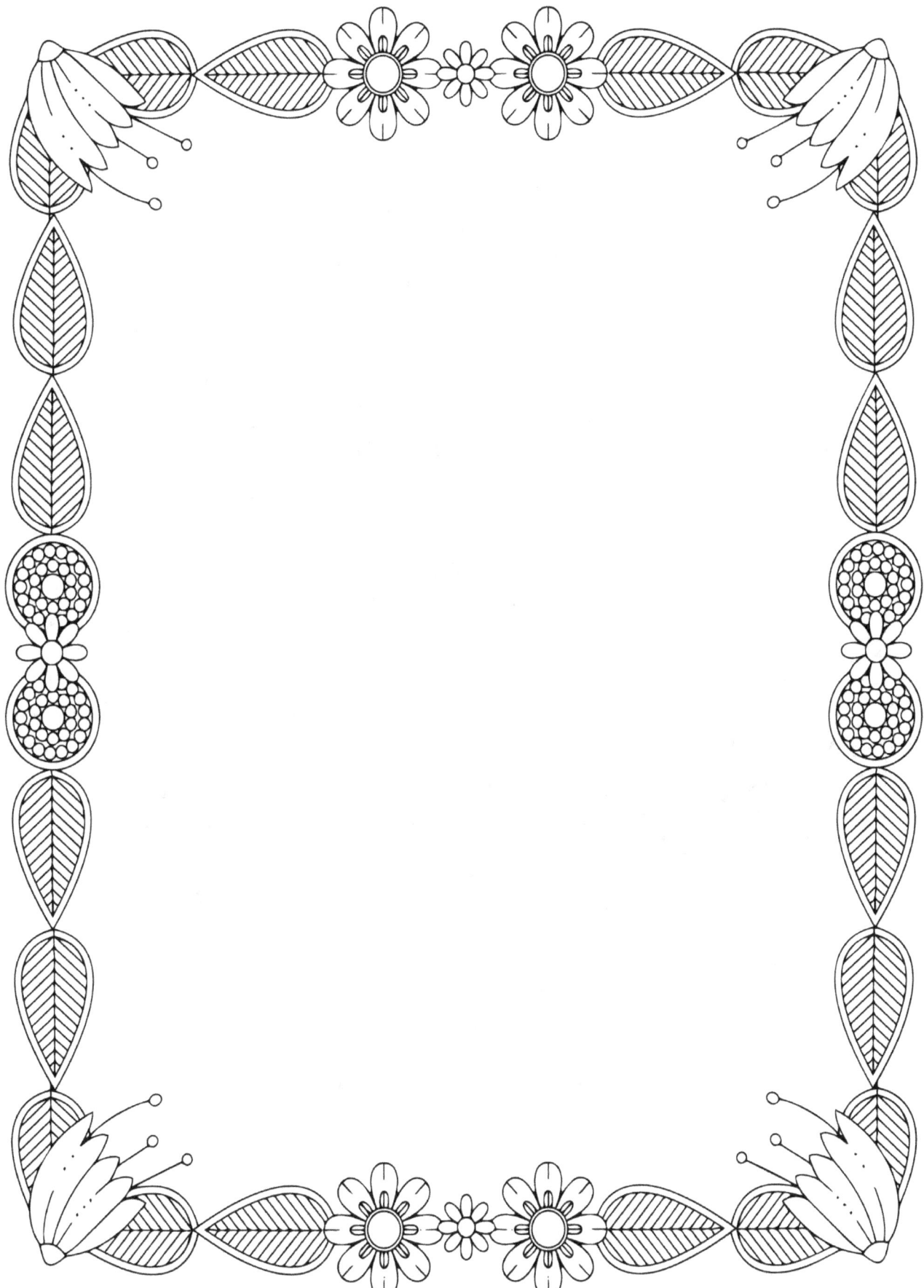

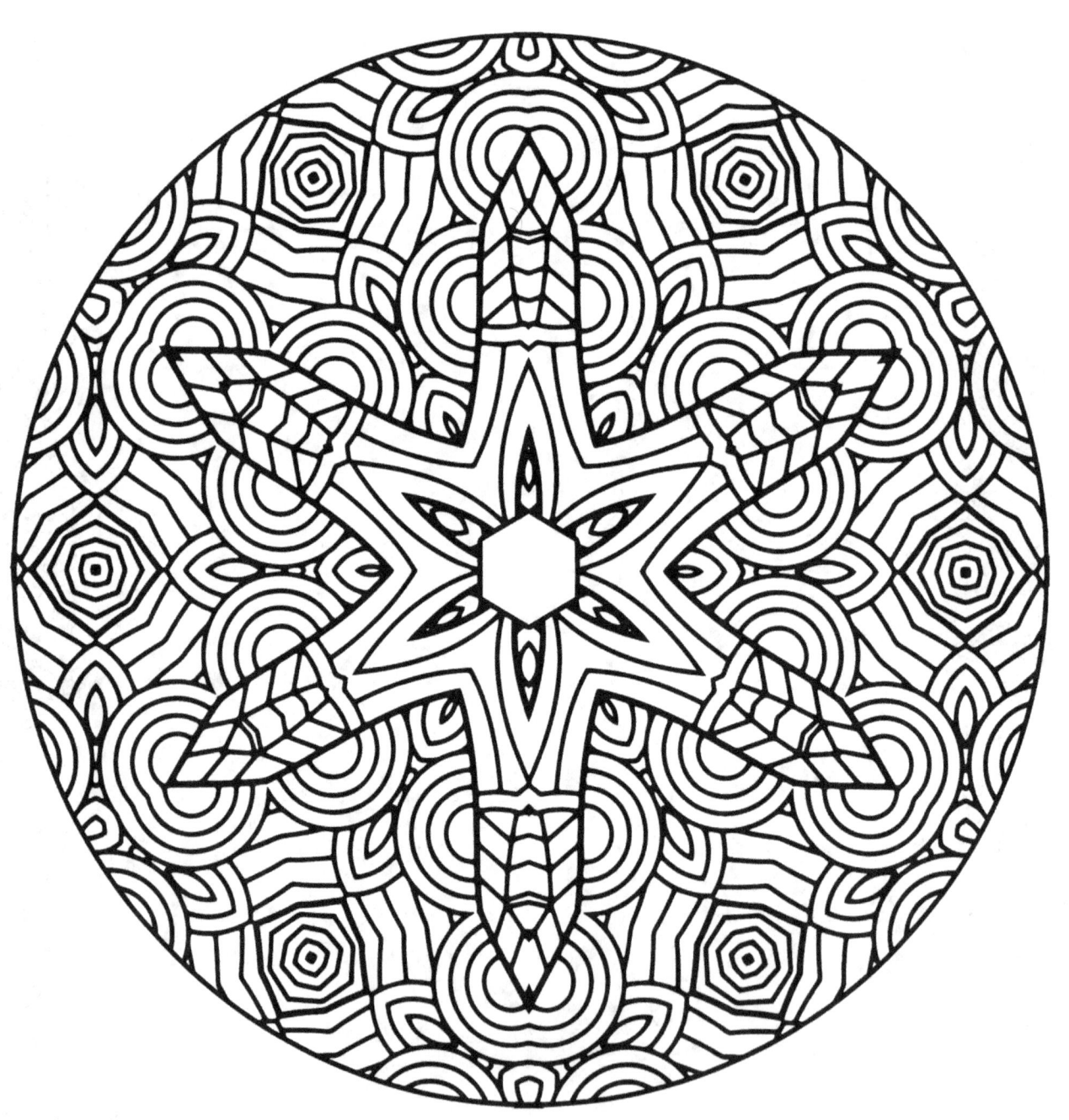

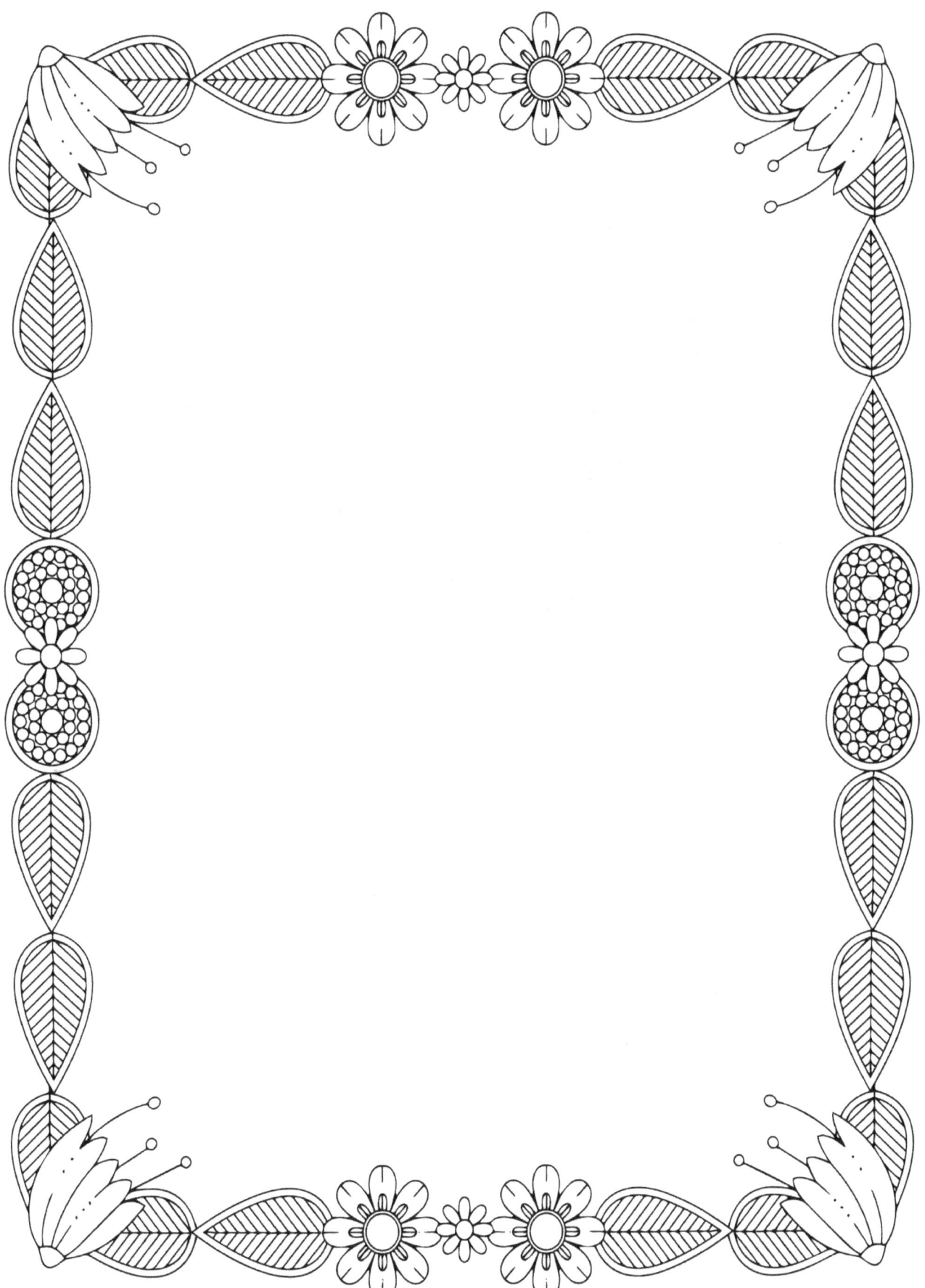

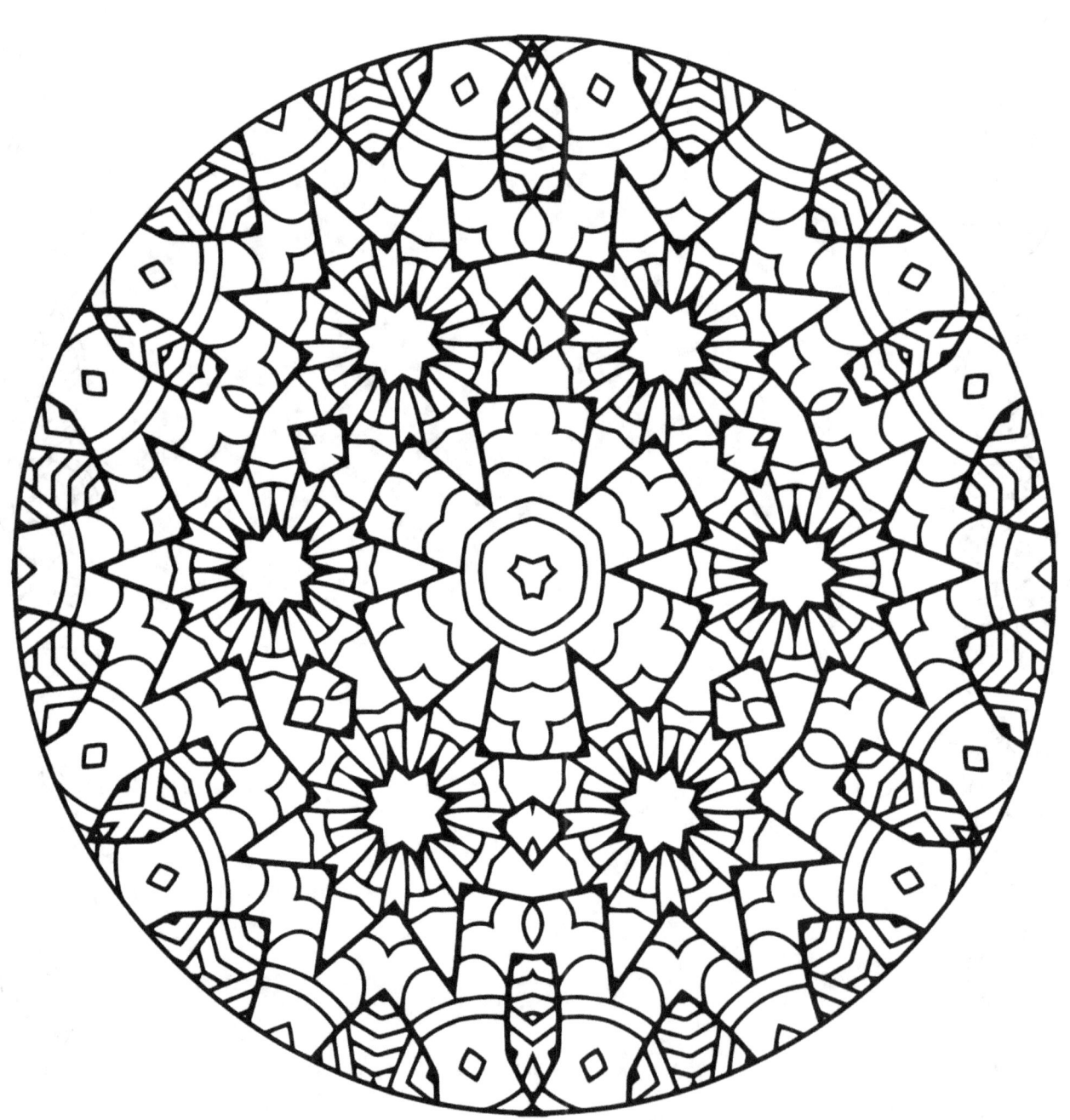

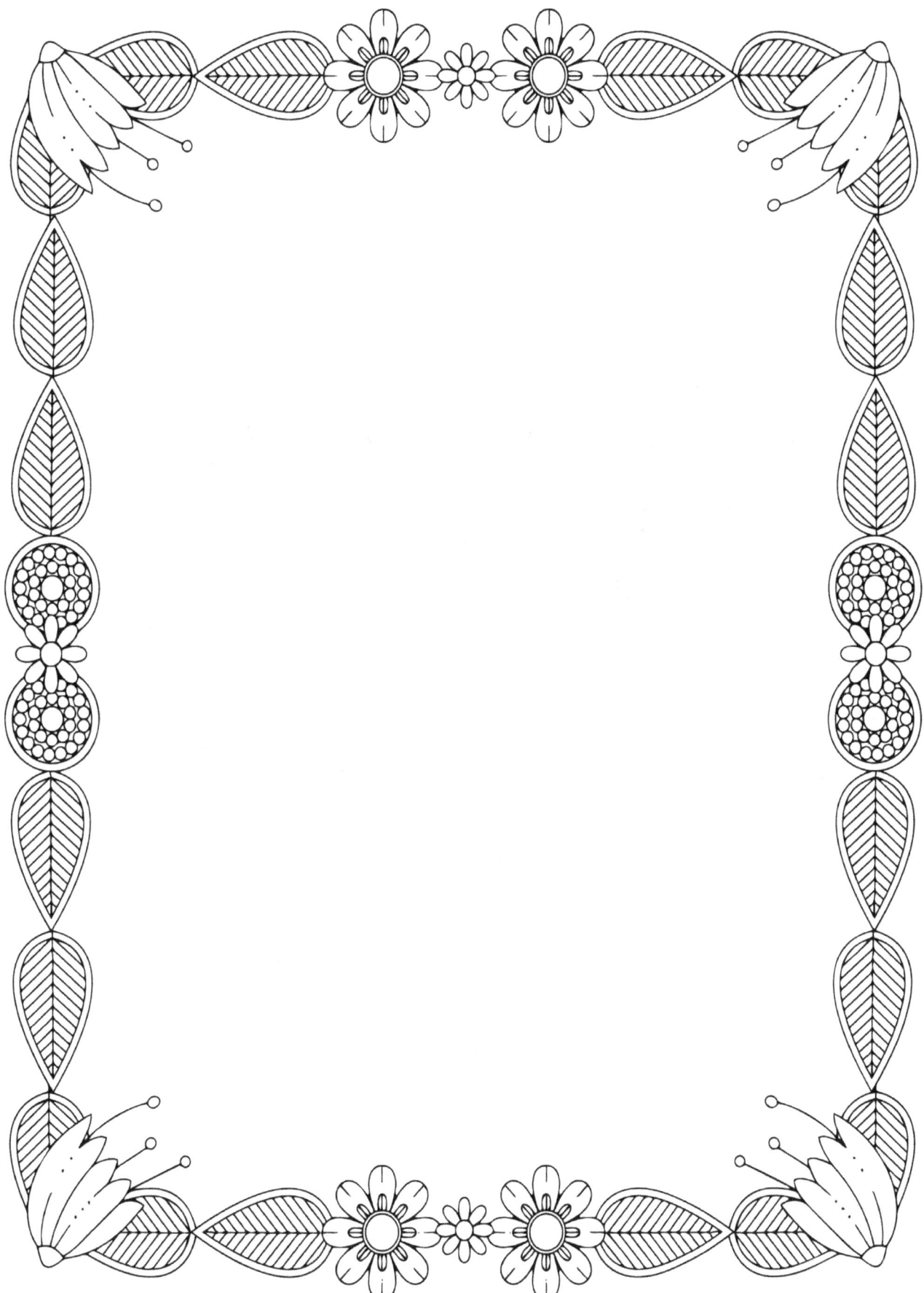

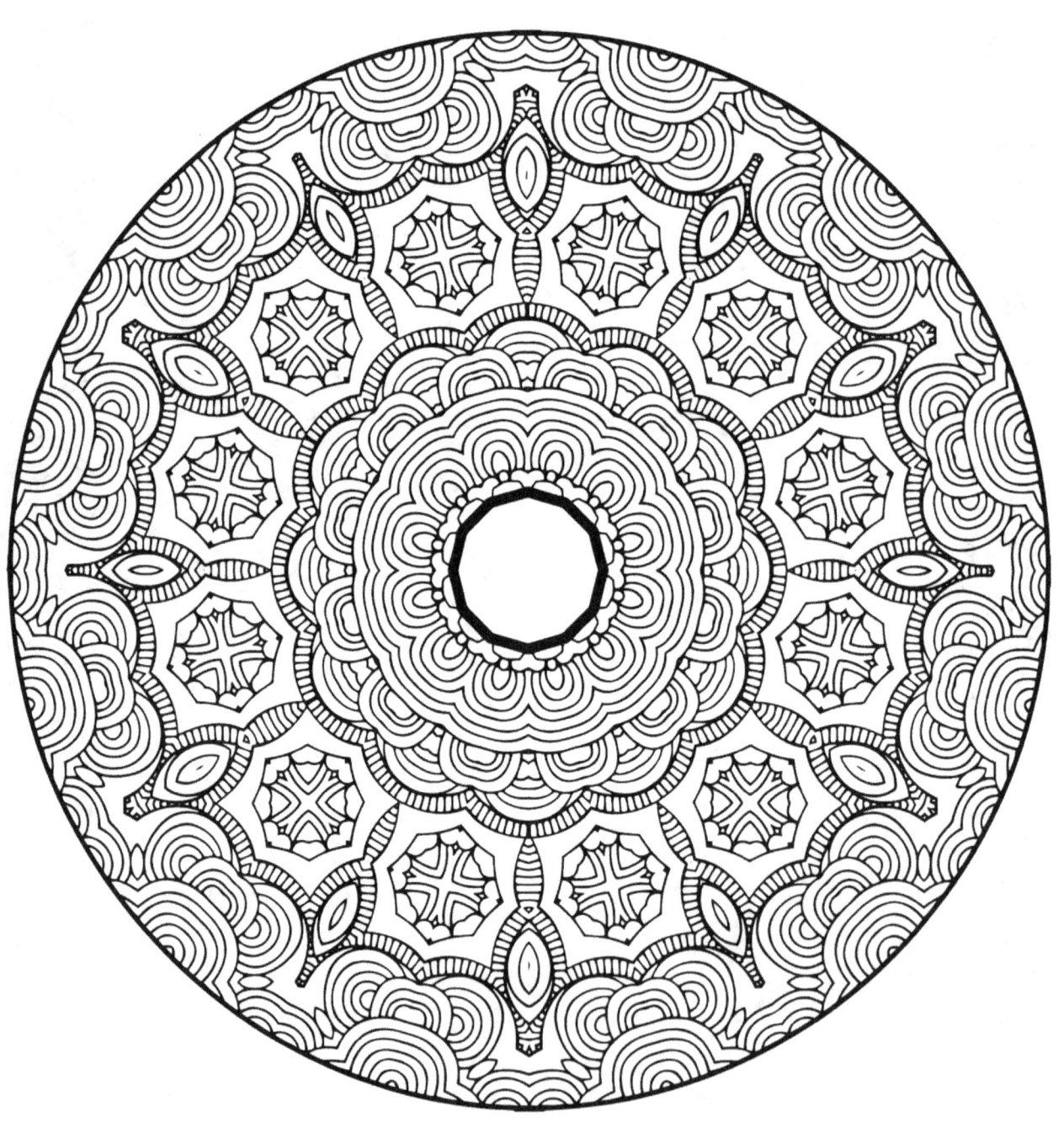

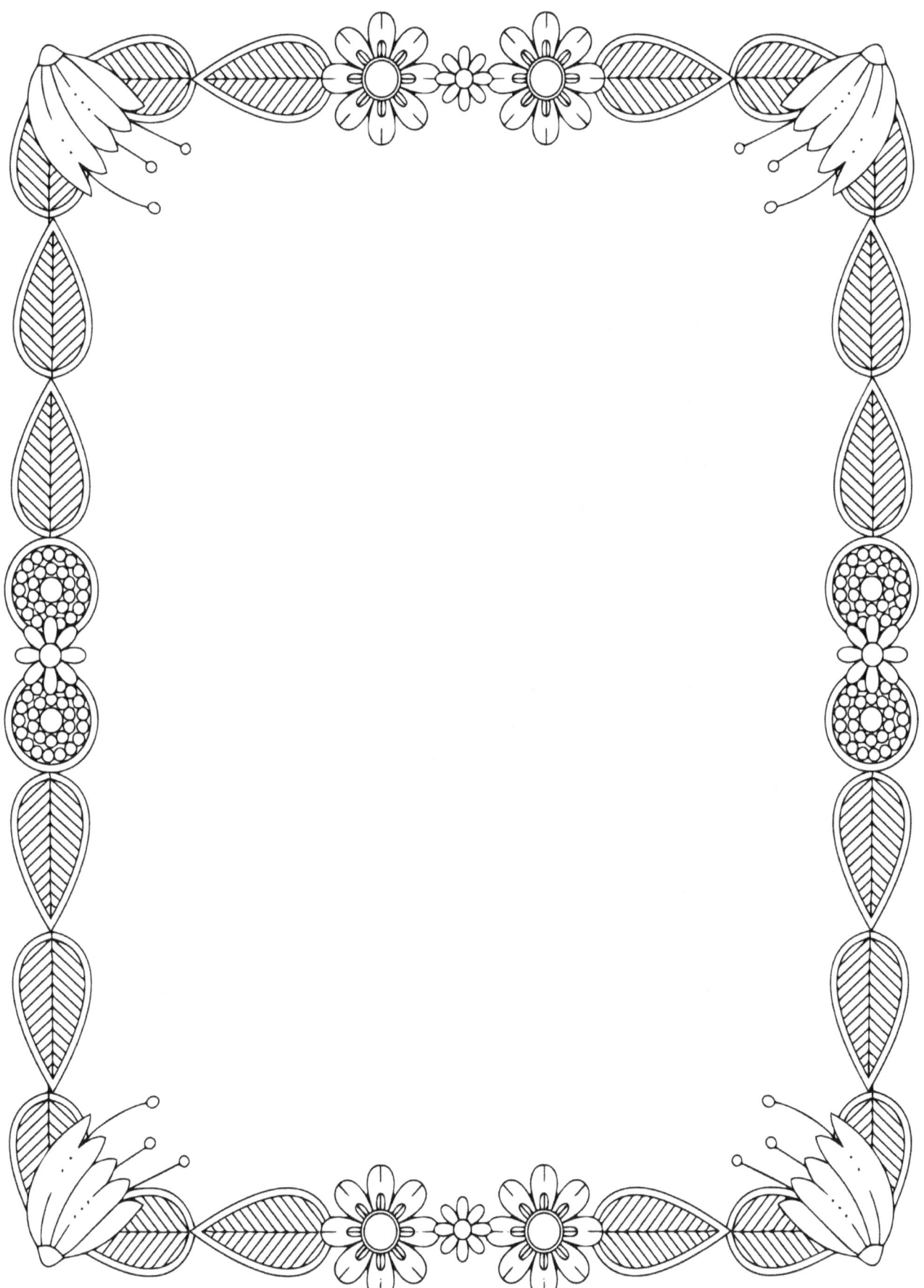

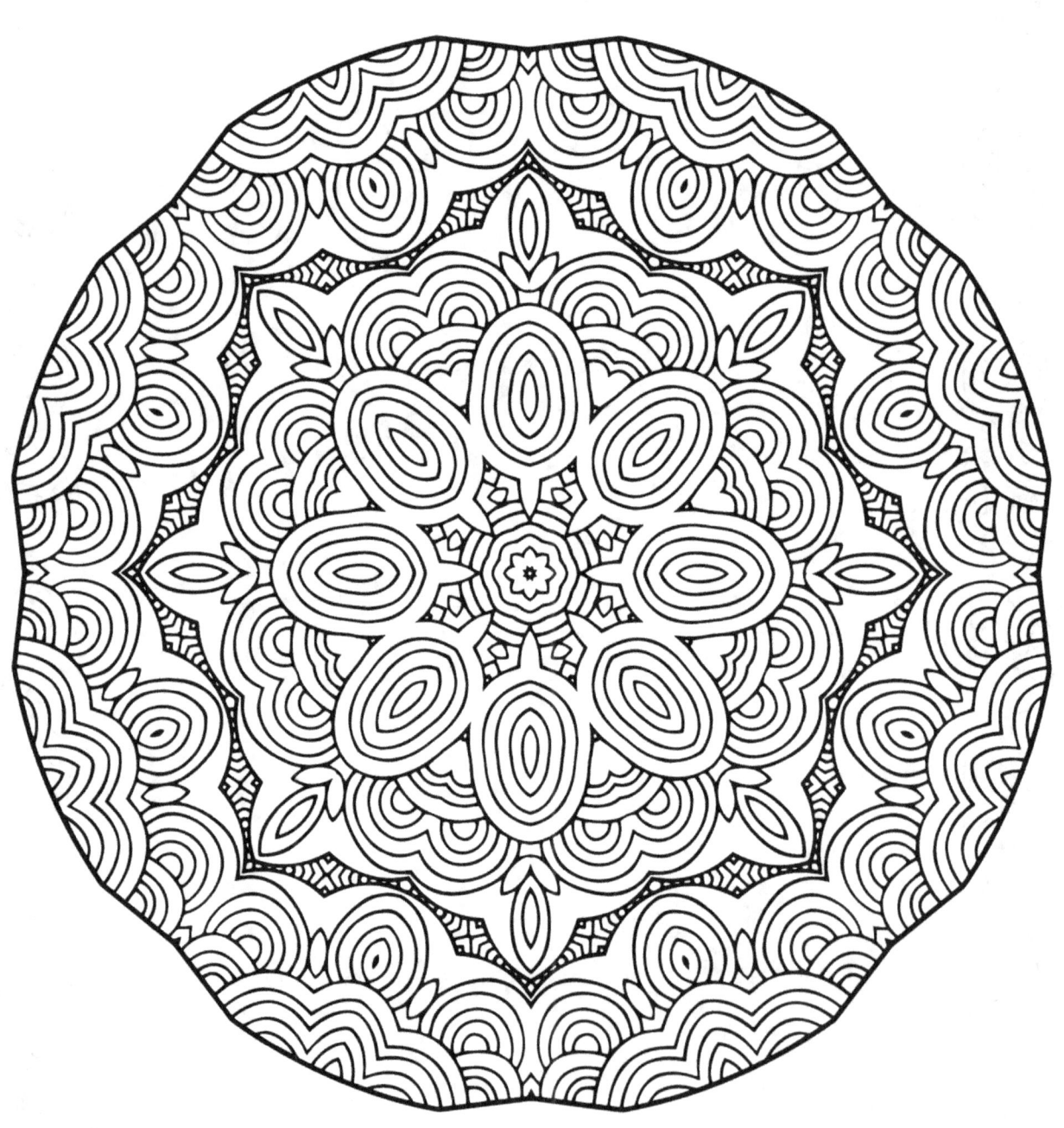

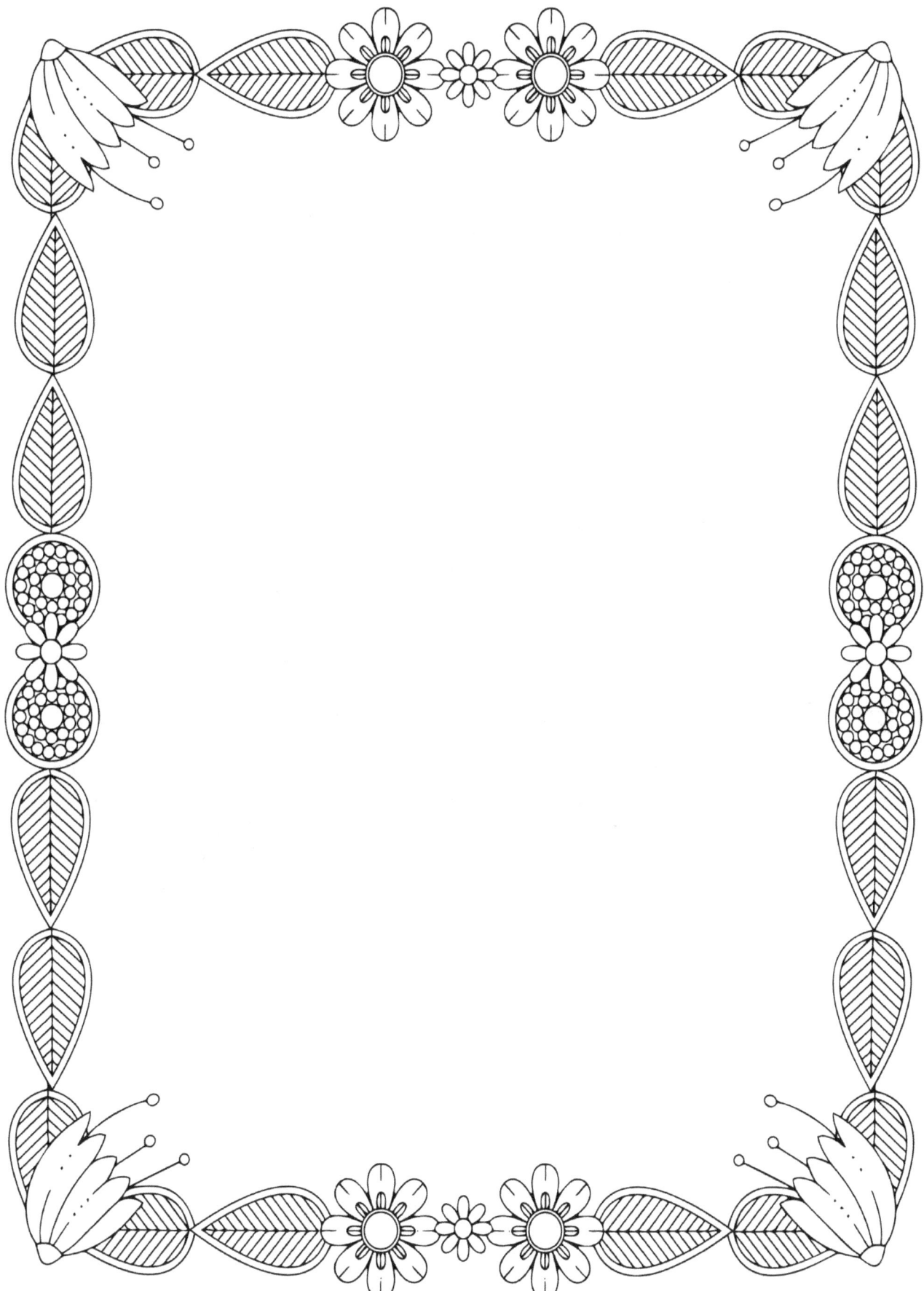

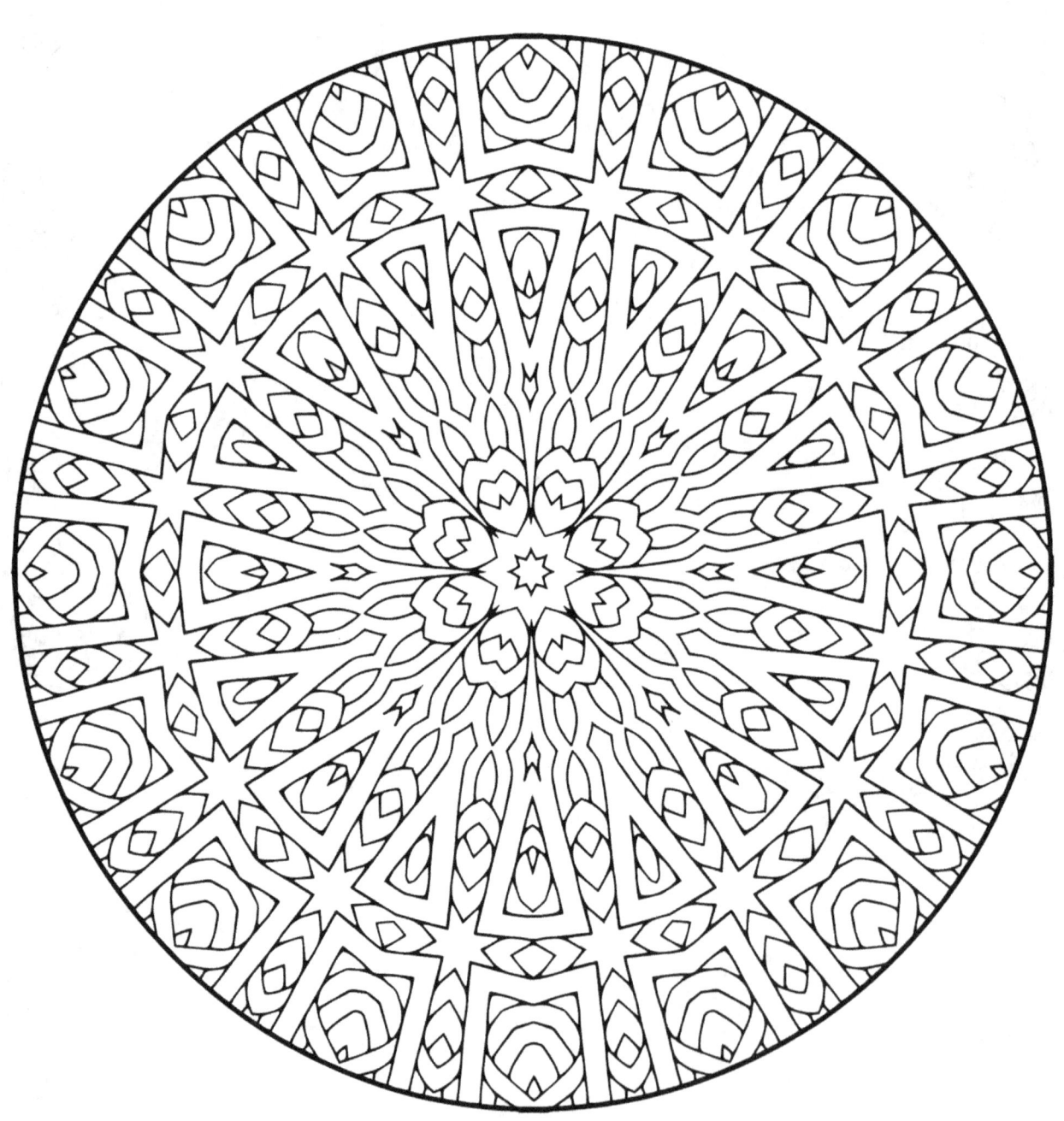

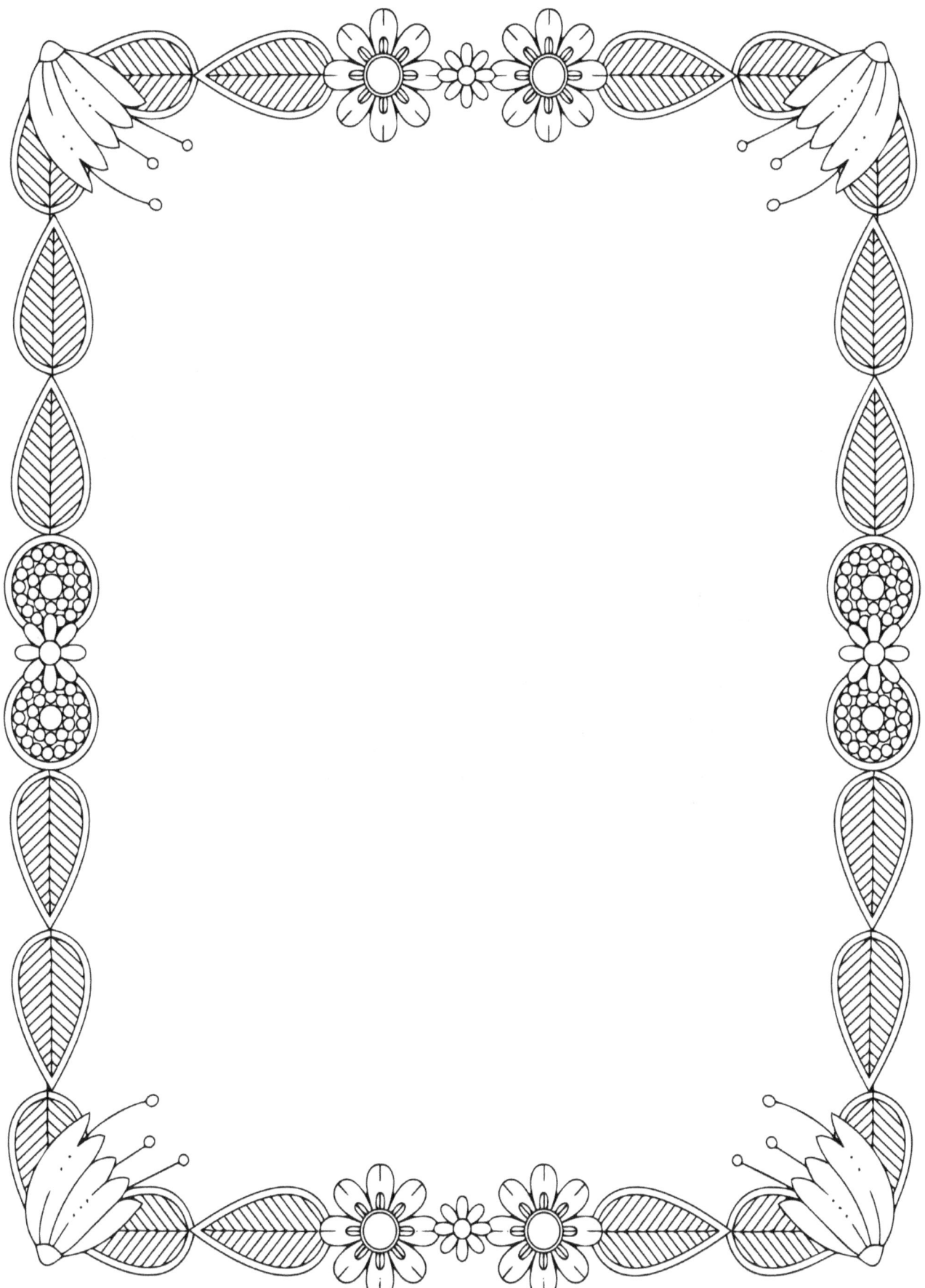

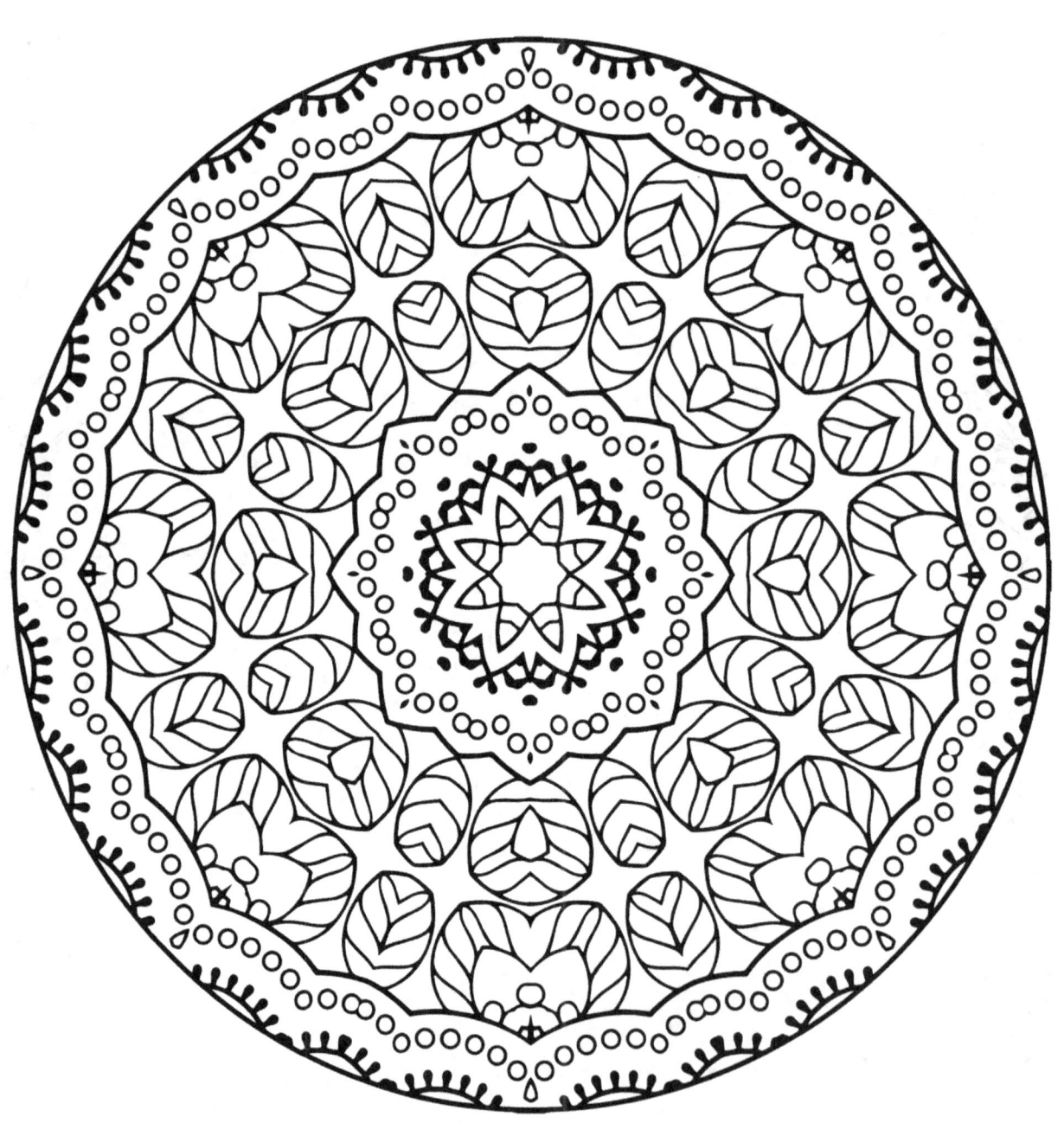

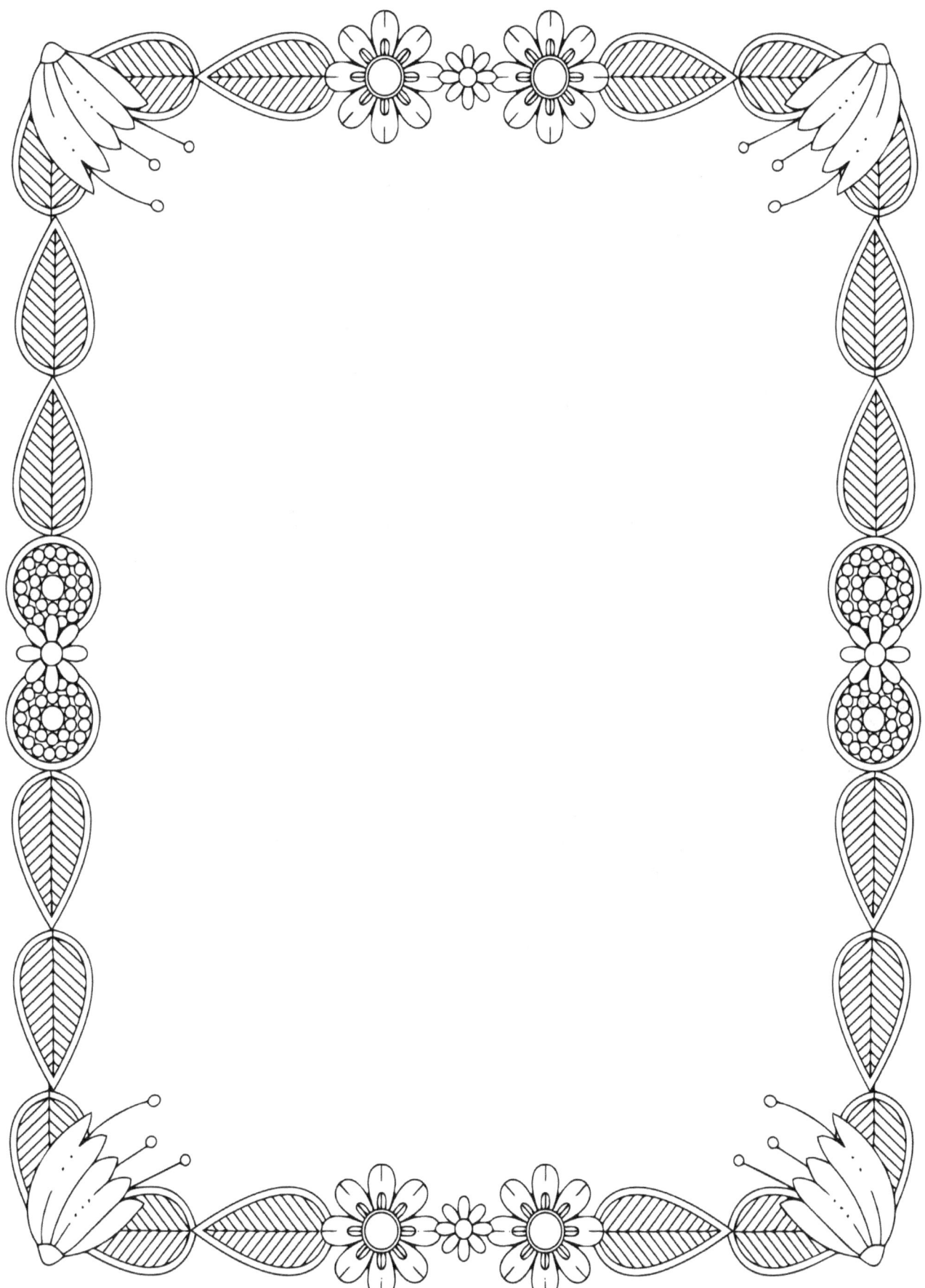

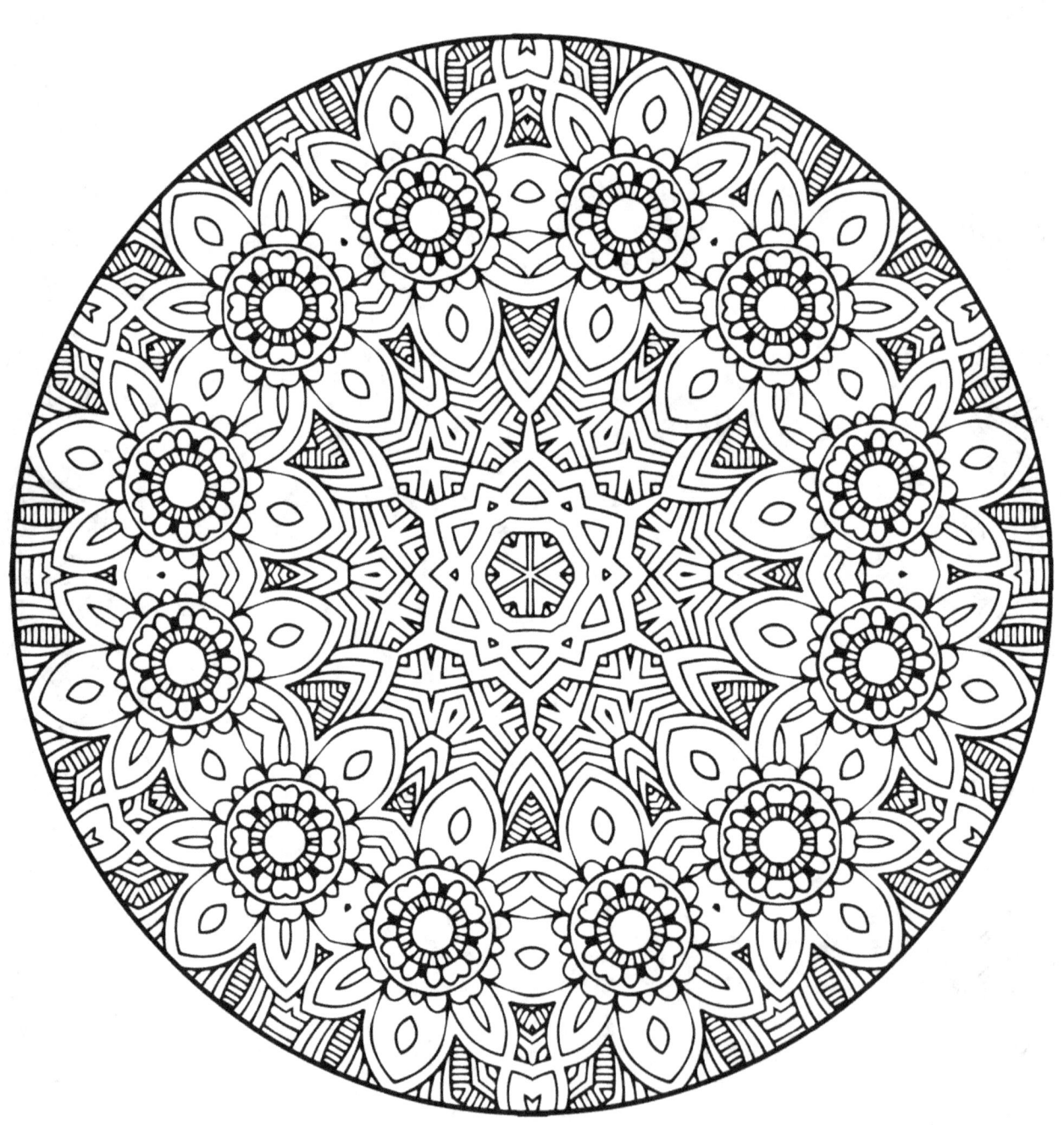

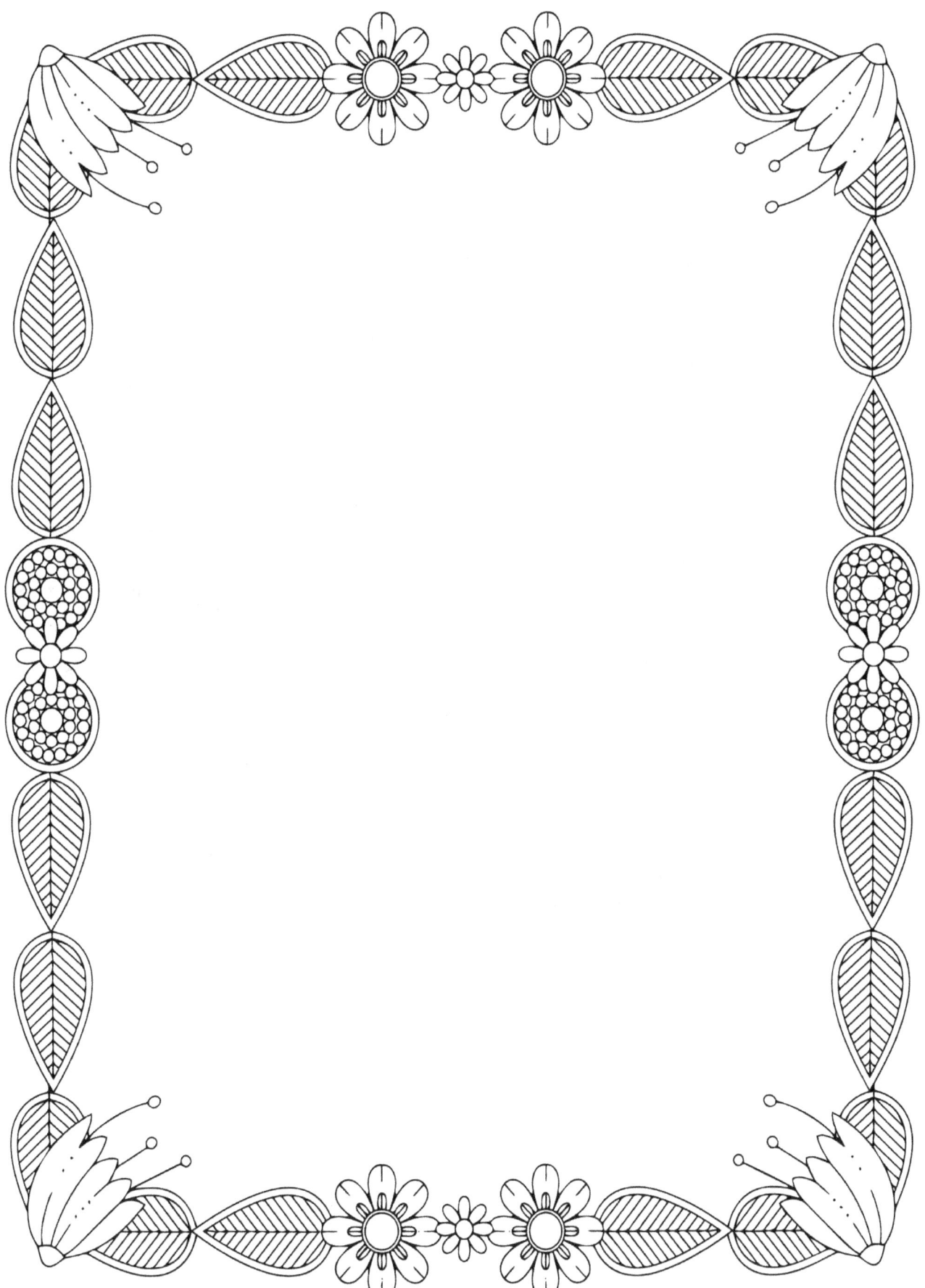

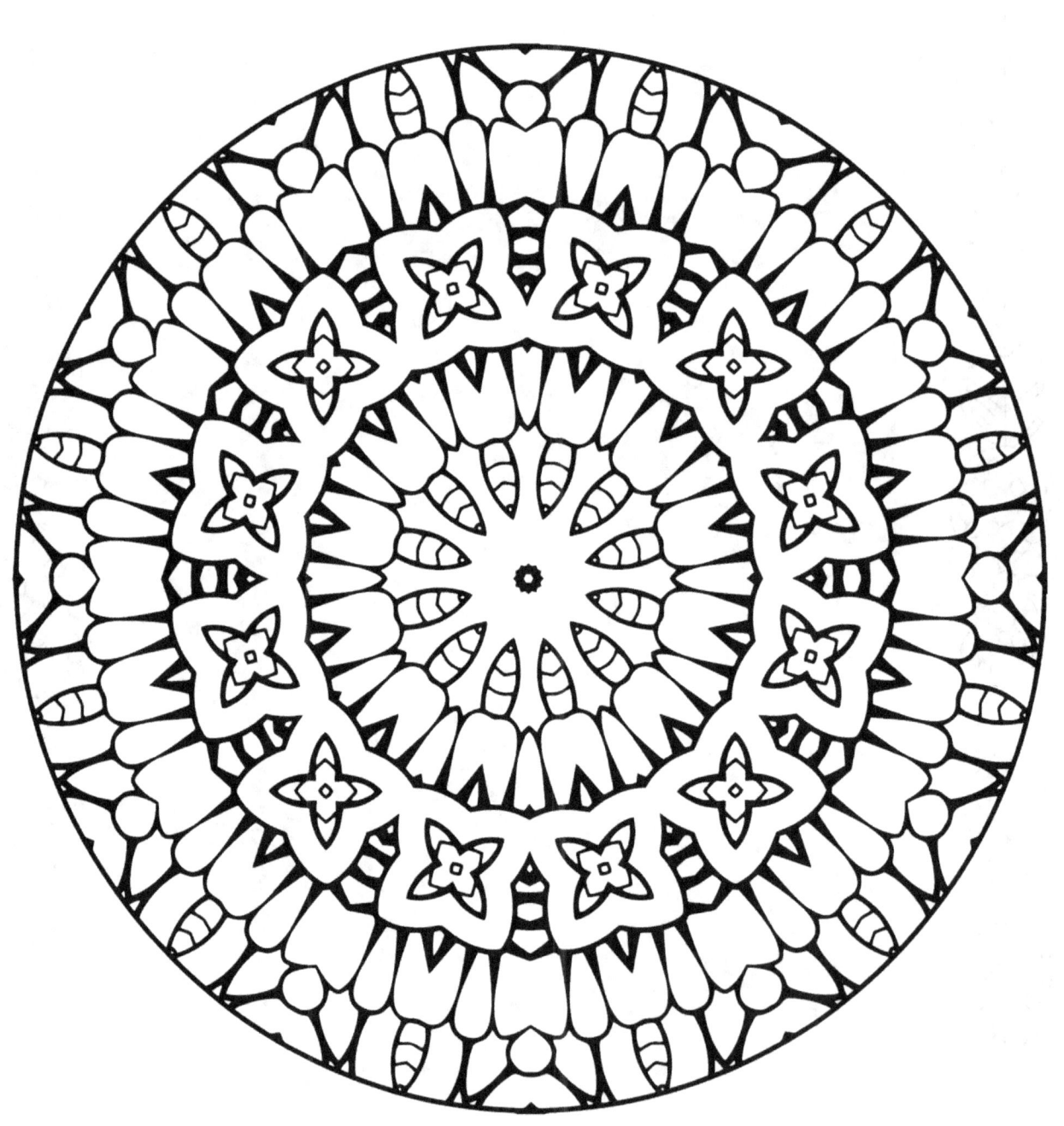

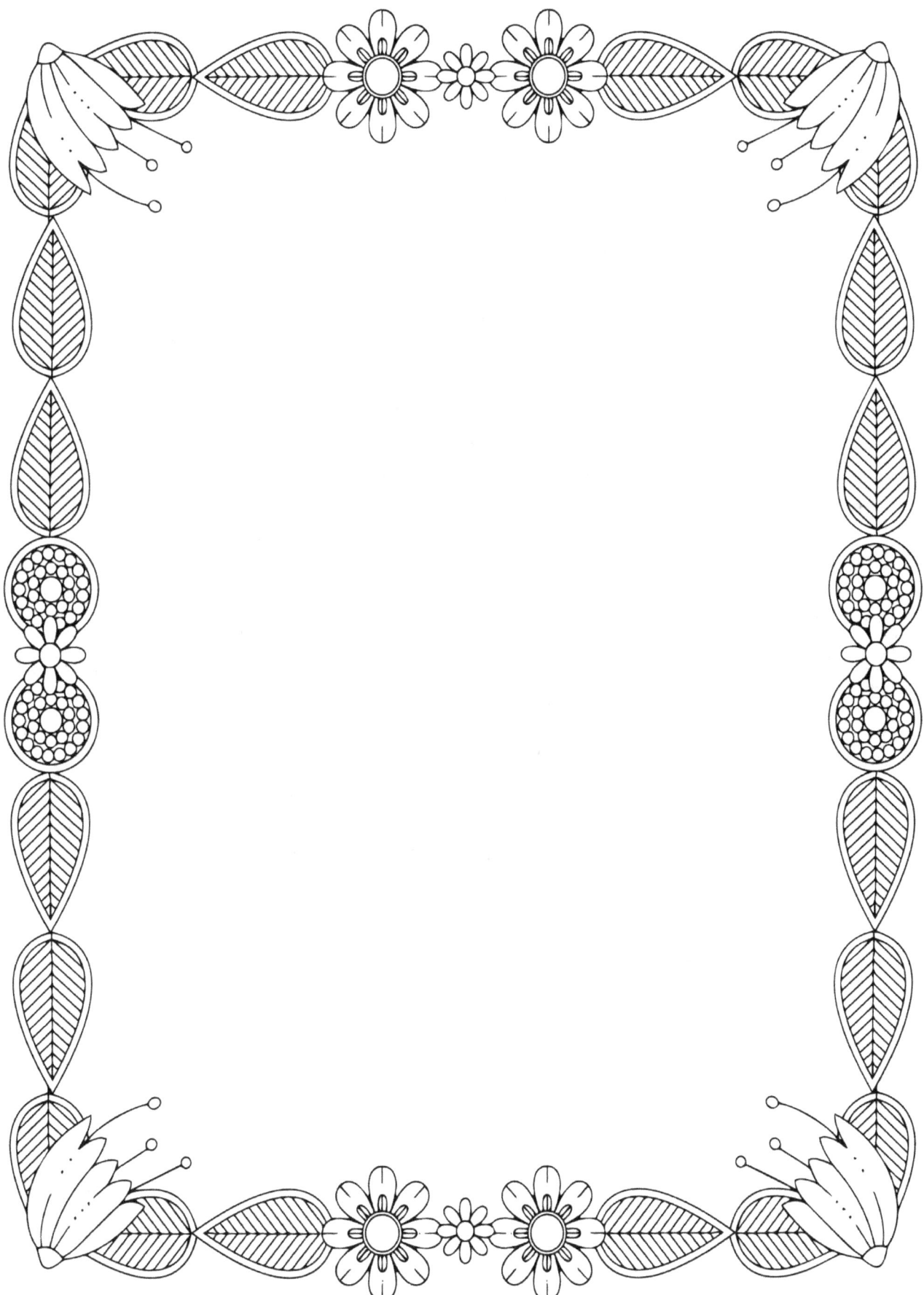

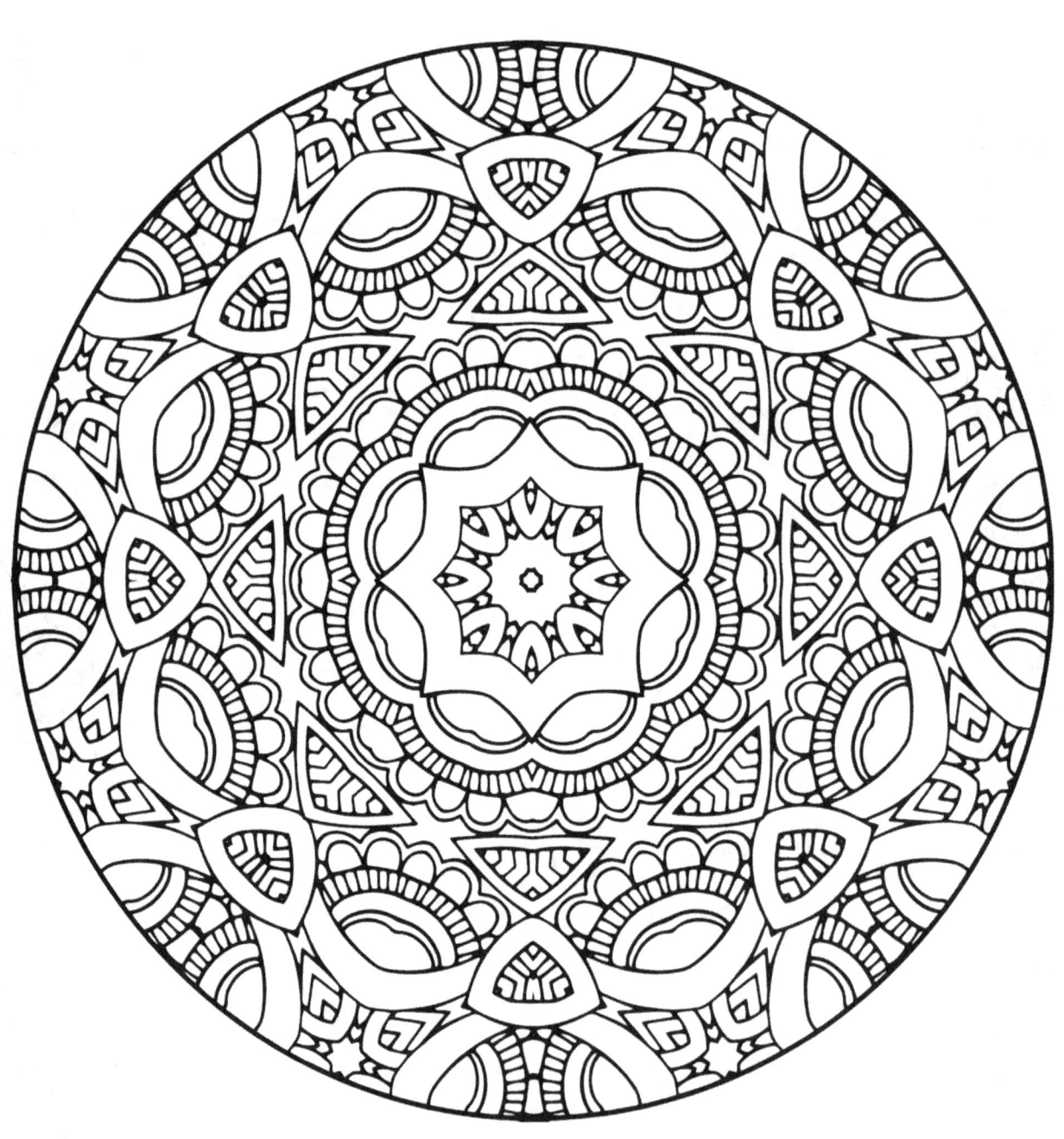

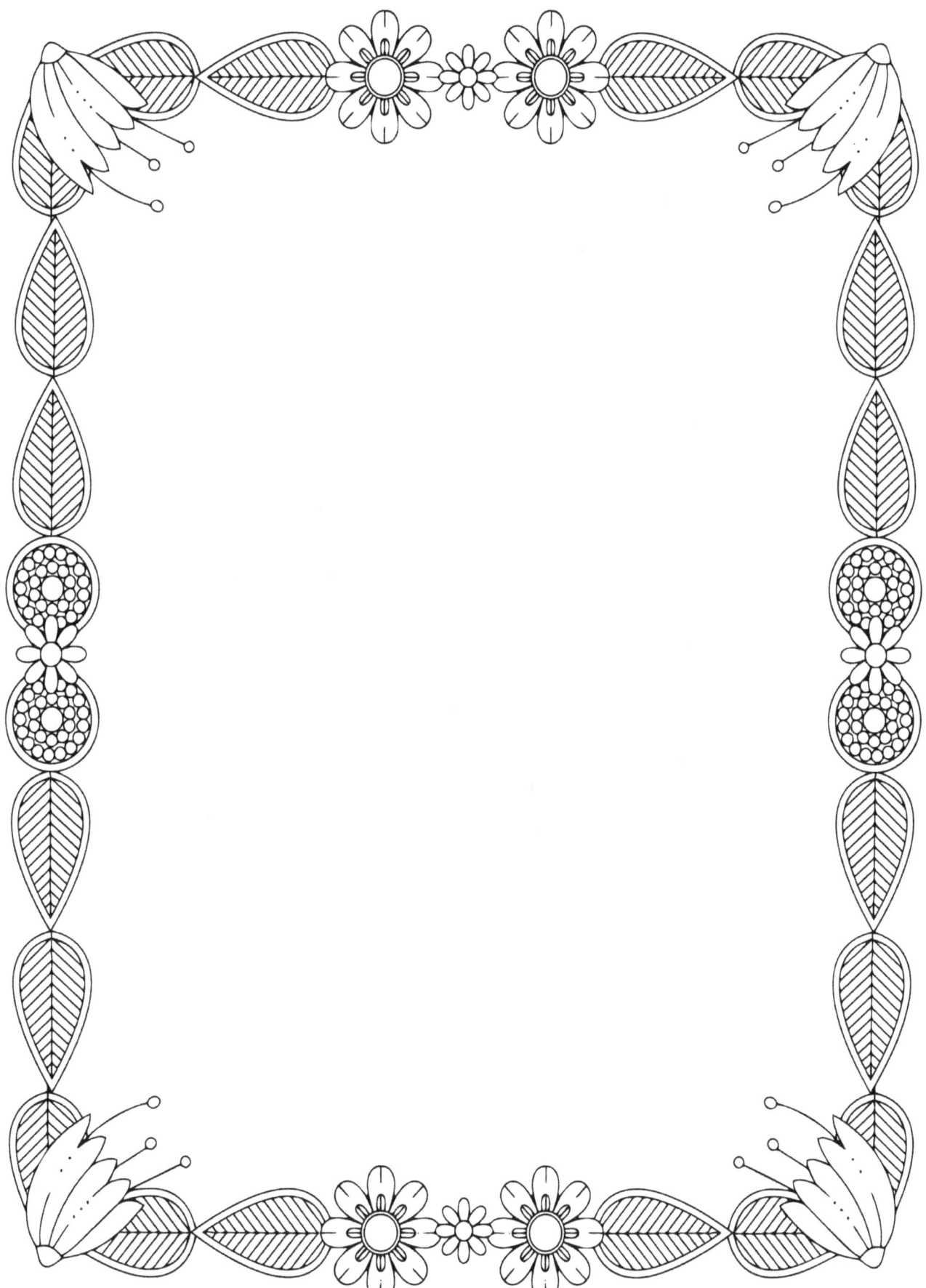

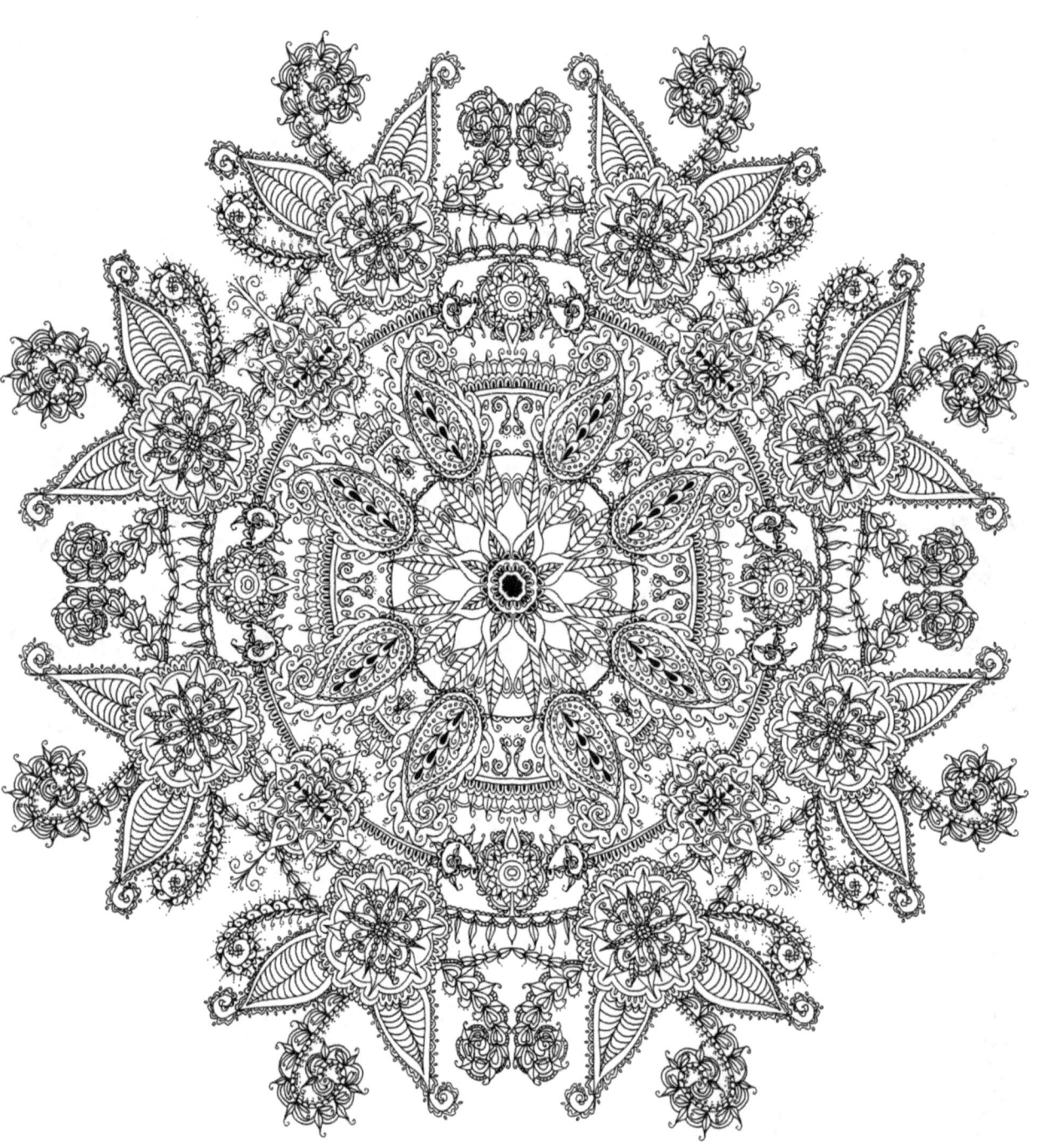

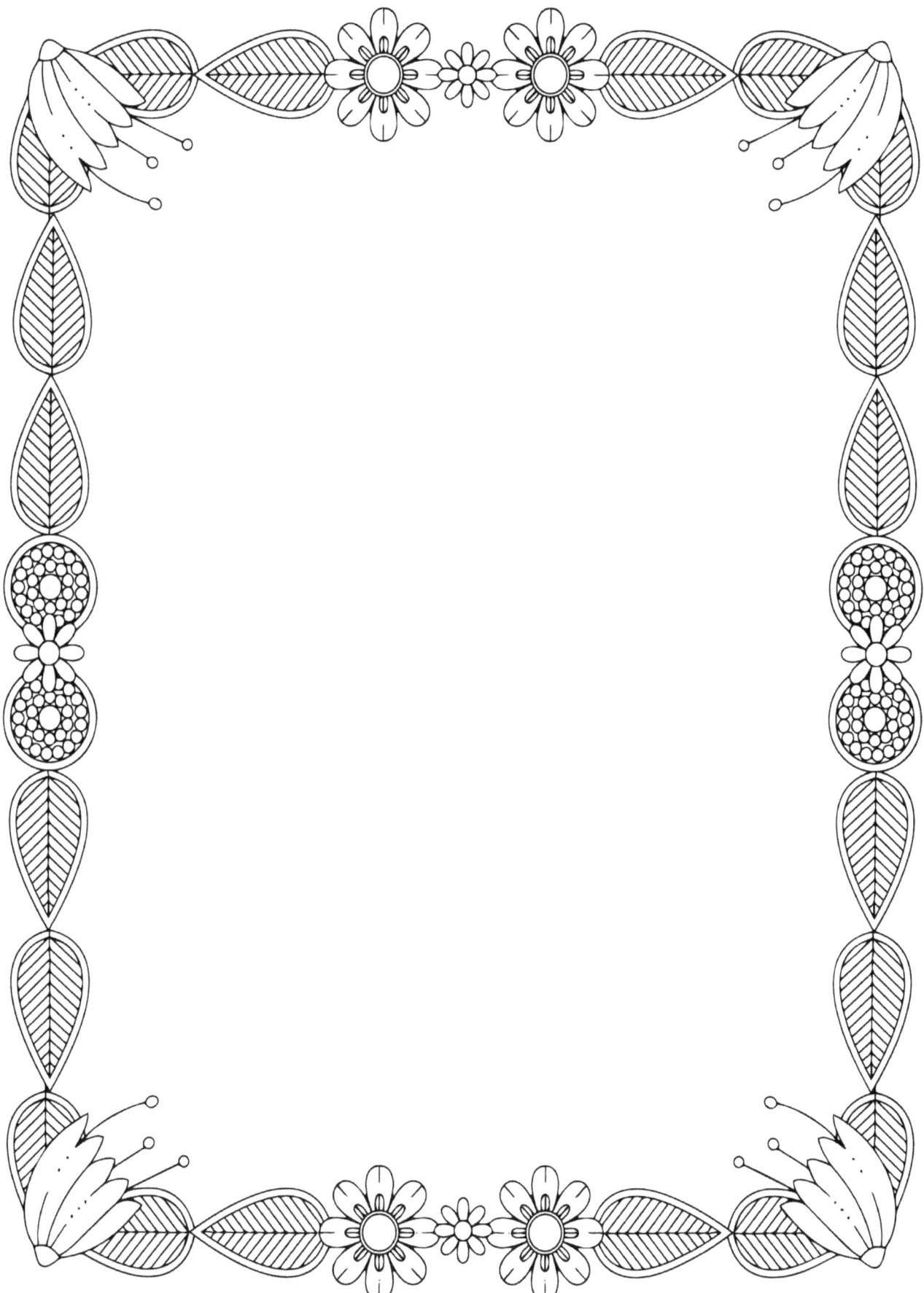

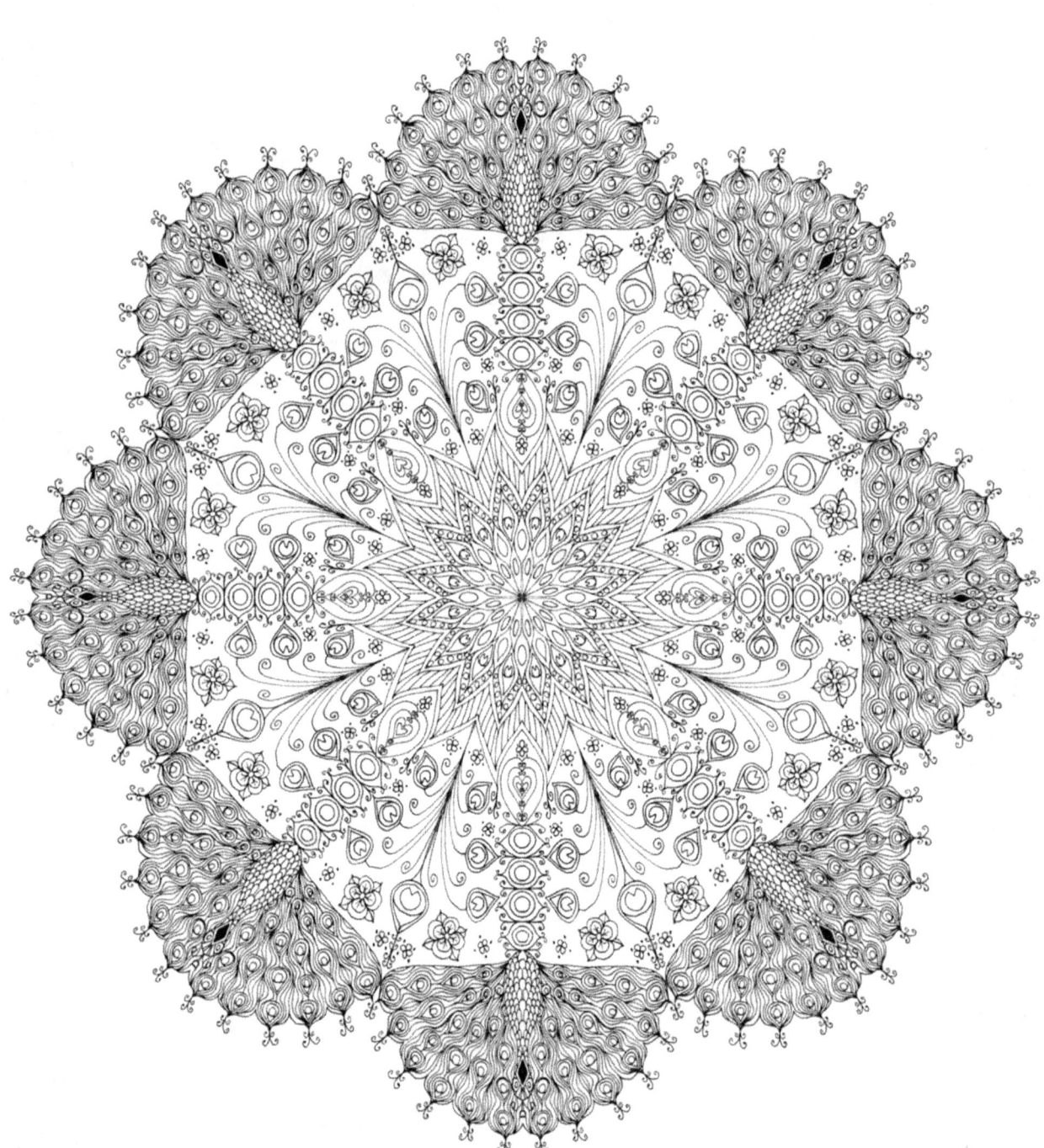

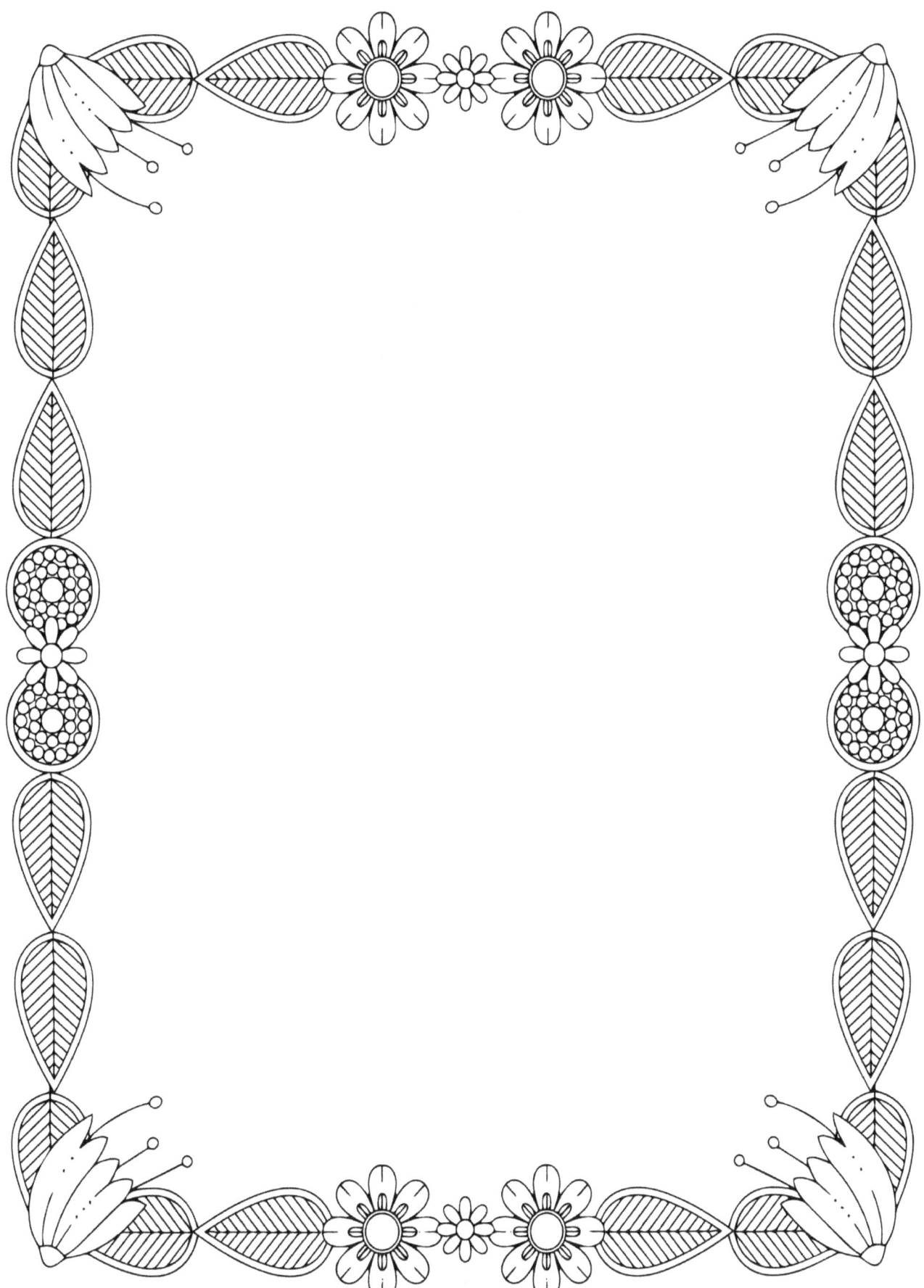

Notes

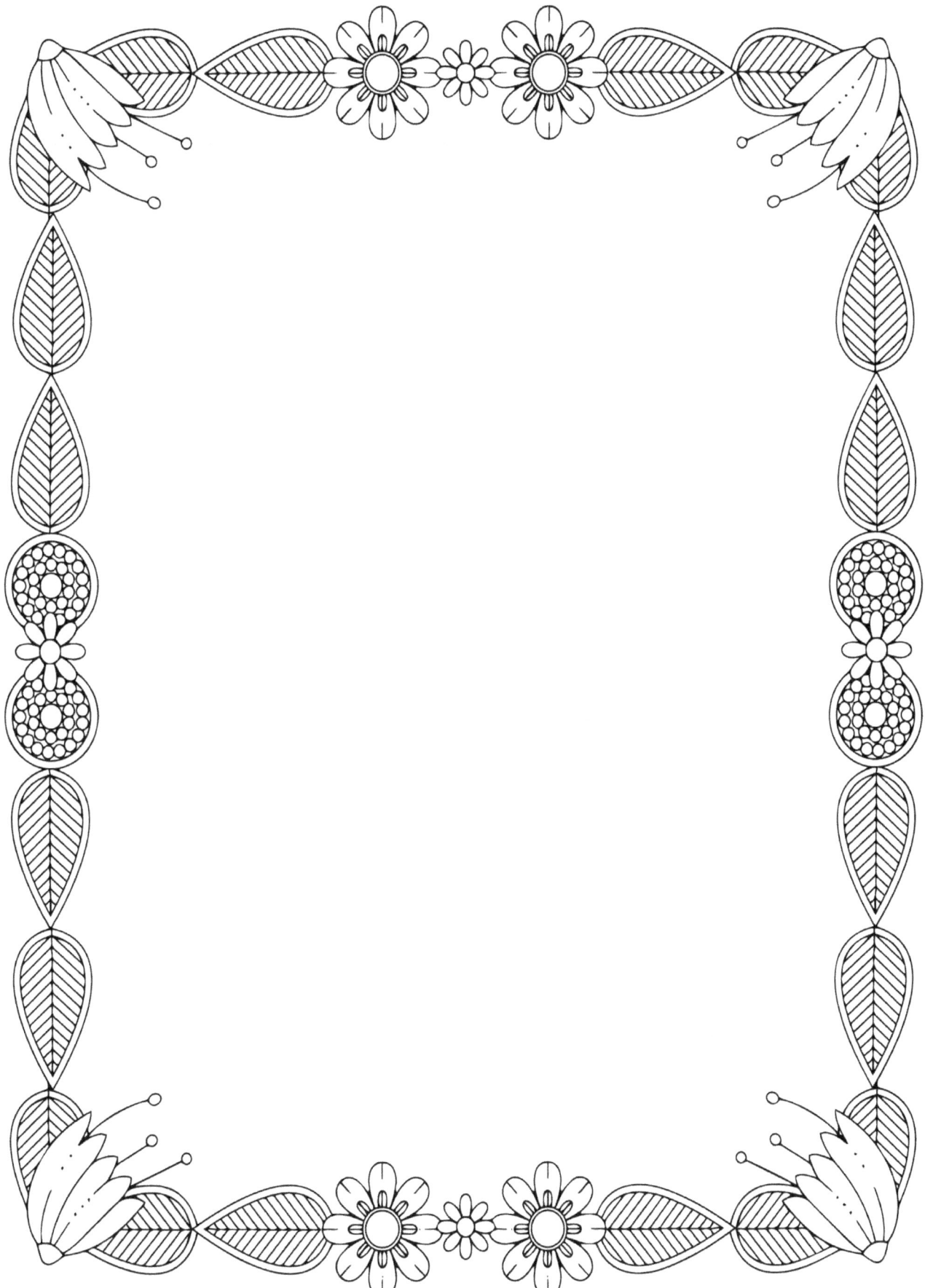

Notes

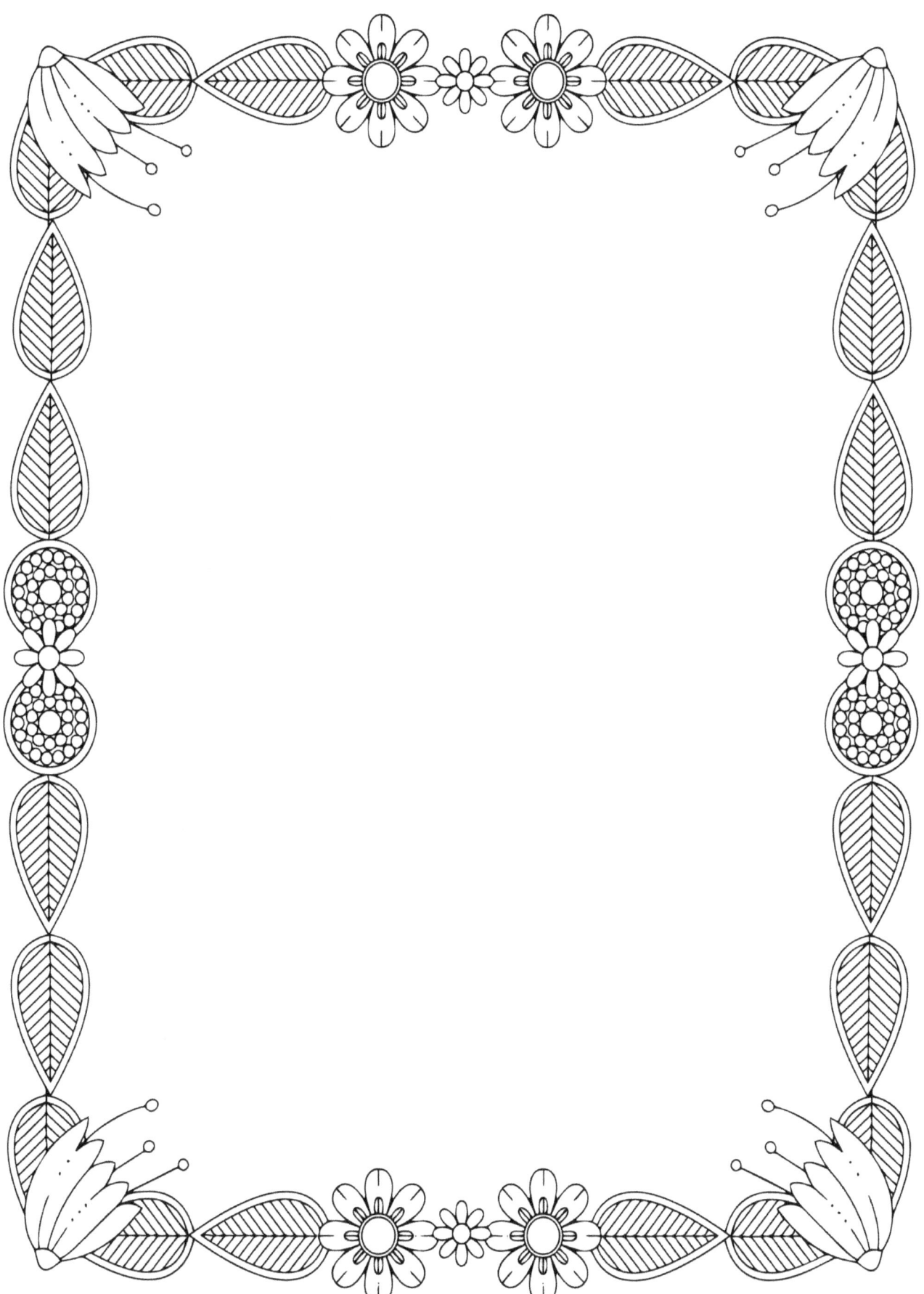

Notes

www.ingramcontent.com/pod-product-compliance
Lightning Source LLC
Chambersburg PA
CBHW081734220526
45468CB00008B/2089